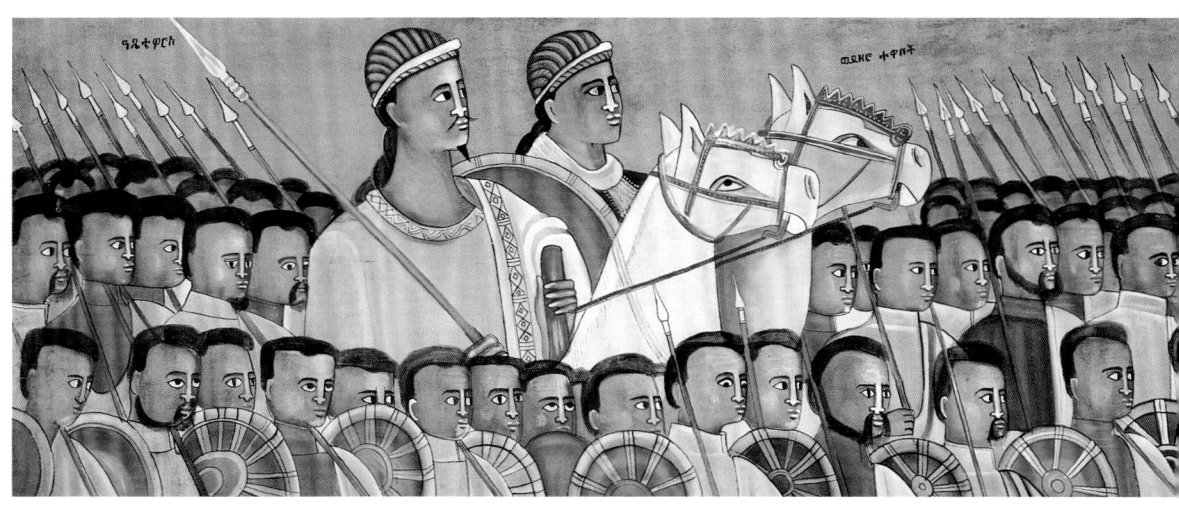

Painting Ethiopia

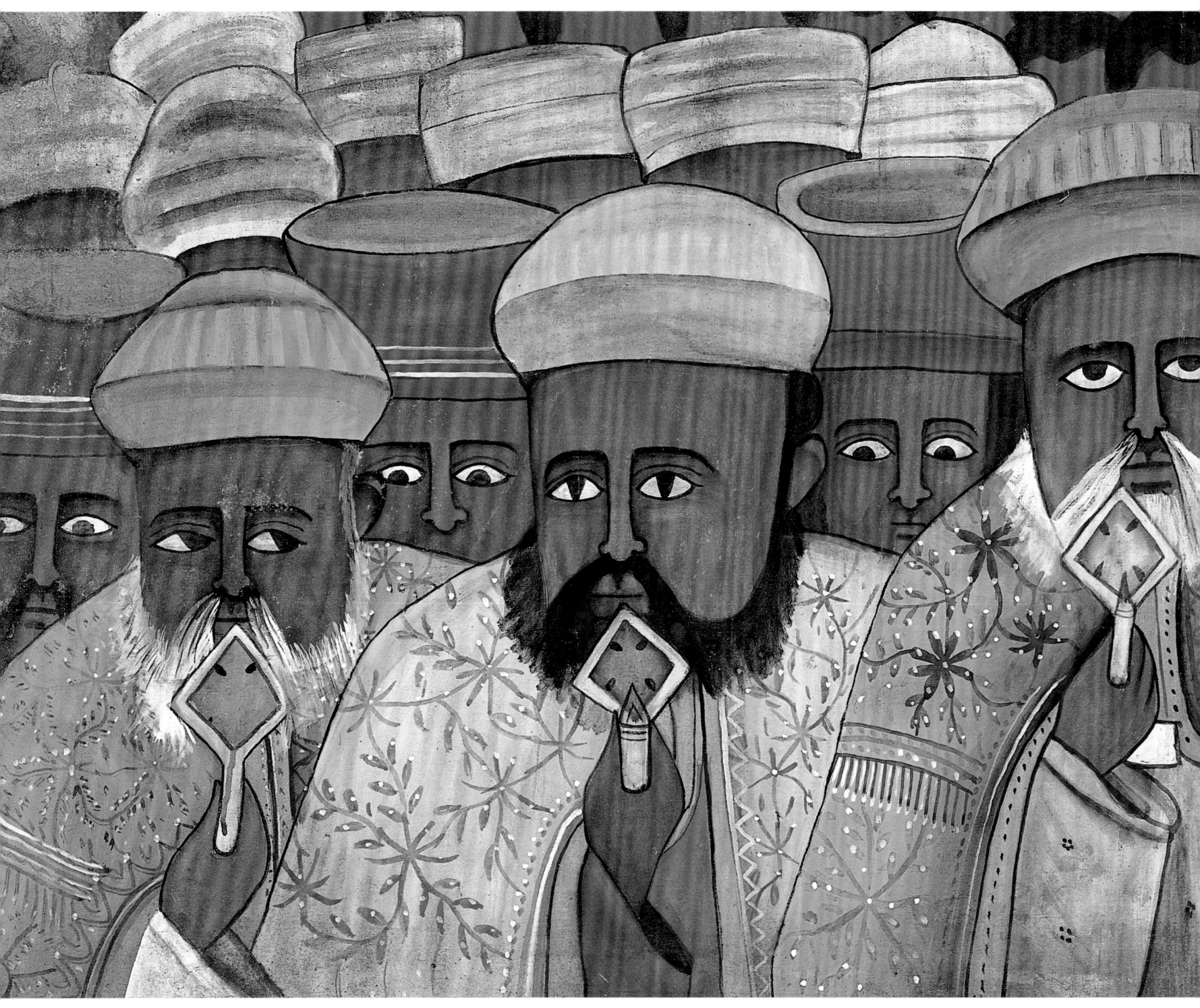

UCLA FOWLER MUSEUM OF CULTURAL HISTORY
LOS ANGELES

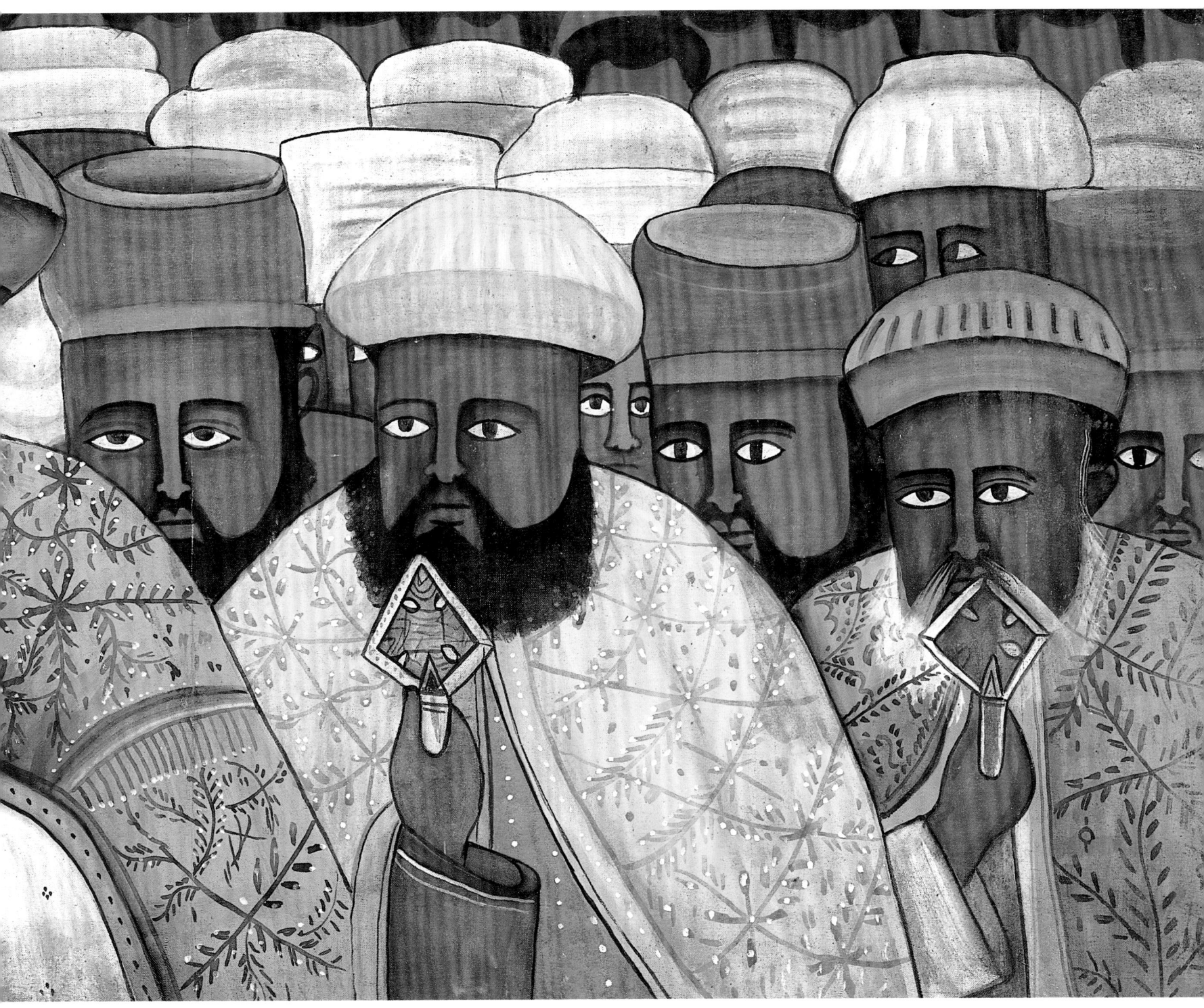

Painting Ethiopia

THE LIFE AND WORK OF QES ADAMU TESFAW

RAYMOND A. SILVERMAN

With contributions by Neal Sobania and Leah Niederstadt

The Fowler Museum is part of UCLA's School of the Arts and Architecture

Lynne Kostman, *Managing Editor*
Danny Brauer, *Designer and Production Manager*
Don Cole, *Principal Photographer*

Printed and bound in Hong Kong by South Sea International Press, Ltd.

Library of Congress Cataloging-in-Publication Data

Silverman, Raymond Aaron.
    Painting Ethiopia : the life and work of Qes Adamu Tesfaw / Raymond A. Silverman; with contributions by Leah Niederstadt and Neal Sobania.
        p. cm
    Includes bibliographical references.
    ISBN 0-9748729-2-X
1. Qåes Adamu Tesfaw—Exhibitions. 2. Christian saints in art—Exhibitions. 3. Orthodox Eastern Church—In art—Exhibitions. I. Qåes Adamu Tesfaw. II. Niederstadt, Leah. III. Sobania, N. W. IV. University of California, Los Angeles. Fowler Museum of Cultural History. v. Title.
    ND1086.3.Q24A4 2005
    759.963—dc22

                                       2004028716

Support for this publication and the accompanying exhibition has been provided by

Ethiopian Art Heritage Project
Packtra Pvt. Ltd. Co.
National Promotions & Advertising
Lufthansa Airlines
Manus, the support group of the UCLA Fowler Museum
    of Cultural History

Front cover—detail of cat. 9; back cover—detail of cat. 12; p. 1—detail of cat. 19; pp. 2–3—detail of cat. 11; pp. 4–5—detail of cat. 35; p. 6—detail of cat. 5; p. 14—detail of cat 8; p. 18—detail of cat. 10; pp. 40–41—detail of cat. 6; p. 42—detail of cat. 1; p. 72—detail of cat. 16; p. 98—detail of cat. 31; p. 120—detail of cat. 27.

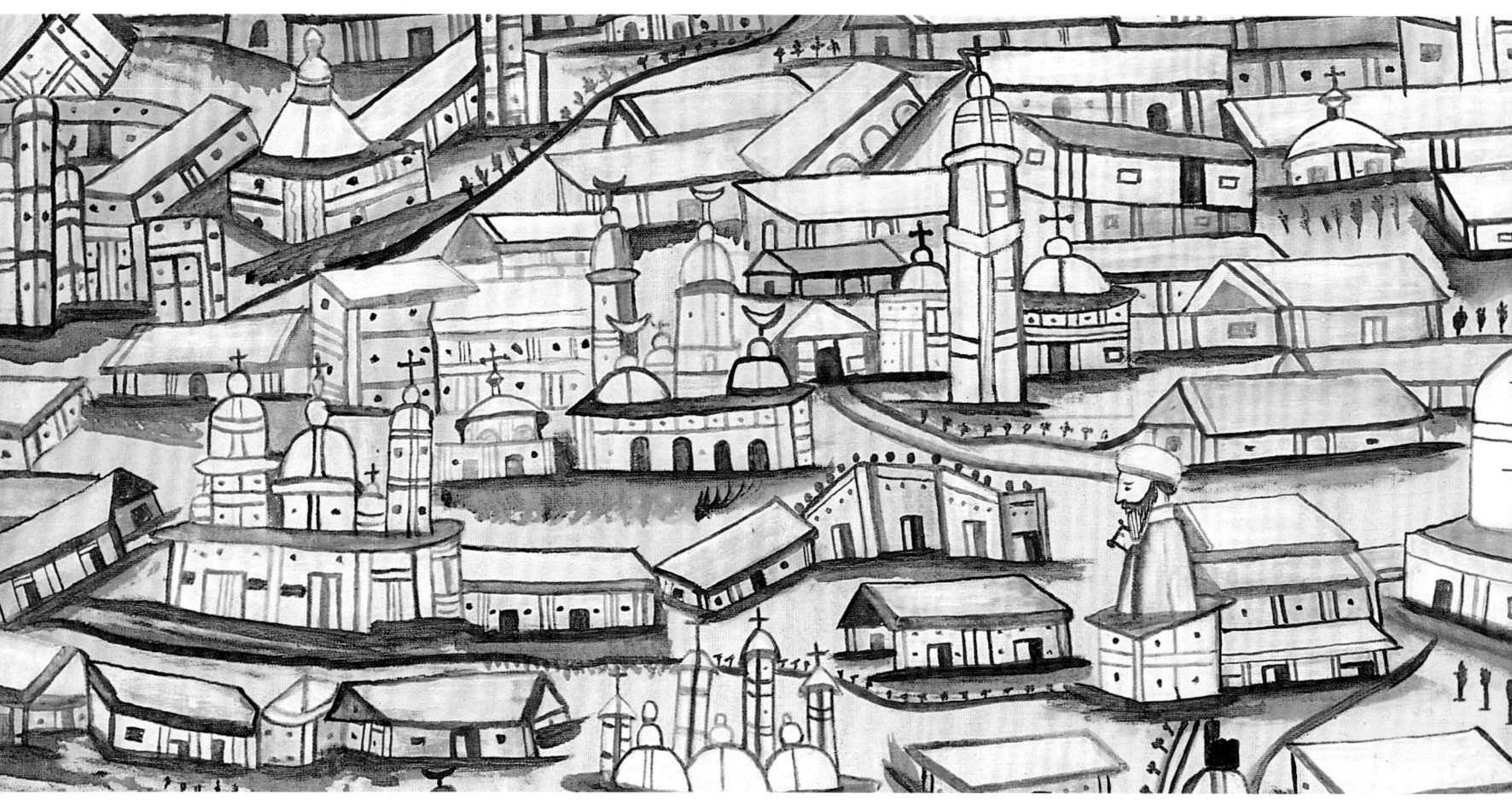

Contents

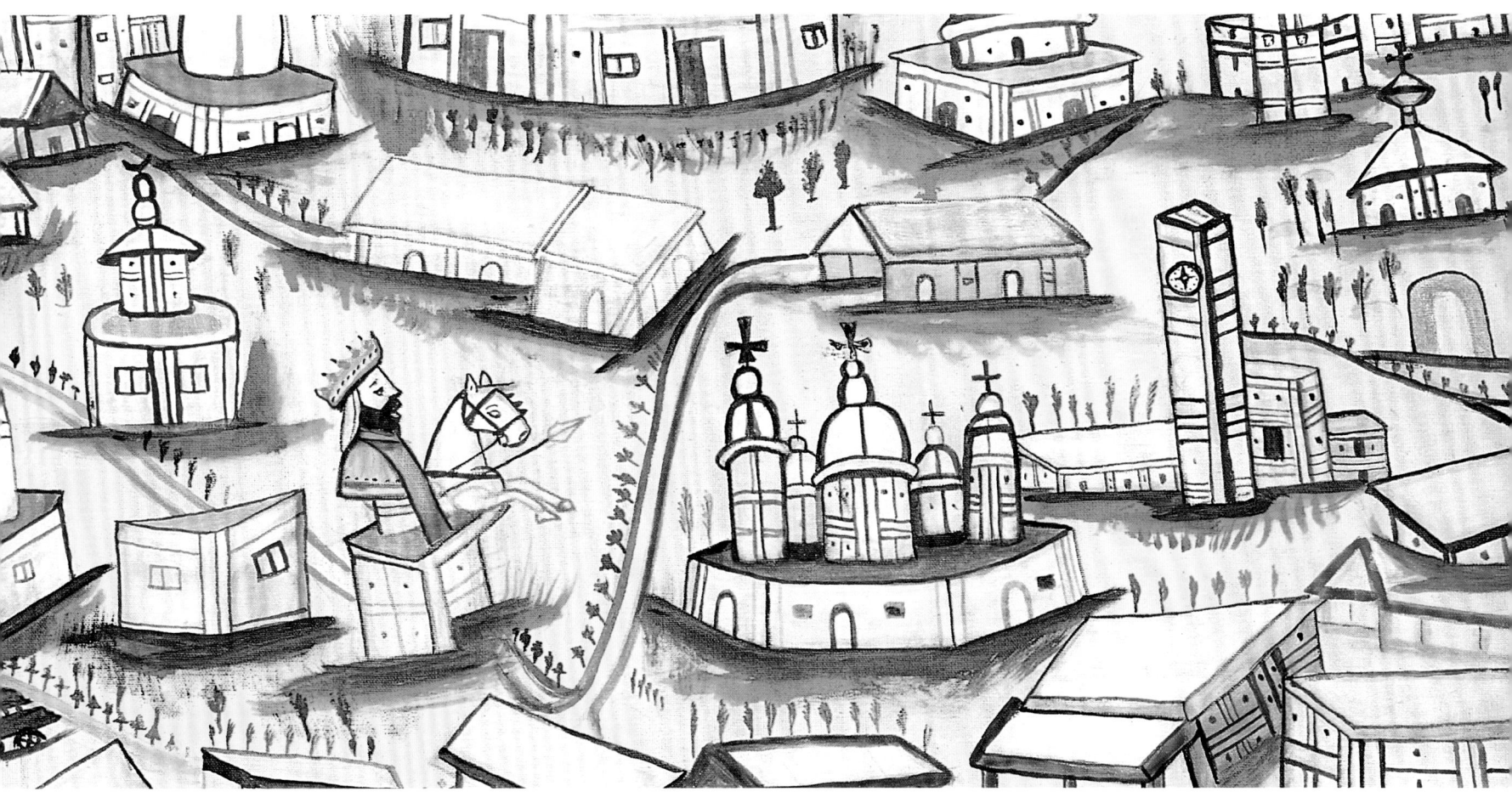

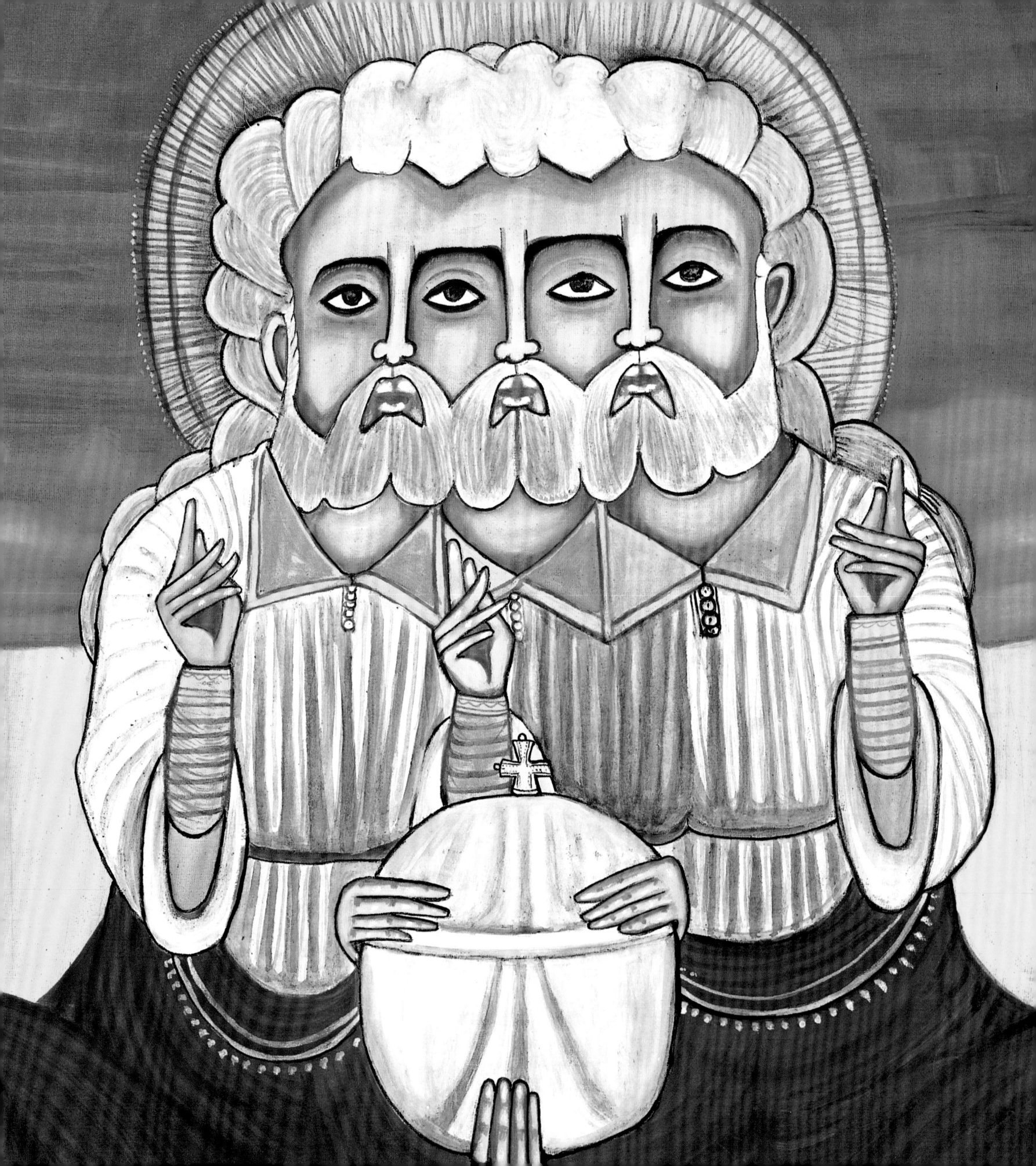

Forewords

It is with great pleasure that the Fowler Museum of Cultural History presents the first exhibition dedicated solely to the work of Ethiopian artist Qes Adamu Tesfaw. The discovery of a new artist is always cause for excitement, and we are especially proud to join curator Raymond Silverman in introducing the strikingly original paintings of Qes Adamu.

Schooled in the fifteen-hundred-year-old painting tradition of the Ethiopian Orthodox Church and ever sensitive to its narrative and iconographic requirements, Adamu has managed to transcend the formulas that tradition requires him to embrace. By giving up the priesthood and turning to painting full-time, the artist has also found the freedom to venture outside the realm of religious subject matter to produce work that chronicles historical events both inside and outside Ethiopia, as well as scenes that depict the everyday life of his native country.

Adamu's remarkable oeuvre includes saints on horseback, soldiers gathered in historic battles, Solomon and Sheba's courtship, and Ethiopians attending church or praying at mosques. His portrayals are marked by a dynamism and monumentality that sets him apart from other artists painting for the urban art market of Addis Ababa. Whether focusing on a few characters in a single episode inspired by a biblical story or painting a raging battle scene, Qes Adamu achieves a psychological intensity that immediately engages the viewer. His bold color choices and unusual compositional strategies only intensify the affectivity of his images and the stories they tell.

Considered within the larger framework of art produced in Africa today, Adamu's paintings do not fit neatly into any one category. As Ray Silverman suggests in his essay, Adamu's work cannot be classified as strictly "traditional" or strictly "modern," a dichotomy critiqued by many scholars for its limitations in adequately capturing the multivalence of artistic expression in contemporary Africa. Adamu's paintings partake of tradition and modernity at the same time—the artist living, as he does, in Ethiopia's urban center and at the same time drawing, as he does, on a deeply held liturgical tradition. As Elsabet Wolde-Giorgis argues in the foreword following mine, finding the right definition for Adamu is further complicated by the fact that he is working for a broad audience of Ethiopians as well as foreign visitors. Because his work encompasses a wider range of subjects than could ever be subsumed within traditional church painting, he can also be described as a popular artist. And, is Adamu not a commercial artist if the content and style of his painting is shaped by market forces? How does an artist maintain his integrity while simultaneously confronting the strictures of a long-standing church tradition and the demands of the potential purchasers of his art? As Sidney Littlefield Kasfir notes in her important study of just these issues, "contemporary art in Africa has built through a process of *bricolage* upon the already existing structures and scenarios on which the older, precolonial and colonial genres of African art were made. It is in this structural sense, and in the habits and attitudes of artists towards making art, rather than in any adherence to a particular style, medium, technique or thematic range, that it is recognizably 'African'" (1999, 9).

Thus Adamu, acknowledges that leaving out certain elements of a biblical episode might get a church painter "in trouble," while also feeling free to use television programs as a source of inspiration. And, while perpetuating a style he himself refers to as *bahilawi*—one having its roots in culture or tradition—he is equally compelled to paint his subjects in the ways *he* believes the eye actually perceives and interprets them. Qes Adamu's own brand of *bricolage* is highly original and as responsive to his own creative instincts as it is to the vagaries of his burgeoning international audience.

I would like to thank Raymond Silverman, professor of the History of Art and Afroamerican and African Studies at the University of Michigan, for preparing the sensitive and insightful text of this volume and for so expertly curating the exhibition that accompanies it. Ray has worked closely with Adamu Tesfaw for more than eleven years, and his extensive knowledge of Ethiopian art history and culture has allowed him to examine Adamu's work within that context and in terms of the particularities of the artist's unique biography. Ray's devotion to his subject is obvious, as is Adamu's trust and affection for him. Without Ray's broad vision for this project and his generous help with complicated international negotiations, it might never have been realized. I would also like to express our gratitude to Neal Sobania and Leah Niederstadt, who collaborated with Ray in writing the catalog entries. All of these scholars are experts in the field of Ethiopian art and intimately acquainted with Adamu and his world. Their contributions have enriched this volume immeasurably.

The assistance and cooperation of the Institute of Ethiopian Studies (IES) at Addis Ababa University, and especially of its former director Baye Yimam and current director Elsabet Wolde-Giorgis, have been critical to the evolution of this project. The IES has generously lent eighteen seminal works by Qes Adamu for the exhibition and has consented to the reproduction of many more in this volume. We are delighted to have had the opportunity to collaborate with this important Ethiopian institution. In addition to the IES, Mrs. Benedetta Riva, Michigan State University Museum, Neal and Elizabeth Sobania, Ian Campbell, Leah Niederstadt, and several private collectors have all graciously lent works to the exhibition. I would also like to express the Museum's gratitude for financial and in-kind support from the following organizations: the Ethiopian Art Heritage Project in Santa Barbara, California; Packtra Pvt. Ltd. Co., Addis Ababa; National Promotions & Advertising, Los Angeles; Lufthansa Airlines; and Manus, the Museum's support group.

Several individuals and institutions in the Ethiopian community of Los Angeles assisted the Museum's Education Department in its efforts to assure that this exhibition reach the widest possible audience. I would like to thank Elias Wondimu, Tsehai Publishers and Distributors; Mesai Haileleul, Addis Art; Esseye Gebre-Medhin, Debre Hayq Ethiopian Art Foundation; Elizabeth Asrat, Ethiopian Community Association; Azeb Tadesse, James S. Coleman African Studies Center, UCLA; the Virgin Mary Ethiopian Orthodox Tewahedo Church; Saint Mary Ethiopian Orthodox Tewahedo Church; and Abune Aregawi Ethiopian Orthodox Tewahedo Church.

As always, the entire Fowler Museum staff contributed to the success of this project. I would like to thank Polly Nooter Roberts, Deputy Director and Chief Curator, for her excellent work in coordinating the many facets of the exhibition's development. The staff of the Registration and Collections Departments—Sarah Kennington, Farida Sunada, Fran Krystock, Jason DeBlock—worked diligently to ensure the prompt delivery and careful handling of Adamu's paintings. Conservator Jo Hill and her assistant Patricia Measures overcame the considerable challenges of mounting and framing these relatively fragile works. The beautiful presentation of the paintings and the sympathetic installation design are testimony to the talents of David Mayo, Director of Exhibitions, and his staff, Mike Sessa and Wendy Phillips. Exhibition graphics were imaginatively conceived by Stephanie Donon. The staff of the Museum's Education Department, under the direction of Betsy D. Quick—enthusiastically assisted by Ilana Gatti and Gina Hall—has once again developed a creative program of interdisciplinary offerings to enrich and extend the exhibition's range, including an artist's residency in Los Angeles and the active involvement of the city's Ethiopian community. Lynne Brodhead and Leslie Denk of the Development Department have been tenacious in their pursuit of funding for the publication and exhibition, and Stacey Ravel Abarbanel has demonstrated her usual flair in developing a handsome publicity package. Karyn Zarubica has ably overseen the development of an exhibition tour in the Museum's effort to share the artist's work with the broadest possible audience. Under the direction of David Blair, Assistant Director, the administrative staff—Marylene Foreman, Jennifer Garbee, Betsy Escandor, and Amy Whittenburg—has supplied timely and efficient support to all.

This elegant volume is the work of Danny Brauer, Director of Publications, who has created a design perfectly suited to the subject matter. The text was edited with sensitivity by Lynne Kostman, and the beautiful photographs were taken by Don Cole.

Once again I express on behalf of the Fowler Museum our profound gratitude to Raymond Silverman for introducing us to Qes Adamu Tesfaw's work and for so tirelessly laboring to ensure the artist's global recognition and enduring legacy. I will always remember my first exposure to Adamu's monumental paintings—their vibrant and unusual color palette, the unexpectedly bold and even quirky compositions, and their intensely personal portrayals of devotion and history. It is an honor to bring the artist's visionary work to the world's attention.

Marla C. Berns
Director
UCLA Fowler Museum of Cultural History

It is with great pride that I join Marla Berns in celebrating the publication of this volume dedicated to the work of Qes Adamu Tesfaw. The Institute of Ethiopian Studies at Addis Ababa University is especially pleased to lend the UCLA Fowler Museum of Cultural History eighteen remarkable paintings by this seminal artist for reproduction in the text and inclusion in the exhibition that accompanies it. Qes Adamu is certainly known within the Ethiopian art world and has recently received attention in exhibitions held in Europe and the United States: *Ethiopia: Traditions of Creativity*, also curated by Raymond Silverman (Michigan State University, 1994); *I santi cavalieri: Arte e leggende d'Etiopia* (Rome, 1996); *Adamu, Kidane, Qanna: Three Painters from Ethiopia* (Leighton House Museum, London, 1998). We applaud the Fowler Museum for introducing Adamu's paintings for the first time to a West Coast audience and for extending the knowledge of this important artist and of the range and depth of art production in Ethiopia today.

The Fowler's book and exhibition take on special import because, in comparison to what has been accomplished in the social sciences concerning Ethiopia—and to what has been written about the art of many other African countries—Ethiopia's rich artistic legacy has received very little attention. This unfortunate situation may be explained in part by the absence of local art historians and the subsequent lack of intellectual discourse on art. To the extent that Ethiopian art has been studied, it has largely been treated by foreign scholars, and in many cases their scholarship has focused exclusively on issues of technique and classification, often relying upon European models and failing to take into account the metaphysical narratives of the art. The cultural and social context of Ethiopian art—wherein the relationship between art and religion, priest and artist, ritual and display are closely intertwined—cry out for appropriate exploration. I am extremely gratified, therefore, that Raymond Silverman, the author of the present volume, is acutely aware of and responsive to this predicament:

> Most art-historical inquiry in Ethiopia has been devoted to searching for the iconographic and stylistic origins of Ethiopian religious art. Most scholars have approached this challenge from *outside* Habesha culture. Their studies leave one with the impression that the sources of creativity, innovation and change always come from *outside* Ethiopia. Scholars have successfully identified various foreign sources, and they duly acknowledge the creative genius required to integrate these ideas into an Ethiopian setting, but there is little written on *how* or *why* these models were assimilated and transformed to become part of a distinctive Ethiopian canon. [Silverman 1999, 147]

The cultural bases of Ethiopian art forms must be fully investigated to insure a complete understanding. If we, for instance, consider the aesthetic underlying Ethiopian traditional Christian art, we find that it is not only value laden but also essentially ideology laden. It is part of the Orthodox Christian mythology, which must be studied in order to comprehend it fully. Language is key to illuminating the obscurity, the ambiguity, and the secrecy of these mythological concepts. Geez, the ancient liturgical script, is intricately related to the image, and at times image and text are continuous.

They originate in the same source of mythic conceptions and beliefs. Like Amharic, the language spoken in present-day Ethiopia, Geez is replete with puns, witticisms, and layered meanings, creating what Donald Levine has referred to as "a cult of ambiguity" (1965, 10).

Ethiopian traditional art embodies the "wax and gold" concept, the most dominant form of poetic expression in both Amharic and Geez. The apparent figurative meaning is referred to as the "wax," while the hidden and significant meaning is termed the "gold." Philosopher Messay Kebede terms "wax and gold" the "art of discovering and reinstating the truth." This corresponds with the Ethiopian conception of the divine. "For the Ethiopian," according to Messay "there is a fundamental duality in the nature of God" and "the mystery of God and His omnipotence constitute the dyad appearance-essence." Thus

> Despite its relative technical sophistication, its bare and skimpy aspect—as compared with European painting (which is full of flesh, color, volume and form)—is evidence of a deliberately impoverishing conception of sensuous reality. God is signified not so much by magnificence as by contrast of the kind which makes physical presentations poorer than their contents. [1999, 182, 183, 191]

Ethiopian traditional art is, therefore, more symbolic than representative or descriptive. And in focusing on redundancy, overfamiliarity, distortion, and classification, existing studies misconstrue the mystification inherent in traditional art forms, attempting instead to fit them into a Western art historical paradigm.

Qes Adamu Tesfaw is an especially interesting artist in light of the foregoing. On the one hand he is church-trained and, therefore, has ties to traditional art and its underlying metaphysics. On the other hand, he is a successful popular artist, painting for a far wider audience than ever envisioned by traditional religious painters. Unlike traditional art, popular art assumes some of the traits of realism in reflecting culture and history. It comprehends, nonetheless, the distinctive intellectual, spiritual, and aesthetic aspects of life, as well as narrating the value systems and beliefs that characterize the group. Thus the same multidimensional dynamics that are important to an understanding of traditional art—ideology, identity, and historical development around the concept of culture—remain critical elements in analyzing Ethiopian popular art forms.

Raymond Silverman has worked closely with Qes Adamu Tesfaw for many years and has closely studied the nuances and complexities associated with his paintings. He is keenly aware of the importance of context and language in defining and interpreting traditional paintings, realizing that like the work of Qes Adamu, they are social products expressive of a myriad of values. We are extremely fortunate to benefit from Raymond's sensitivity to both context and content. His scholarship is tantamount to the comprehensive view of Ethiopian art that has heretofore been missing. It is my hope that publications like this one and exhibitions like the one accompanying it will set a precedent for future transformative scholarly dialogues on Ethiopian art and that, as in the Fowler exhibition, the wax will be made to yield way to the gold.

Elsabet Wolde-Giorgis
Director
Institute of Ethiopian Studies
Addis Ababa University

Acknowledgments

Painting Ethiopia is the product of a relationship with Qes Adamu Tesfaw that began in 1993 when my colleague Neal Sobania and I first met this remarkable man. We have continued to meet with him over the last eleven years. Each visit has been an education, and I shall be forever indebted to Qes Adamu for sharing his time and so many marvelous insights into his work, as well as into the visual traditions of the Ethiopian Orthodox Church and the commercial art world of Addis Ababa.

The impetus for this project came from Ahmed Zekaria, the head of the Museum of the Institute of Ethiopian Studies (IES) at Addis Ababa University, in 2001. The museum had recently acquired close to one hundred of Qes Adamu's paintings, and aware of my previous work with the artist, Ahmed asked if I might curate an exhibition of Adamu's paintings at the IES. I suggested that the IES Museum team up with a U.S. museum to develop an exhibition that would tour in the United States, and perhaps Europe, and would then be installed in the IES Museum. Roughly a year later, I approached Marla Berns and Polly Nooter Roberts at the UCLA Fowler Museum of Cultural History with the project. I showed them some reproductions of Adamu's paintings, and they were immediately impressed.

Painting Ethiopia, like most exhibition projects, is the product of a wide range of expertise, countless hours of hard work, and a significant amount of good will. Over half the paintings in the exhibition come from the IES. I would like to thank the staff of that institution and, in particular, Ahmed Zekaria, Derege Berehanu, and Ketsela Markos, for their assistance at various stages of the project. They were particularly instrumental in preparing the loan paintings for shipment to Los Angeles. *Painting Ethiopia*, of course, would not have been possible without the support of the director of the IES—many thanks to both Professor Baye Yimam, who helped launch the project, and his successor, Elsabet Wolde-Giorgis, who has overseen the project's implementation. We are grateful to Leah Niederstadt, who has participated in this project in a number of capacities, for her efforts in insuring that the IES paintings were safely shipped from Addis Ababa to Los Angeles. I would also like to thank two special friends Berhanu Wolde-Amlak and his son Bruk for the logistical support that they have generously provided during my various sojourns in Addis Ababa.

Over the last ten years, several research assistants—Degefa Etana Rufo, Tibebe Eshete, Daniel Berhanemeskel, and Makda TekleMichael—have played a critical role as translators at our meetings with Qes Adamu. Dealing with Amharic and its mother language, Geez, is no easy task. Of special note, Tibebe Eshete masterfully translated Qes Adamu's autobiography. I also would like to acknowledge Heran Serekebrhan who offered her expertise in interpreting some of the more subtle nuances in Adamu's self-reflections. We very much appreciate the efforts of Grover Hudson, an expert on the languages of Ethiopia, who accepted the challenge of establishing transliteration guidelines for the Ethiopian names and vernacular (primarily Amharic) terms presented in this book.

In addition to the research in Ethiopia, I was very fortunate to have had the opportunity to travel to Rome to speak with Benedetta Riva who was both a patron and mentor to Adamu for the better part of fifteen years in the 1960s and early 1970s. I'd like to thank her for sharing with me her memories of working with Qes Adamu. I would also like to thank her daughter, Renata Riva, for making the arrangements for and participating in my meetings with Signora Riva. Another member of the family Margot Parra, Signora Riva's granddaughter-in-law, assisted with transcontinental communication, and my friend Livio Crescenzi graciously offered his hospitality during my stay in Rome.

The paintings that comprise the exhibition are drawn primarily from the collections of the IES, the Fowler Museum, and Michigan State University Museum. But many of the key works displayed in *Painting Ethiopia* were lent by individuals, namely Ian Campbell, Leah Niederstadt, Benedetta Riva, Neal and Elizabeth Sobania, and two anonymous lenders. I would like to thank all of them for generously agreeing to participate in this important project.

In addition to the financial and in-kind support mentioned in Marla Berns's foreword, I would like to acknowledge Michigan State University, the University of Michigan, and the Fowler Museum for supporting the research in Ethiopia that is presented in this publication and the exhibition.

Thanks also must go to the eminent scholars of Ethiopian art and history Stanislaw Chojnacki and Richard Pankhurst, who generously shared their expertise regarding queries that arose in the preparation of my essay. I very much appreciated the feedback I received on an early draft of the essay from my colleagues and friends David Doris, Leah Niederstadt, and Neal Sobania.

Special thanks are reserved for Neal Sobania and Leah Niederstadt who have been important partners in this project, Neal since 1993 and Leah since 2002. In addition to assisting with writing the entries for the catalog, Neal and Leah have participated at various times in discussions with Qes Adamu. Working with them has been an enriching and fulfilling experience.

The Fowler Museum has been a part of my life for almost thirty years. My first experience of the Museum was as an undergraduate at UCLA when I volunteered to do some pretty mundane (but I like to think important) work with the Fowler's registrar. Since then I have been involved in a number of Fowler exhibition projects. Curating an exhibition at the Fowler has always been a dream. It has been a real pleasure working with the Fowler's superb staff on *Painting Ethiopia*. I would like to thank them all, but especially Marla Berns and Polly Nooter Roberts, for making this publication and the accompanying exhibition such a success.

Raymond A. Silverman

Note on Orthography

A variety of systems exist for the transliteration of Ethiopia's Semitic languages, and at present there is no general agreement as to which should be considered the standard. We have made every effort to regularize the transliteration of Ethiopian names and terms throughout the text that follows without resorting to the use of diacritical marks. Our goal has been to try to assure that the reader will have some sense of how the words in question are correctly pronounced. We have departed from the aforementioned practice only when quoting published material, and for authors' and other proper names, such as Haile Selassie, for which a different practice is established in usage.

Long consonants are written as double letters, for example, *Kassa*. The Ethiopian glottalized consonants, which our readers would not be able to pronounce, are simply written identical to unglottalized consonants. Vowels, for which English letters are insufficient, are particularly problematic. These we have converted as follows: *e* for the Amharic "first-order" vowel (approximately that of English *sun*), *u* for the "second-order" vowel (Eng. *soon*), *i* for the "third-order" vowel (Eng. *seen*), *a* for the "fourth-order" vowel (Eng. *sod*), *e* for the "fifth-order" vowel (Eng. *sane*), *i* for the "sixth-order" vowel (not in English but close to that of *sin*), and *o* for the "seventh-order" vowel (Eng. *sown*).

Many Ethiopians use two names, the first being a given name and the second the name of the person's father. The first name is that primarily used to address a person and in citations, and that is the practice that we have followed in this volume. In the list of References Cited, Ethiopian authors are alphabetized by their first names, and in textual references to published material by Ethiopian authors the full name has been used.

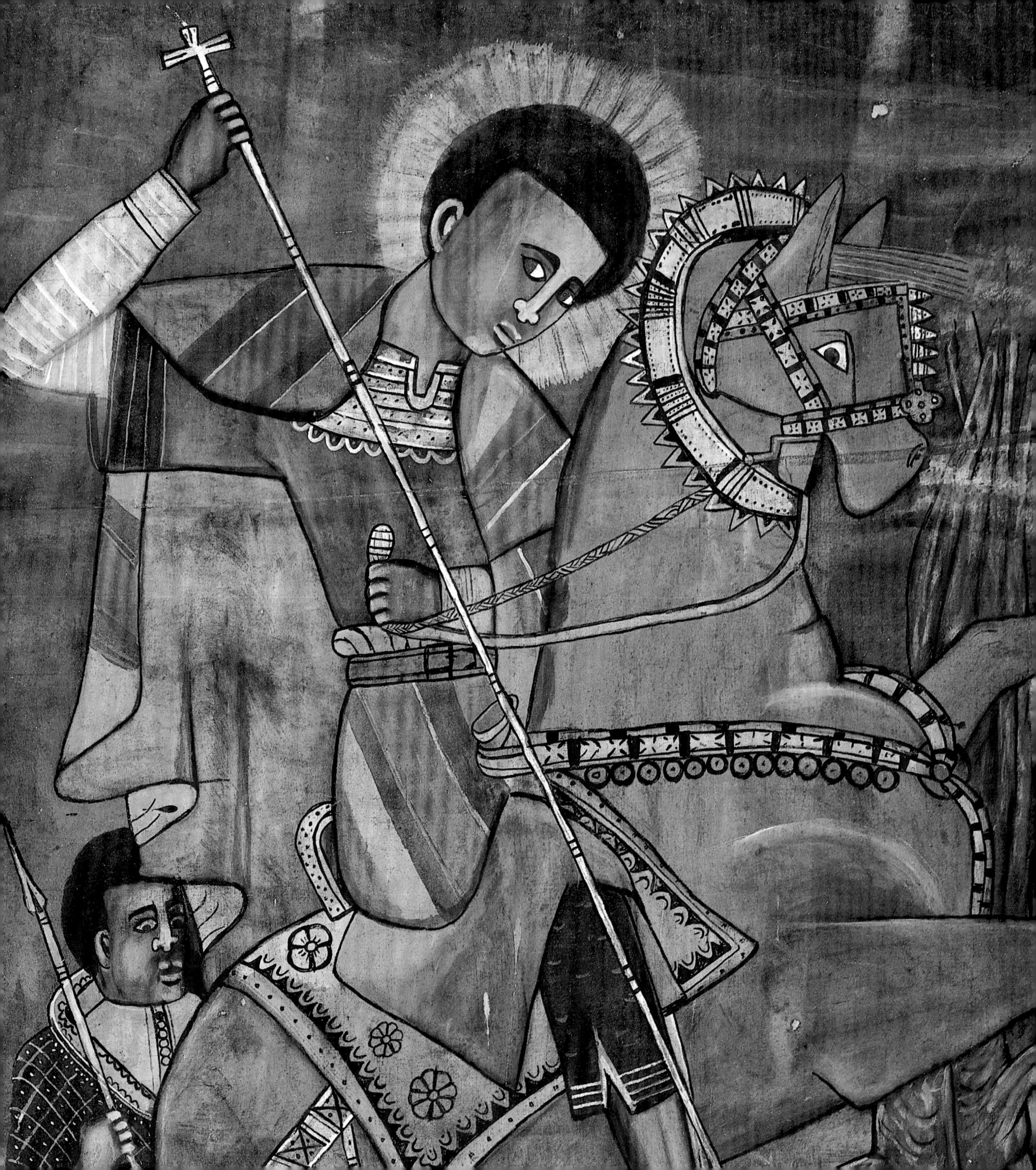

A Brief Account of My Life

QES ADAMU TESFAW

Translated by Tibebe Eshete

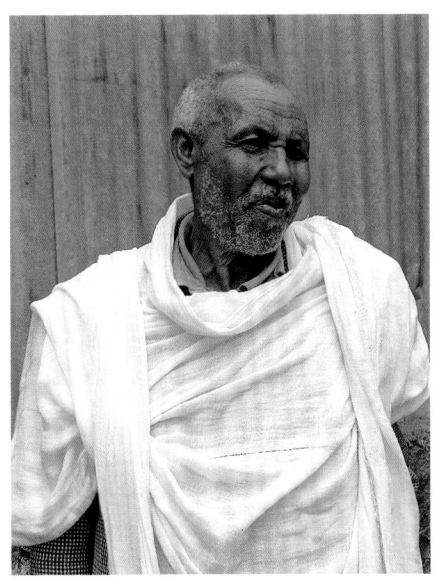

A Qes Adamu Tesfaw. Photograph by Raymond Silverman, Addis Ababa, 2003.

In the name of God the Father, the Son, and the Holy Spirit, One God. Amen! Oh God, the One who causes the day to come and to pass, our Creator and Holy Savior, let glory be to you. You provide the food we eat, the water we drink, hence, praise be to you. I present my history in due recognition of your presence.

I was born in Ethiopia, a country that always stretches its hand toward its Creator, in Gojjam Province, in Bichena District, Enemai Subdistrict, near Bichena Qiddus Giyorgis church. My mother's name is Weizero Mellesech Negusse, and my father's name is Qes Gebez Tesfaw Getahun. I was born in 1922 [EC] and was the third child for my parents.[1] Since I was only one year old, the people of my parish, old and young, showed me considerable affection, cuddling me and carrying me in their arms. The neighbors were so attached to me, they were reluctant to let me out of their sight for long. In my childhood I liked to swim and play *genna*.[2]

As I grew older, because of the yearning I developed to learn, I started my primary lessons with *fidel,* studying with the known Deggwa teacher, Merigeta Webetu Gebru.[3] I completed my lessons up to the level of Dawit.[4] Thereafter, whenever I visited the church, I was enraptured by the paintings on the walls. They inspired awe in my heart. I studied images of saints, martyrs, emperors, and nobles with wonder and never thought they were created by human beings. Gradually, a strong passion for the arts began to take shape within me. Those who noticed my new interest began to express their admiration and encouragement. I even heard people saying, "This child is going to become just like his uncle." So, I asked my father about his brother, my uncle, that is. My father told me that Aleqa Kassa Getahun was a well-known artist in Gojjam,[5] whose paintings could be found in Gojjam in the churches of Adet Medhanealem, Yewesh Mikael, Dese Medhanealem, Yeduha Kidane Meheret, and Bichena Giyorgis. Learning about my uncle and his work added to my passion.

Qes Gebez Anteneh Gebru, a friend of my father's, recognized my keen interest in painting and began giving me more attention. Though I was not aware at the time, I later came to know that he was an accomplished painter himself. One day, he invited me to his home where he showed me all his works. That was when I realized that paintings were created by human beings. I felt enlightened and proceeded to create art on virtually any available material. I used fragments of ceramics, broken bones, which I softened with an axe, and pieces of flat and soft stone. There were no pens and pencils, so I used *qesel* or *tintag,* for drawing.[6] That was the moment I really began creating works of art.

While painting, I continued to pursue my education, moving from one monastery to another to study with different *liqawnt* and attain knowledge of Zema and Qine.[7] I continued my church education though I had to beg for food and withstand the barking dogs.[8] In 1937 [EC], due to my father's initiative, I came to Addis Ababa from Gojjam, traveling on foot for seven days. I went back to Gojjam together with my father after having received my ordination as a deacon from Abuna Qerlos at the Qiddist Maryam Church.[9] Again, the journey from Addis Ababa to Gojjam, took us another seven days. Soon after my return, I began to serve as a deacon in Bichena Giyorgis while creating paintings and carvings. My younger brother was good at carvings. He liked to make engravings on stone and wood. I acquired some ideas from him. Soon enough, I also started to do carvings and basket weaving.[10] My brother, Abba Menberu Tesfaw,[11] because of his deep interest and proven ability in making wood engravings and sketches, found employment at the Ministry of Education. He still lives in Bale Province, in Adaba District. Overall, I can say that fine art is a trait that has been shared by members of our family.

So in this manner, I continued serving the church while painting and sculpting, combining my duties and art without problem. I created sculpture by mixing mud and water and kneading the two together. I also used *biha* stone to make sculptures.[12] I gradually improved and began to use wood. I used to make portrait carvings of men, domestic and wild animals. I introduced my creations to the various churches in the district [of Bichena], which helped me acquire confidence in my skill. In this way, I began to promote my artwork, I also began to expand and diversify my artwork, like producing wooden carvings and drawing paintings in books and on parchment. In that manner, I boosted my morale and encouraged myself to do more. I committed myself to doing several things at the same time, such as basket weaving, engravings of the cross, church bells, and the like. I used cloth to draw and paint on. I sewed the cloth and stuffed it with hay to provide shape for the pieces. I nurtured and improved my skills and continued to provide service to the church.

Through family arrangement, I got married in 1946 [EC] in a formal *teklil* ceremony.[13] Soon after, I was ordained a priest in Debre Marqos by Abuna Marqos, the bishop of Gojjam. Even while serving my church as a priest, my love and interest in art remained, and I followed the painter and priest Qes Anteneh Gebru. I traveled with him wherever he went to make paintings. With his mentoring, I practiced and gained much experience. Eventually, he explained that I had enough skill and experience to paint independently. I rejoiced in my heart. I then decided to come to Addis Ababa to meet with my godfather Ato Yohannis Tesemma,[14] a well-known artist, to improve my newfound profession. He was then working at Empress Menen Handicraft School. Staying and working with him while I was in Addis Ababa allowed me to learn more about artwork, which gave a significant boost to my career. After staying with him for a while I went back to my hometown.

Upon reaching Bichena, I learned that my wife had violated her marital vows. Saddened by the unfortunate situation, I returned to Addis Ababa.[15] I shared the sad story with my godfather who comforted and advised me. My godfather allowed me to stay with him and continue painting. I worked diligently for five years. My godfather incessantly advised me to marry and have children. After serious deliberations over the idea of marriage and the need to have children, I heeded his advice and took action. In 1956 [EC], I married my current wife, Weizero Mulu Berqe, with whom I have been graced with seven children. As God wills it, we have lost four of them, while we have successfully raised the remaining three (fig. B). Nowadays, my wife and I have taken communion.[16]

Marriage and children brought increased financial challenges, I worked hard to earn money. An Italian-Ethiopian named Signor Riva [and his wife] was a long-standing client of ours. The couple had a souvenir shop, which sold a variety of Ethiopian cultural artifacts. They were well acquainted with my paintings, and I agreed to work with them producing paintings. This began a long and happy business relationship. The couple were like family, constantly encouraging and constructively criticizing my works. Our ties went beyond business relations. They advised me to buy land and build my own house. With their encouragement, I purchased land, built and furnished my house in the area of Weira Sefer. I painted at home and delivered my work to the Riva's shop to sell. Unfortunately, because of the change of government, my most helpful and favorite clients had to leave Ethiopia and go to

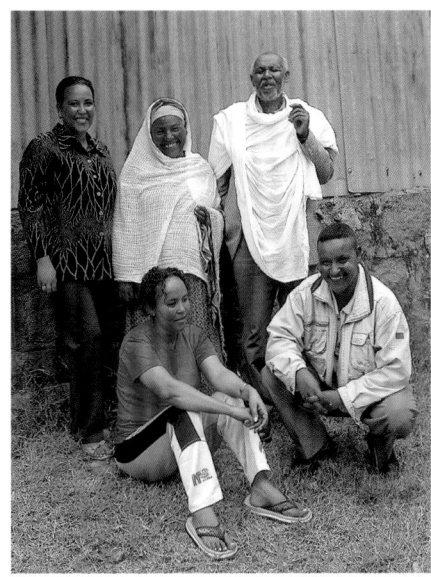

B Adamu with his family. Photograph by Raymond Silverman, Addis Ababa, 2003. Standing (left to right): Wineshet Adamu (eldest daughter), Mulu Berqe (wife), and Adamu. Seated at left: Hanna Adamu (youngest daughter); seated at right: Hizb Adamu (son).

Italy. I continued to work diligently from my home, and new clients began to visit me. I started to receive commissions for a variety of work. For a long time, I have been doing paintings on cloth, parchment, and *gendi*.[17] In addition to that, I have also been doing basketry, carvings, and a variety of sculptures. Among my works are *azmari*, *baltet*, and *kahin*.[18] I also make wooden carvings [and] basketry, like the cross and church bell, once in a while.

While I was doing my work in this manner, Ato Wondimu Wonde, a painter and a friend, introduced me to two American scholars who are lovers of fine arts.[19] Through our close working contacts, I learned more about the world of art and introduced them to my work. They even traveled [with me] as far as Gojjam and my hometown Bichena to see my works. They were impressed and expressed desire to establish a working relationship with me. I agreed and happily accepted their requests to create paintings of various saints, martyrs, and kings. They provided me with needed paint. Especially after their 1989 [EC] visit when they viewed my works on the walls and ceiling of the *qine mahilet* in Bichena Giyorgis church, they showed high regard for [my] talent.[20] Following that, they organized an exhibition in America at the museum of Michigan State University, where different international and American citizens were able to view my works. My life story was written in *Ethiopia: Traditions of Creativity* in a chapter entitled "*Qes* Adamu—A Priest Who Paints."

By publishing my story and my paintings, the scholars have contributed greatly to introducing my work to my fellow countrymen as well as to people from other countries. As a result of this, I had the opportunity of being invited for an interview in the nationally acclaimed Ethiopian TV program *Meto Haya* [meaning "120"] and on Radio Fana. Though I am currently engaged in creating diverse artworks, such as paintings, sculpture, and basketry, I have given painting major concentration and focus. I happily continue to live and work, singing and listening to the sweet melodies of the songs of Yared, painting saints, martyrs, and the works of kings and nobles.[21] Glory and praise be to God who inspires beginnings and accompanies till the end. Amen.

May 2003

Notes

Every attempt has been made to translate Adamu's autobiography as accurately as possible. Minor editorial changes have, however, been made for the sake of clarity. A brief biography of Qes Adamu may be found in the artist profile produced by Raymond Silverman for the Michigan State University exhibition *Ethiopia: Traditions of Creativity* (1994), organized by Michigan State University Museum (Silverman 1994). This profile was the source of biographical information that Stanislaw Chojnacki used in his essay of 1996 on Adamu's paintings of equestrian saints (Chojnacki 1996, 56–58). A brief biography was also included in an essay about Qes Adamu that Silverman published in the book also called *Ethiopia: Traditions of Creativity* (Silverman 1999, 135–36). In it, he erroneously indicated that Qes Adamu was born in 1933.

1. Qiddus Giyorgis is Amharic for Saint George, a popular saint in Ethiopia. *Weizero* is an Amharic term equivalent to "Mrs." *Qes* is the title for a "priest" in the Ethiopian Orthodox Church, and *gebez* is the title given to the chief priest. The designation "EC" refers to a date conforming to the Ethiopian calendar, which begins each year on Meskerem 1, the equivalent to September 11 (September 12 if a leap year) in the Gregorian calendar. The Ethiopian calendar is seven years behind the Gregorian calendar. Thus, the year 1922 EC is equivalent to 1929–1930 CE. Bichena is a large town situated in eastern Gojjam, about 200 km north of Addis Ababa.
2. *Genna* is a game similar to field hockey that is played in the Ethiopian highlands, especially around Christmas.
3. *Fidel* is the Ethiopic alphabet; *Deggwa* are the hymns sung during church services, *merigeta* is a church title for the leader of the *debteroch* (sing., *debtera*), who are lay clerics in the Ethiopian Orthodox Church.
4. Dawit is Amharic for the Psalms of David.

5. *Aleqa* is the church title for the chief priest of a parish church.
6. *Qesel* and *tintag* are Amharic terms for sticks of charcoal.
7. *Liqawnt* are learned elders of the church; Zema is church music; Qine is church poetry.
8. Adamu is here relying on a common metaphor to indicate how young students in the Orthodox Church were expected to learn discipline and piousness through the humbling process of begging for food, etc., while studying scripture.
9. *Abuna* is the title for the leader (patriarch) of the Ethiopian Orthodox Church.
10. Adamu is referring to the woven straw sculptures that he has made. He produces bells, crosses, picture frames, etc., (see fig. 5, p. 20).
11. *Abba* is an honorific meaning "father."
12. *Biha* is a soft stone that is easy to carve.
13. When the bride and groom partake in Holy Communion.
14. *Ato* is an Amharic word meaning "Mr."
15. Adamu is implying that his first marriage was over. Church law, however, dictates that anyone married in the Ethiopian Orthodox Church cannot divorce. Doing so, only four years after his ordination, Adamu relinquished his position as a priest.
16. *Qurban* is the term Adamu uses, which refers to the taking of bread and wine. In this case, however, it is a euphemism for abstention from sexual relations.
17. *Gendi* is heavy parchment sometimes used for paintings destined for the export market.
18. An *azmari* is a musician/singer; *baltet* is an elderly woman; *kahin* is a priest.
19. Adamu is referring to Raymond Silverman and Neal Sobania.
20. The *qine mahilet* is the choir of an Ethiopian Orthodox church.
21. Saint Yared, who lived in the sixth century, is remembered for introducing music into the Ethiopian Orthodox liturgy.

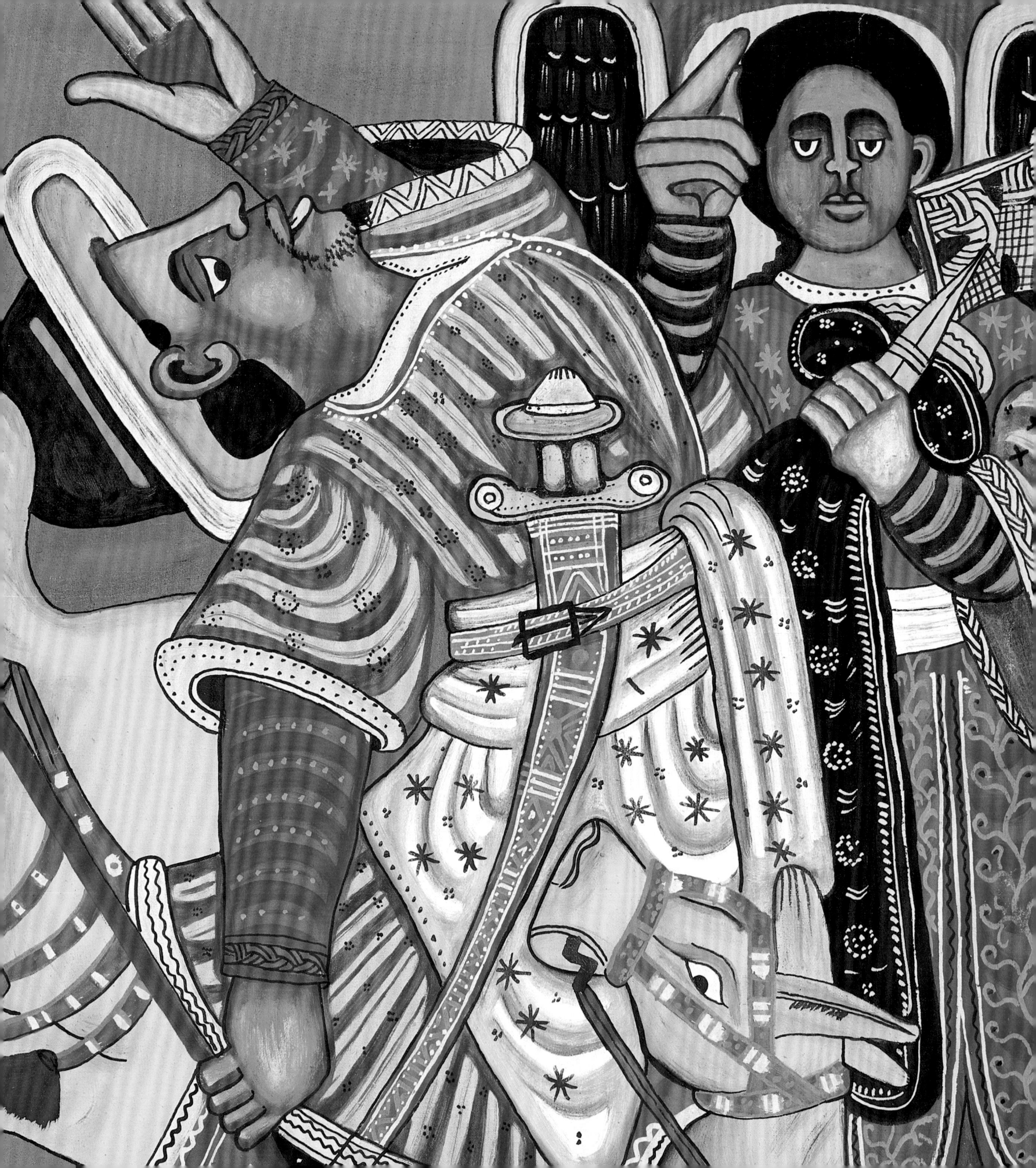

Painting Ethiopia

THE LIFE AND WORK OF QES ADAMU TESFAW

RAYMOND A. SILVERMAN

It was on my first visit to Ethiopia in 1991 that I encountered the work of Qes[1] Adamu Tesfaw. I was at the Institute of Ethiopian Studies (IES) viewing paintings of religious and historical subjects and scenes of everyday life executed by Ethiopian artists in what is sometimes described as a "traditional idiom" when I was struck by a single canvas by Qes Adamu. Although the precise subject of the painting has receded from my memory, I will never forget the boldly drawn composition; the elongated heads, hands, and bodies; the distinctive treatment of the faces—their foreheads and long straight noses drawn on the same flat plane with the brow running perpendicular to create a sharply angular, almost faceted effect. The figures were possessed of a strength, a monumentality, that is rarely encountered in twentieth-century "traditional" Ethiopian painting.

Two years later, I again found myself in Ethiopia, this time with my colleague Neal Sobania, conducting research for an exhibition dealing with a number of Ethiopian visual traditions.[2] It was on that visit that I decided to locate Qes Adamu. We had been told that he lived in Addis Ababa, but no one seemed to know exactly where. Further, rumor had it that he was something of a recluse. Pursuing our investigation, we contacted the artist Wondimu Wonde,[3] a close friend of Adamu's,

1 Exterior of Qes Adamu's house in the Weira District of Addis Ababa. Photograph by Raymond Silverman, 1993.

2 Mural portrait of a priest painted by Adamu on a wall at the entrance to his house. Photograph by Raymond Silverman, Addis Ababa, 2002.

3 Adamu's paintings of *Saint George Slaying the Dragon* and the *Madonna and Child* on one of the walls of his house. Photograph by Raymond Silverman, Addis Ababa, 2003.

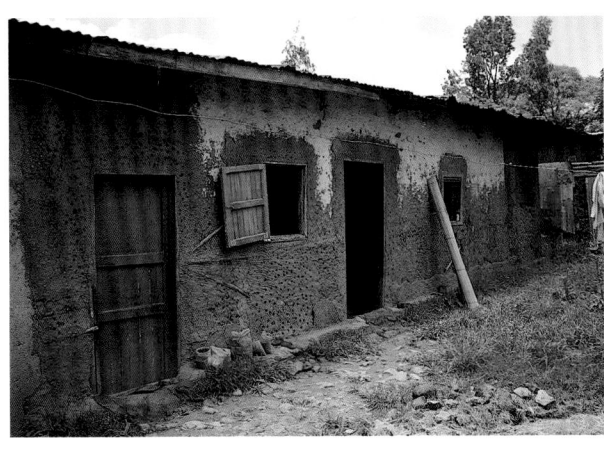

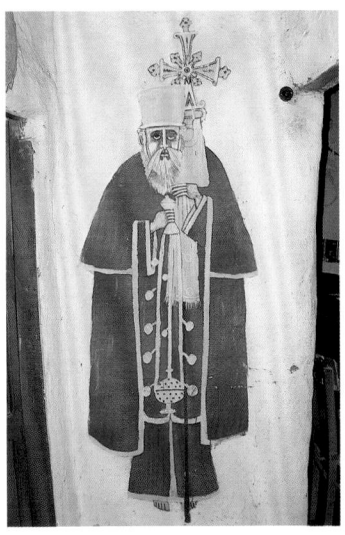

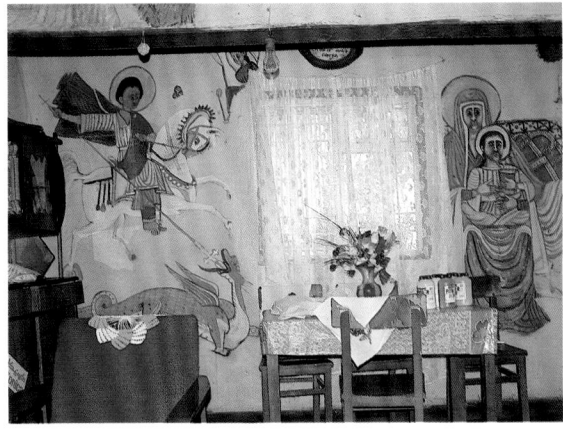

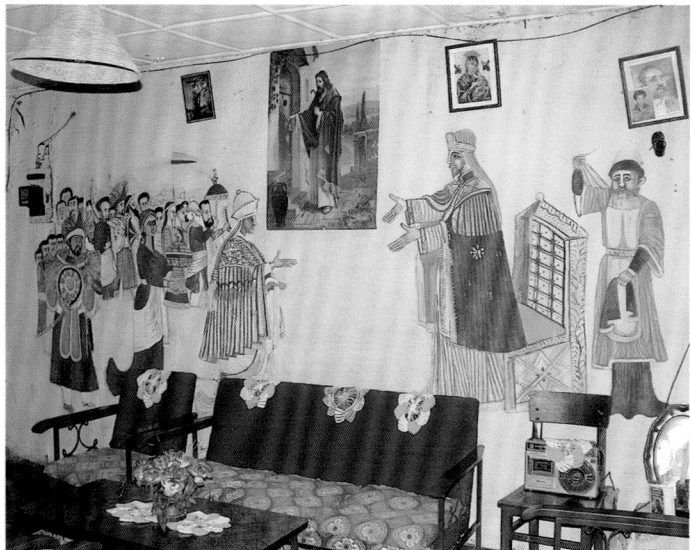
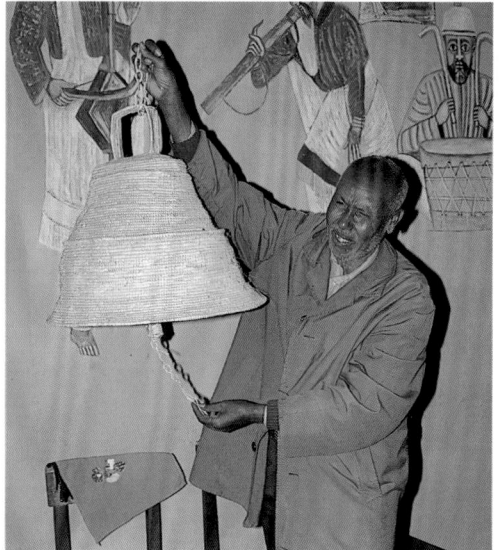
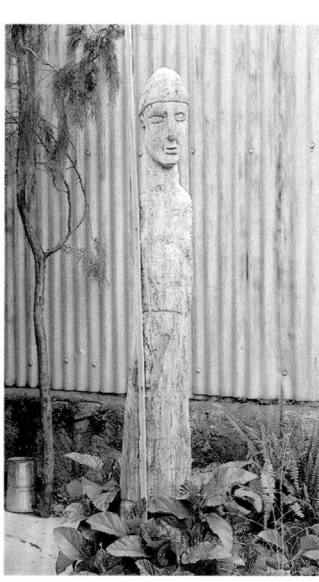

4 A painting by Qes Adamu of *King Solomon Receiving the Queen of Sheba* on a wall inside his home. Photographs of members of Adamu's family and commercial prints of Christian religious figures also decorate the wall. One of Adamu's woven straw bells hangs from the ceiling in the upper-left corner. Photograph by Raymond Silverman, Addis Ababa, 2003.

5 Qes Adamu displaying one of his woven straw bells. Photograph by Neal Sobania, Addis Ababa, 2002.

6 A warrior carved by Adamu from the trunk of a tree stands in his yard. Photograph by Raymond Silverman, Addis Ababa, 2004.

and although he either could or would not reveal Adamu's address, he did volunteer to arrange a meeting with him. This was our first experience with the relationships of painters and their agents in the Addis Ababa art market, a dynamic that I will explore further below with reference to its impact on the reception of Qes Adamu's paintings.

After several attempts to connect, Neal finally managed to meet Adamu at Wondimu's house one afternoon in May 1993 and then drove Adamu home. Returning from this initial meeting, Neal enthused "you're not going to believe this guy's house!" A few days later we visited Qes Adamu's home located in the Weira District of southwest Addis Ababa. Walking up to the house for the first time, an unexceptional wattle and daub structure (fig. 1), I wondered what Neal had meant, but as soon as I stepped inside I was stunned. Every wall was covered with figurative paintings—a life-size image of an Ethiopian Orthodox priest greeted me on first entering (fig. 2), images of Saint George Slaying the Dragon, the Madonna and Child (fig. 3), the Queen of Sheba's visit to King Solomon (fig. 4), Saint Yared,[4] and musicians and clergymen in procession covered the walls of the living-dining room, or "salon," as it is known in Ethiopia.[5] Never before had I seen domestic mural painting. Eleven years and many visits later, I have yet to encounter such paintings in another Ethiopian home.[6] Furthermore, each of the compositions exhibited a monumentality—a distinctive manner of rendering human and animal figures that had captured my eye two years earlier.

On each of the many subsequent visits that I have paid to Adamu's home, the images on the walls have changed. Sometimes Qes Adamu has "refreshed" the paintings, other times he has altered their compositions, adding or removing figures.[7] A truly creative spirit, he possesses a passion bordering on obsession for "making things"(figs. 5, 6). He once related that he has a "love for painting" and "dreams about it most of the time" (Silverman 1999, 135). As he recounts in his autobiographical statement (see pp. 15–17), even as a young boy, he was consumed with a desire to draw and would sketch with charcoal on virtually any surface, including rocks and shards of broken pottery.[8] "When I was walking along and found a piece of charcoal," he once recalled, "I would sketch something on the rocks. If someone was walking on a path that I had been down, they would know that I had gone down that path!"

Qes Adamu Tesfaw is an artist whose work defies easy categorization. He is at once a devotional painter, a popular painter, a traditional painter, a genre painter, a history painter, and a commercial

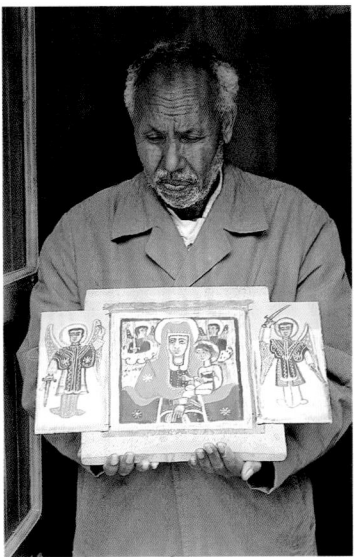 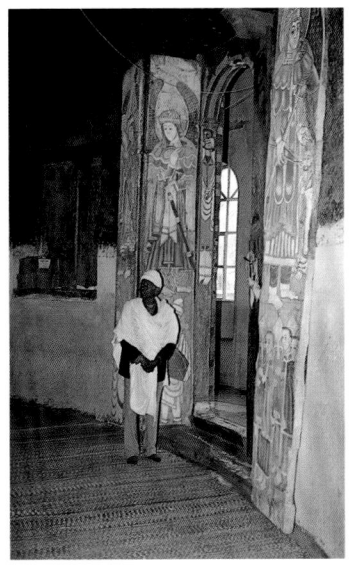 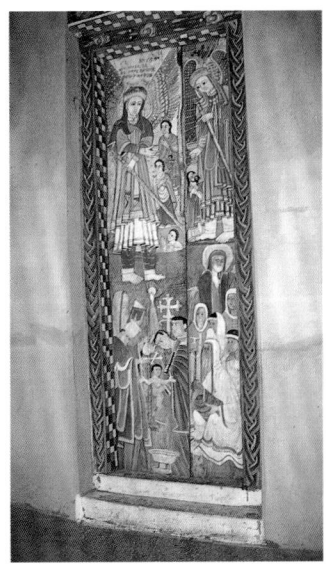

7 Adamu holding one of his icons, a triptych. Photograph by Raymond Silverman, Addis Ababa, 2001.

8 Qes Adamu's large paintings on cloth adorn the doors and windows of the *qine mahilet,* or choir, in the church of Bichena Giyorgis. A priest, Meleake Berhan Ayalew Wasse, stands in front of the door at the left. Photograph by Raymond Silverman, Bichena, 1997.

9 One of Adamu's large painted doors in the church of Bichena Giyorgis. Depicted are Saints Rafael and Urael, above, and a baptism, below. Photograph by Raymond Silverman, Bichena, 1997.

painter. On one hand, he is an artist schooled in the philosophy and aesthetics of a fifteen-hundred-year-old tradition associated with the Ethiopian Orthodox Church.[9] His artwork, on the other hand, is often eccentric and individual—sometimes in response to the vagaries and complexities of the Addis Ababa art market—and Adamu has thus in some ways transcended the confines of his artistic education.

Students of twentieth-century African art have long struggled with artists like Qes Adamu, not knowing exactly how to classify them or their work. A good deal has been written about postcolonial urban art and its association with the concept of modernity. But recently the basic premise upon which these discussions have been based—that the art of twentieth- and now twenty-first-century Africa must be classified as either "traditional" or "modern"—has been reexamined.[10] Is Qes Adamu a "traditional" or a "modern" artist? This is a tough question, one that raises complex cultural and historical issues concerning the nature of tradition and modernity in Ethiopia, and perhaps more significantly, the nature of how Western scholarship has engaged the visual cultures of not only Ethiopia, but the entire continent. An examination of Adamu's complex and visually compelling paintings reveals much about this complicated debate, while at the same time providing significant information about Ethiopia and Ethiopians.

Religious Imagery in Ethiopian Art

Religious imagery of the sort found in Qes Adamu's paintings has historically appeared in three contexts: illustrations (i.e., illuminations) on parchment in religious manuscripts; wood panel paintings (i.e., icons); and murals on the walls of Orthodox churches. Qes Adamu has worked in all three media (fig. 7).[11] Most of his energy, however, has been spent producing large paintings on cloth, which are associated with the mural tradition (figs. 8, 9).

Mural paintings have long been situated in churches and monasteries in highland Ethiopia, and before the twentieth century, the primary patrons of such institutions were members of the aristocracy, who alone possessed the means to sponsor these projects.[12] To this day, members of the Ethiopian Orthodox Church believe that making such gifts is a means of attaining God's protection and of ultimately securing a place in heaven. Once installed, paintings of the saints, especially the Virgin Mary and Saint George, become a medium through which individuals can seek spiritual intervention in their lives. In a society with a historically high rate of illiteracy, especially in rural areas, such paintings, which include imagery from both the Old and New Testaments, also serve a didactic end (figs. 10, 11). Qes Adamu is very much aware of this extremely important educational

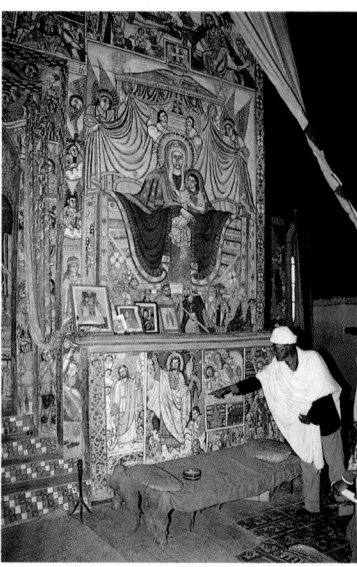 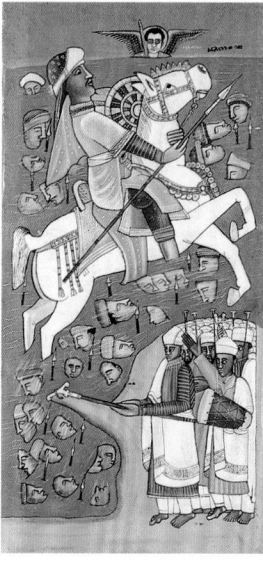 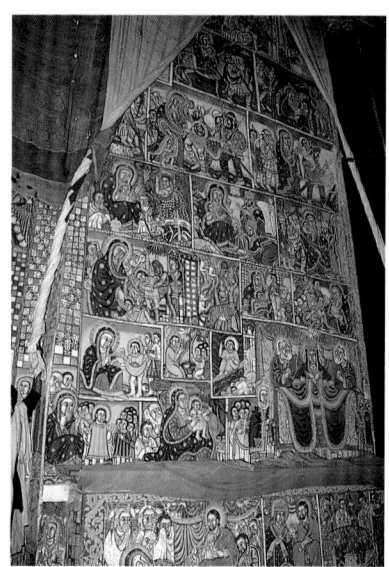

10 A priest, Meleake Berhan Ayalew Wasse, explains the paintings on the west wall of the *meqdes,* or sanctuary, of the church of Bichena Giyorgis. Devotional mural paintings serve an important didactic function in the Ethiopian Orthodox Church. Photograph by Raymond Silverman, Bichena, 1997.

11 Qes Adamu Tesfaw. *Pharaoh Crossing the Red Sea,* circa 1980–1995. Paint on cloth. 198 x 90 cm. Collection of the Institute of Ethiopian Studies, Addis Ababa University, no. 10321. Photograph by Raymond Silverman. This is an example of one of Adamu's Old Testament Paintings

12 Paintings on the south wall of the *meqdes* in the church of Bichena Giyorgis depicting the life and miracles of Saint Mary. Photograph by Raymond Silverman, Bichena, 1997.

function, one that today extends well beyond the teachings of the church. As he once pointed out, in the course of discussing his painting dealing with the subject of HIV/AIDS (cat. no. 34), "This painting is my gift to help teach. I am a painter, so I teach through my paintings."

The limited biographical information available for artists, like Adamu, who work in Addis Ababa reveals that many of them originally came from Gojjam, a region where there was a rich tradition of painting churches and the palaces of provincial rulers. The period from the last quarter of the nineteenth century to the early twentieth century was particularly fertile for church painting and painters in Gojjam. Negus Tekle Haymanot (r. 1881–1901), who ruled the province during this peaceful period, was known for building new churches and refurbishing old ones.[13]

Ethiopian art historian Abebaw Ayalew (2002, 18, 20) informs us that Bichena Giyorgis—the central church in Bichena where Qes Adamu began his religious education and was first introduced to painting—was rebuilt and decorated (i.e., painted) first under the patronage of Ras Hailu I (r. 1777–1795) during the second half of the eighteenth century and again, roughly one hundred years later, by Negus Tekle Haymanot. The latter's son and successor, Ras Hailu II (r. 1901–1932), continued his father's program by engaging one of Gojjam's leading painters, Aleqa[14] Hailu, who worked with three other local church-trained painters, Desta, Wudu, and Adamu's uncle, Aleqa Kassa Getahun, to paint the four exterior walls of the church's *meqdes.*[15] It was these paintings that inspired the young Adamu Tesfaw, who initially thought them to be the work of angels (figs. 10, 12). Adamu continues to regard them as the finest paintings he has ever seen.

The decorative programs of churches often included secular elements as well. It is generally held that the first non-religious elements to appear in religious paintings, probably in the eighteenth century, are representations of the donors who commissioned the works. At that time, such figures were usually depicted prostrate in a gesture of supplication. Later, in the nineteenth century, however, donors began to be portrayed standing, first by themselves, then accompanied by a spouse, and finally, by the end of the century, in the presence of the entire family (Abebaw Ayalew 2002, 125). During the first half of the nineteenth century, paintings documenting the military exploits of the country's rulers appeared in the churches of Gojjam, and by the turn of the century, these scenes had become quite prominent. In Bichena Giyorgis, for instance, a magnificent processional featuring Negus Tekle Haymanot and Ras Hailu II occupies the entire lower register of the east wall of the *meqdes* (fig. 13).

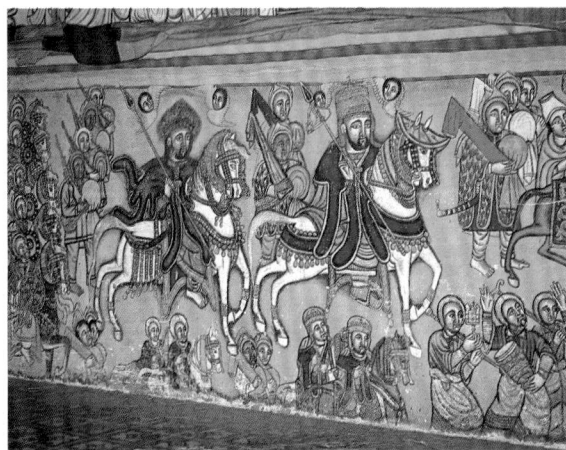

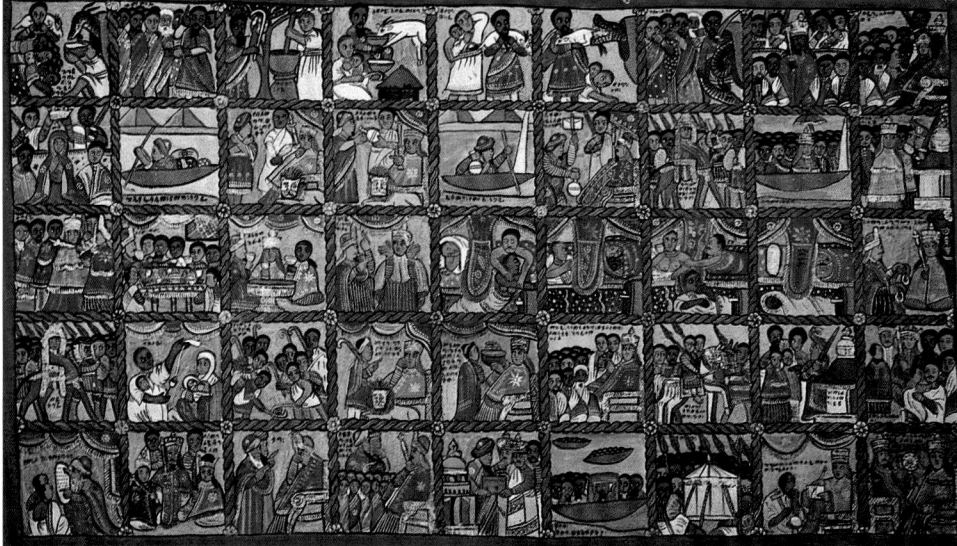

13 Detail of a painting depicting Negus Tekle Haymanot and Ras Hailu II located at the base of the east wall of the *meqdes* of Bichena Giyorgis. Photograph by Raymond Silverman, Bichena, 1997.

14 Artist unknown. Story of the Queen of Sheba, circa 1930. Paint on cloth. 81 x 142 cm. Collection of Suzanne Oliver-Miers, on loan to Michigan State University Museum, no. L202.9. Photograph by Raymond Silverman. This painting relates in serial form the story of the Queen of Sheba (known as Makida in Ethiopia). The painting is unsigned, and the artist's name was not recorded when it was collected.

Bahilawi and *Zemenawi* Painters

The urban-based painting tradition in which Qes Adamu participates grew out of practices associated with the Ethiopian Orthodox Church. Painters who had first learned their art while receiving a church education in towns like Bichena came to Addis Ababa as early as the end of the nineteenth century. There they developed a new genre of painting, one directed at a recently developed market: foreign visitors to Ethiopia. Richard Pankhurst, a historian of Ethiopian culture and society, notes that "Little or no commercialization of traditional art appears to have taken place until the very end of the 19th or beginning of the 20th century, in other words, until after the establishment of Addis Ababa, the advent of the foreign legations and the emergence of a sizeable foreign community" (1966, 23). Some of these artists continued to receive commissions to paint churches, while also producing paintings on cloth and parchment for sale to foreigners. Until quite recently, there remained a community of church-based painters in Addis Ababa, most of whom had come from the provinces of Gojjam, Begemdir, and Shewa.[16]

Belatchew Yimer (c. 1894–1957), who had painted churches in Gojjam and Begemdir before moving to Addis Ababa in the late 1910s or 1920s was one of the pioneers of urban painting (Pankhurst 1966, 39). He was famous for his serial (comic strip-like) interpretations of the story of the Queen of Sheba, who is known in Ethiopia as Makida (fig. 14). This was and still is the most popular genre of urban painting, and Belatchew was one of its first and best painters. He was also known for his hunting scenes and portraits of Ethiopian and foreign dignitaries. The latter are particularly interesting because they reveal the impact that photography had on painting at this time. Images of contemporary political figures were often inspired by official photographic portraits, and they typically utilized increased modeling (i.e., the play of light and shadow to define three-dimensional surfaces) in order to achieve a greater degree of naturalism than had previously been encountered in Ethiopian painting (fig. 15).[17] Like Belatchew, a number of urban artists worked in multiple idioms.[18]

Significantly, Adamu Tesfaw chose not to pursue "modern" modes of visual representation. Though he has worked from photographs in magazines for some of his compositions, including *Haile Selassie Receiving Queen Elizabeth* (cat. no. 24) and *Haile Selassie's Visit to Jamaica* (figs. 16, 17), he has consciously chosen not to emulate the photographic realism that one encounters in the work of some Ethiopian painters. He refers to those paintings that he does model after photographs or reproductions of paintings found in books as "photocopies." When asked why he does not produce naturalistic portraits, Adamu states that it was a conscious decision. He believes that he could easily

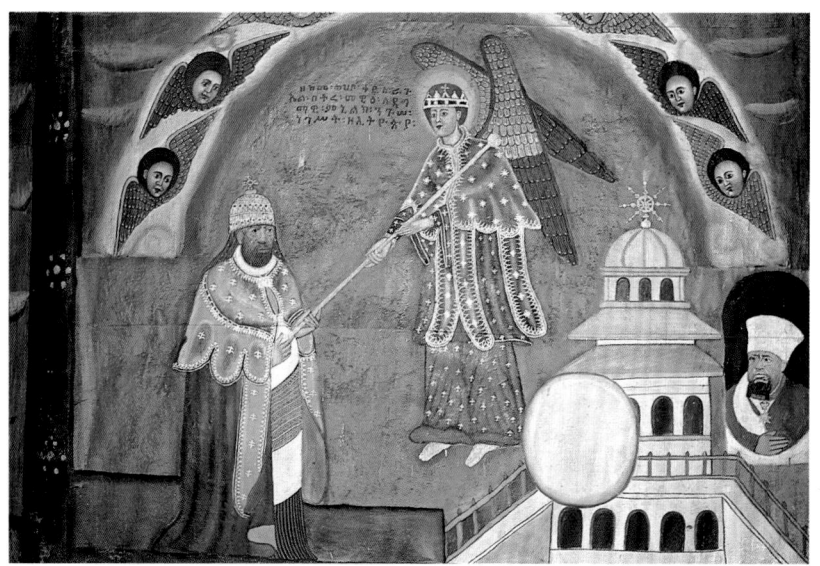

15 This painting of Emperor Menilek II and Saint Raguel is found inside the Church of Saint Raguel on Entoto, a mountain located at the northern edge of Addis Ababa. The church was built in the late nineteenth century by Menilek II. In the painting, Saint Raguel (the winged figure on the right) has been rendered in the traditional style by the painter Aleqa Lukas, while the standing figure of Menilek II, especially his face, has been painted more naturalistically by Aleqa Lukas's son, Sahlu. A contemporary photograph was used as the basis for Sahlu's portrait of the emperor. Photograph by Raymond Silverman, 1991.

develop the skill to produce more naturalistic, or as he refers to them, "modern," paintings. But, Qes Adamu perceives himself as a "traditional" painter. He knows there are various idioms of visual expression, and he differentiates between approaches to painting that one may loosely equate with the Western notions of "traditional" and "modern." In making this distinction, he uses the Amharic expressions *bahilawi* and *zemenawi* respectively. Significantly, the root of *bahilawi* is *bahil*, meaning "culture" or "tradition." *Zemenawi* is derived from *zemen*, the word for "era" or "period," and conveys a sense of that which is current, of the moment, contemporary. These terms are more specific than "traditional" and "modern" and actually offer a more accurate sense of how Adamu understands the production of art in Ethiopia at the turn of the millennium.[19] Qes Adamu sees himself as a *bahilawi* painter—a painter grounded in his culture. He explains that he paints primarily subjects that one finds in the Ethiopian Orthodox Bible and other religious texts, and in a style that has deep roots in Ethiopia.

Adamu speaks about *bahilawi* painting being more difficult ("more tiring" is the expression he uses) than *zemenawi* painting, indicating that if he did not know "cultural" painting, he would be painting in the modern style because it is easier. *Bahilawi* painting is "tiring" because one must create imagery that tells a specific story in a way that can be read or understood by everyone.

His godfather and former mentor, the well-known painter Yohannis Tesemma, advised Adamu to stick with the idiom he had learned as a youth and to develop it into his own distinctive style because there was a better market for this sort of painting among foreigners. Qes Adamu believes that he made the right decision and that he has made a contribution to sustaining a beautiful and important tradition.

He has noted, however, that within the idiom of *bahilawi,* producing paintings of religious subjects is particularly difficult because of their tightly defined "histories." Today, he prefers, in fact, to paint secular subjects and has explained that in

> the past, my interest was making paintings of saints or things of that sort. Nowadays, my interest has shifted. I like to make paintings having to do with culture, social life, politics [i.e., affairs of state], palace decorum, and daily life. I may still produce more paintings related to the former, but if the circumstances were different, I would focus more on the latter. It has a lot to do with creativity. Making paintings of secular subjects gives me the freedom to introduce creativity to my work. It gives me more room, more flexibility, to apply new features, deal with more themes, in short, I can expand, for these subjects are not static. You do not have this opportunity when working on

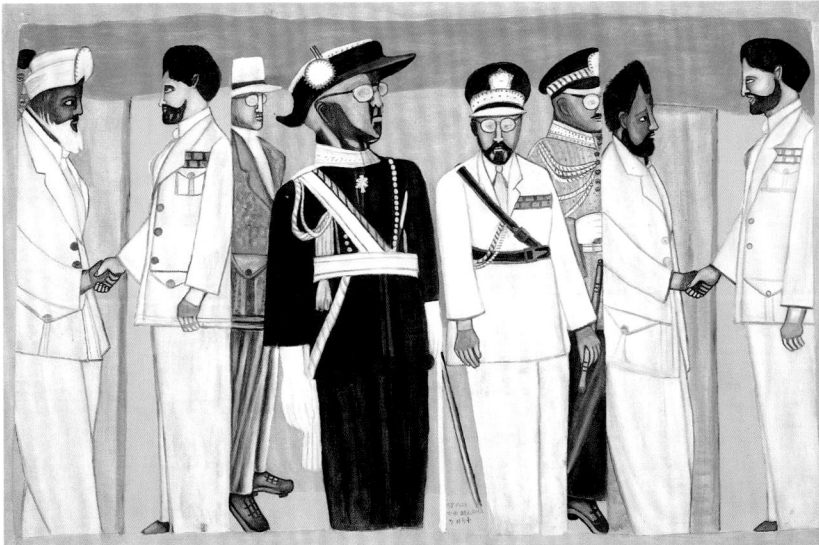
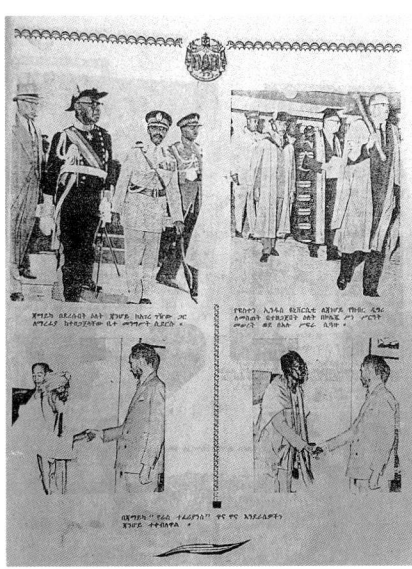

16 Qes Adamu Tesfaw. *Haile Selassie's Visit to Jamaica*, 2003. Paint on cloth. 100 x 152 cm. Collection of Leah Niederstadt. Photograph by Don Cole.

17 Photographs documenting Haile Selassie's visit to Jamaica in 1966, taken from a popular publication chronicling the emperor's life. Adamu owns a copy of the book and used these photographs in painting *Haile Selassie's Visit to Jamaica* (fig. 16). Photograph by Raymond Silverman, Addis Ababa, 2004.

religious paintings. You can't introduce even the slightest changes in paintings that convey sacred messages. Doing so may have serious consequences [i.e., may be construed as blasphemy].... Whereas working with secular subjects does not impose such limitations. You can use your imagination and make changes. In terms of importance, church-related paintings are held in higher esteem, but non-religious themes provide the best setting for creative work and stir more creativity and interest in me. It is like [the excitement and pleasure derived from] riding a horse or swimming in a river.

Inspiration, Individuality, and the Realities of the Marketplace

Much of Qes Adamu's inspiration derives from observation. Over the course of his life, he has viewed paintings in many Orthodox churches, he has studied countless religious texts, many of them illuminated, and has lived for over seventy years—during the first part of his life, in Bichena, and for the last forty-five years, in Addis Ababa. He draws upon all this experience as he formulates ideas for his paintings.

> Old paintings have always brought new light to me, they move me. Whatever aspect of an old painting I may attend to—it could be the rendering of an eye, a forehead, a countenance, or an eyebrow—I receive new inspiration, especially when I want to draw or paint the images of saints. For other things, including natural or social themes, I use my own imagination and creativity based on observations. Old paintings are also a source from which I get information, for instance, about costumes for my paintings. When I am telling a story from an earlier period, I need to depict clothes that are no longer worn today, no longer part of our culture. Knowledge of this sort can only be obtained from the books that contain paintings [and paintings in churches]. But I also add new features if the need arises, like using new styles of clothing. I am open to using the old and incorporating new elements.

Apropos the inspiration he has drawn from various religious texts, especially for painting sacred imagery, Adamu notes: "When I read books, I take interest in the stories, and these somehow produce images and visions, which I later use to make paintings. Stories in the scriptures help me to visualize things in my mind, which, as a result, provide the substance for making paintings. There are sometimes pictures that accompany the stories that might provide the initial basis for my work. I develop them further, based on the narratives, to provide a fuller picture."

In 2002, we gave Adamu a notebook containing reproductions of roughly one hundred and fifty of his paintings and asked him to select thirty that he would like to see in the current exhibition of his work. We made it clear that his choices would inform the exhibition team but that there were other criteria we needed to consider when making the final selection for *Painting Ethiopia*.[20] This proved an extremely revealing exercise. Seven of the thirty paintings Adamu chose were selected for the exhibition.[21] In almost every case, his rationale for selecting a specific work concerned the subject and not the painting's formal qualities. It is the significance of the stories that Qes Adamu insists is the most important feature. For example, when I asked why he selected the painting of sheep being sold at a rural market (cat. no. 30), he explained, "This is about sheep. Sheep represent simplicity, sacrifice, innocence, saintliness, righteousness. Sheep, on the other hand, also have a lot of [practical] significance for Ethiopians. We buy sheep from the market and slaughter them during holidays, they hold a central place in that collective experience. So they are doubly important, their symbolic significance and their utilitarian value [as a source of food]." Indeed, when asked on numerous occasions to comment on the formal qualities of his paintings—for instance, composition or color—Adamu has only rarely offered any insight into his visual thinking. One such occasion occurred when he learned that we had selected a painting depicting *Haile Selassie Receiving Queen Elizabeth* maintained in the IES collection. He was adamant that we had not made a good decision and that the painting in the Sobania collection (cat. no. 24) was a much better example of the subject. He pointed out that there was a great deal more detail and the palette was much livelier in the Sobania painting. For the most part, however, he either cannot or chooses not to articulate why he does what he does.

Attempts at engaging Adamu in comparing his work to the work of other artists have proven futile. He basically refuses to comment on the quality of the work of other painters. When shown the work of one of his peers, he usually remarks that it is a good painting because it successfully tells such and such a story and leaves it at that. In 1993, the first time we asked him about three paintings, which we had purchased from the artist-merchant Solomon Belatchew and which we suspected to be Adamu's work (this was before we learned he had a business relationship with Solomon; see below), he was reluctant to say much about them.[22] He wouldn't even acknowledge they were his own.

It is curious that on several occasions Adamu has observed that he must have produced thousands of paintings over the years, always adding that he probably would not be able to recognize many of them. This comment may be an expression of a cultural environment that basically eschews individuality.[23] Indeed, prior to the nineteenth century, there was a general proscription against signing paintings, especially those destined for the walls of churches. Creating religious imagery was an act of piety, and as a result, the priests and monks who produced paintings for churches seldom identified themselves; to do so was regarded as a conceit in the eyes of God.[24] For the last hundred years, the impetus for signing paintings—specifically those produced for foreigners—has come from the people who have purchased them. Adamu explains that some people would not buy a painting from him unless it was signed. Interestingly, there are others who required that he not sign his paintings— a situation that will be discussed at length below.

Qes Adamu possesses a genuine modesty that also contributes to this situation. He does not see himself as an exceptional painter, although he is aware that his paintings are different from the work of others. "There are differences in our approach, design, selection of colors, and the way we paint, though the history [i.e., subject matter] is the same." He does not view the work of other artists in any sort of comparative or competitive light. It is his own expressive impulse that motivates him to create his exceptional, often unique, visual narratives.

There have been a few occasions when Qes Adamu has commented on the formal aspects of his paintings. In a November 2001 conversation, he noted, "My weakness is height, I can't overcome that.... I tend to exaggerate the height of the figures in my paintings. I also tend to turn circles into

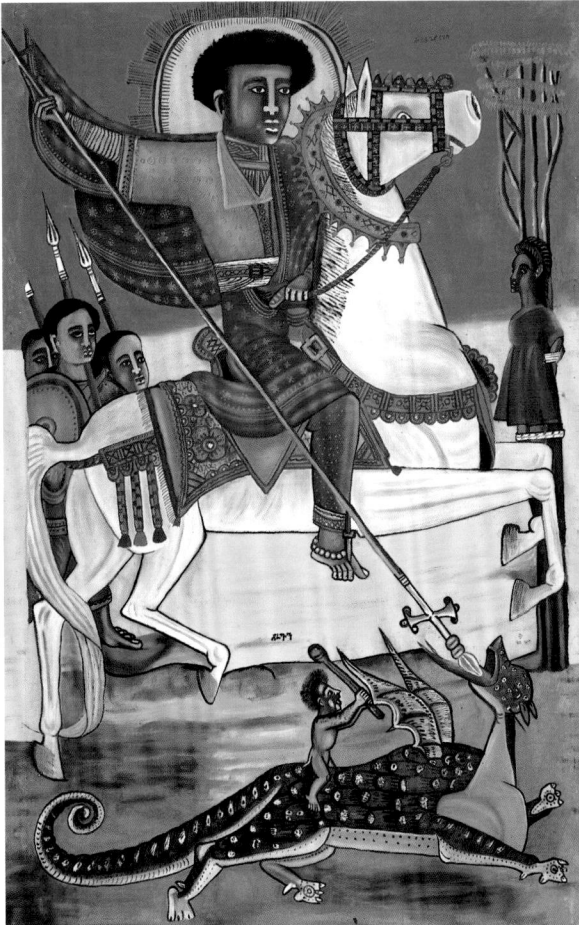 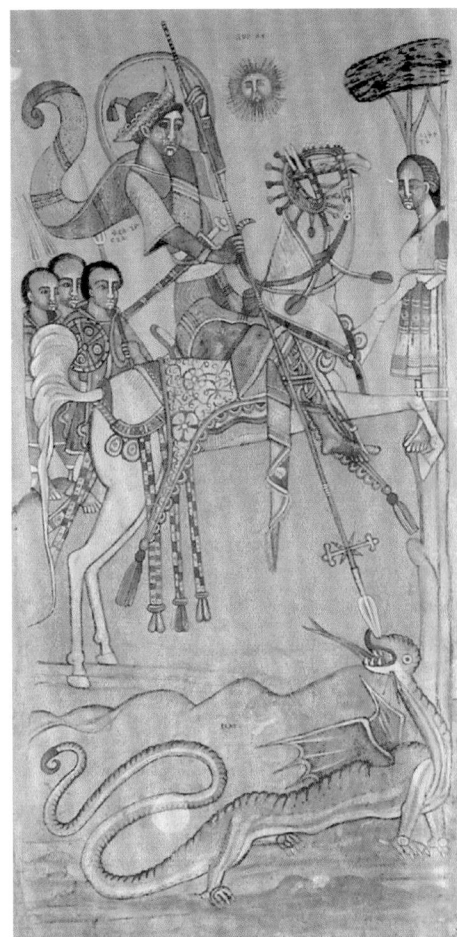

18 Qes Adamu Tesfaw. *Saint George Slaying the Dragon,* 2001. Paint on cloth. 156 x 100 cm. Collection of Leah Niederstadt. Photograph by Don Cole.

19 Qes Adamu Tesfaw. *Saint George Slaying the Dragon,* circa 1980–1995. Paint on cloth. 185 x 91 cm. Collection of the Institute of Ethiopian Studies, Addis Ababa University, no. 10326. Photograph by Raymond Silverman.

ovals, to make things bulge out a bit." Two years later, Adamu elaborated on this, "It all depends on the 'gifts' you have. I can't help it, this is the way I intuitively do it.... No matter how hard I try to overcome this, I cannot get away from it. It is embedded in me. It is my natural inclination. Artists have different inclinations. Some tend to exaggerate while others do not. It is a question of artistic identity." Adamu has always appreciated the critical feedback he has received from fellow painters, patrons, his wife, and his children, but he highlights the importance of listening to his own inner voice or spirit. "It is not bad to listen to people's ideas but it is also not a good thing to ignore your intuition that compels you to do things in certain ways."

Qes Adamu does not copy other paintings, even his own, unless he is commissioned to do so. Indeed, one of the truly amazing aspects of his work is that despite his having painted any number of religious subjects hundreds of times, no two compositions are the same. He treats each painting as a new problem. One can begin to appreciate this creative energy looking at the three interpretations of *Saint George Slaying the Dragon* presented in the exhibition (cat. nos. 6–8), the mural painting in Adamu's home (see fig. 3), and several other examples of this popular subject (figs. 18–20).

Static compositions are characteristic of the painting tradition in which Qes Adamu was trained. There is usually little sense of movement in either religious or secular narratives. One of the hallmarks of Adamu's paintings, however—one that sets him apart from other artists working in the same idiom—is a dynamism, a sense of what he refers to as "movement and action." It is apparent, for example, in his painting of *Saint Gigar Slapping King Herod,* in which the composition is comprised of two figures on horseback galloping across the picture plane (cat. no. 9). Once again, Adamu explains

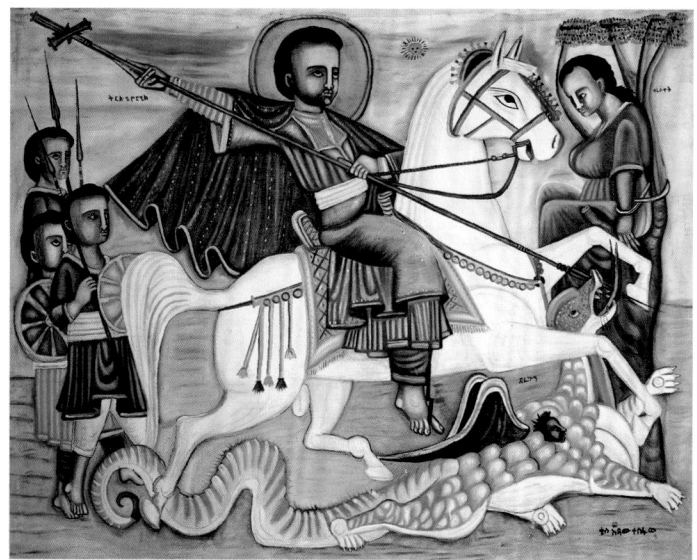

20 Qes Adamu Tesfaw. *Saint George Slaying the Dragon*, 1993. Paint on cloth. 135 x 173 cm. Collection of Michigan State University Museum, no. 7557.35. Photograph by Kim Kauffman.

that his interest in finding ways to portray movement and action is innate, part of who he is, "some sort of movement must be expressed in painting, it must express life."

This painting of Saint Gigar also projects a "presence" that is again exceptional. Adamu actually works in two distinctive idioms. One may be called his monumental style and presents narratives with a limited number of large figures, often just one or two. In addition to *Saint Gigar Slapping King Herod*, we might consider *Solomon and Sheba Embrace* (cat. no. 15) or *Descent from the Cross* (cat. no. 1) as examples of this approach. Adamu also produces compositions with many small figures engaging in a common activity or historical event—his miniature style. Many of his paintings of the Battle of Adwa are presented in this manner (cat. nos. 20, 21 and fig. 21). Interestingly, he also creates monumental compositions depicting this important historical event, such as *Menilek and Taitu at Adwa*, which emphasize the power and majesty of the emperor, and especially of the empress, as they lead the Ethiopian troops in the decisive battle against the Italians (cat. no. 23).[25] Other examples of Adamu's miniature style include *Returning to the Church* (cat. no. 12), *Gugs* (cat. no. 28), *Entering Addis Ababa* (cat. no. 25), and *The City of Addis Ababa* (cat. no. 35).

Looking at paintings that Qes Adamu has completed over the last forty years, it is apparent that he has used many color schemes. Sometimes he employs bright, vibrant colors, at other times the hues are dark and somber. Sometimes the pigments are opaque, at other times they are applied so thinly that they are almost transparent. Some of this variation is due to the nature of the paints Qes Adamu has had at his disposal.[26] Often the darker paintings—those that use brown and toned-down red or magenta—are compositions that are intentionally painted to look old. These are produced on pieces of old *netela* (a gauze-like cloth used for women's and men's clothing) that he has prepared with *muq* (a wheat paste used to transform the cloth into a viable painting surface) mixed with ash and soil. These paintings are sometimes torn or frayed at the edges to enhance the illusion of age (fig. 22). When asked why he produces these paintings, he replied simply, "there is a market for them." This is what merchants like Solomon Belatchew have asked him to produce because this is what foreigners often want—old paintings. In fact, the first paintings by Adamu that I acquired were purchased from Solomon at his shop in 1993 and looked to be old paintings (cat. no. 9). Significantly, most of Adamu's paintings in the IES collection were recently purchased from the same shop and appear to be old paintings as well. Adamu has even produced painting fragments, such as images of angels that appear to have been torn from the walls or ceilings of churches (fig. 23). His skill at creating this aura of age and "authenticity" was poignantly demonstrated when we took the eighteen paintings from

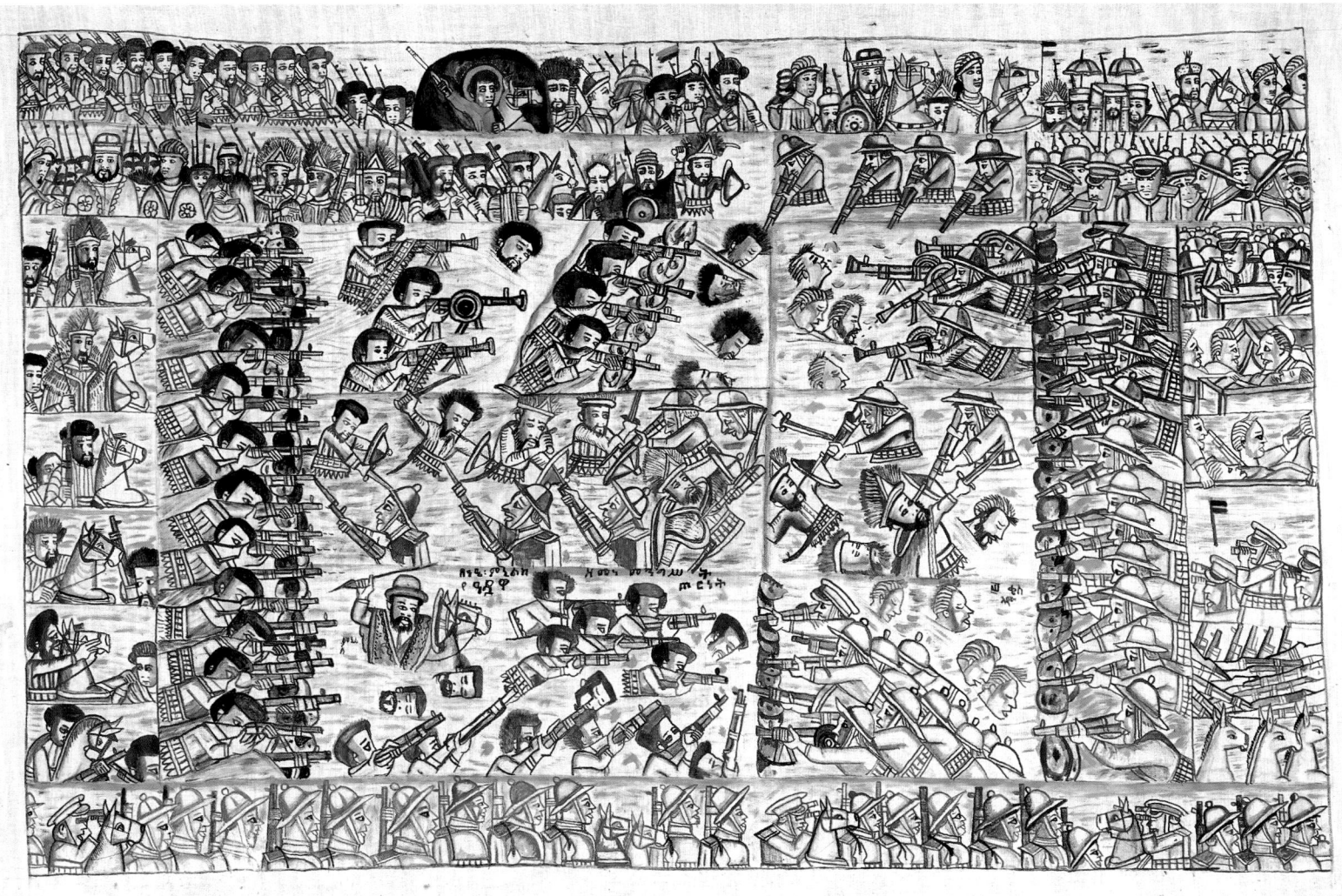

21 Qes Adamu Tesfaw. *Battle of Adwa,* 2002. Paint on cloth. 102 x 154 cm. FMCH X2003.13.4; Anonymous Gift. Photograph by Don Cole.

the IES collection that are included in the catalog section of this volume to the National Museum in Addis Ababa to obtain a permit required to ship them to Los Angeles. Initially, the inspectors refused to issue the permit because they thought the paintings to be historic works that should not leave the country. The tradition of creating "antiquities" for the art market is a phenomenon found all over Africa—indeed, all over the world.[27]

While accommodating the demands of the market, Adamu has employed a variety of palettes. One of his more striking experiments is a basically monochromatic composition in which he uses a single color with the occasional touch of other colors to accentuate important aspects of the composition. A good example is his recent painting of the *Battle of Adwa* in which he uses mostly brown with touches of green for the entire composition, but then draws the viewer's attention to the presence of Saint George at the top of painting with the use of blue and red (fig. 21). This is a very effective and unusual treatment of the popular subject. Most of the paintings we have seen at Adamu's home over the last ten years, as well as those that I have commissioned from him, employ a much brighter palette than those that Solomon Belatchew ordered for sale to tourists in his shop (see below). Adamu actually prefers to use more vibrant colors. Indeed, he says that his favorite color is yellow.

During one of our visits to Qes Adamu's home, he pulled out a pile of paintings he had recently completed. Among them was a stunning scene of people traveling to a rural market (fig. 24).

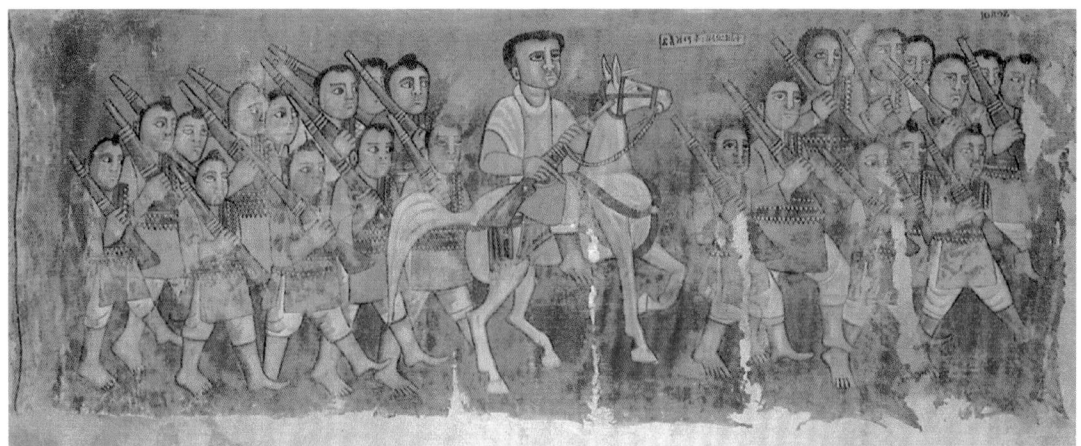

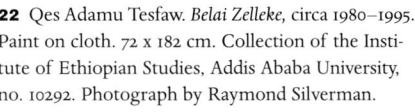

22 Qes Adamu Tesfaw. *Belai Zelleke,* circa 1980–1995. Paint on cloth. 72 x 182 cm. Collection of the Institute of Ethiopian Studies, Addis Ababa University, no. 10292. Photograph by Raymond Silverman.

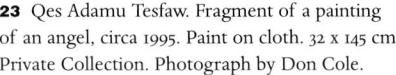

23 Qes Adamu Tesfaw. Fragment of a painting of an angel, circa 1995. Paint on cloth. 32 x 145 cm. Private Collection. Photograph by Don Cole.

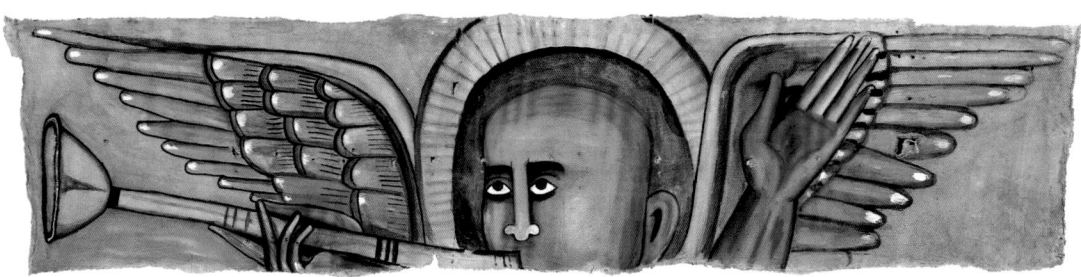

What is remarkable about this painting is that all of the figures in it are viewed from behind—one sees only the backs of people, horses, and donkeys. There are several other paintings in which the artist has used this same approach—his *Jegnoch (Heroes)* is another good example (cat. no. 27). Explaining the origin of the concept, Adamu related, "it just sprung out of me…after all, one doesn't always see things from the front!" He continued, "I had this idea for the first time when I was staying with Yohannis, I imagined doing the painting of *gugs* [a polo-like sport played in highland Ethiopia] from the back. I painted it and when Ato[28] Yohannis saw the painting he asked me to do another one. The second one was just right. What I did was, instead of drawing [the scene] from the side, or front, I reversed it and drew it from behind. I waited without applying color to the picture until Yohannis came and saw it. Later Ato Yohannis came, and the moment he saw the work, he blurted out, 'This is amazing.' He told me not to apply the paint, and in the evening he brought a guest, a famous artist, who took a picture of the sketch. After that, I put colors into the painting. Ato Yohannis asked me to do more and more paintings of this type." Adamu added that it was at that moment that Yohannis had recognized the extent of his ability. Another example of Adamu's use of this device may be seen in *Returning to the Church* in which we view a procession of parishioners walking away from us and up a hill (cat. no. 12).

As noted above, Qes Adamu generally does not copy other paintings, including his own, unless he is asked to do so or he is particularly impressed with an image. In addition to the paintings of dignitaries that he was asked to produce from photographs, he has been shown reproductions of Ethiopian paintings published in various books. In 1961 a large-format book illustrating illuminations from a late-fourteenth- or early-fifteenth-century manuscript of the Gospels maintained in the Debre Kebran Monastery on Lake Tana was published by UNESCO. The imagery from this book circulated in the arts community in Addis Ababa, and many artists, including Qes Adamu, have copied various images from the manuscript. Adamu's *Adoration of the Magi* is a copy of folio 11 (cat. no. 4).[29] Not surprisingly, Adamu has taken considerable license in his "interpretation." The original, which is on

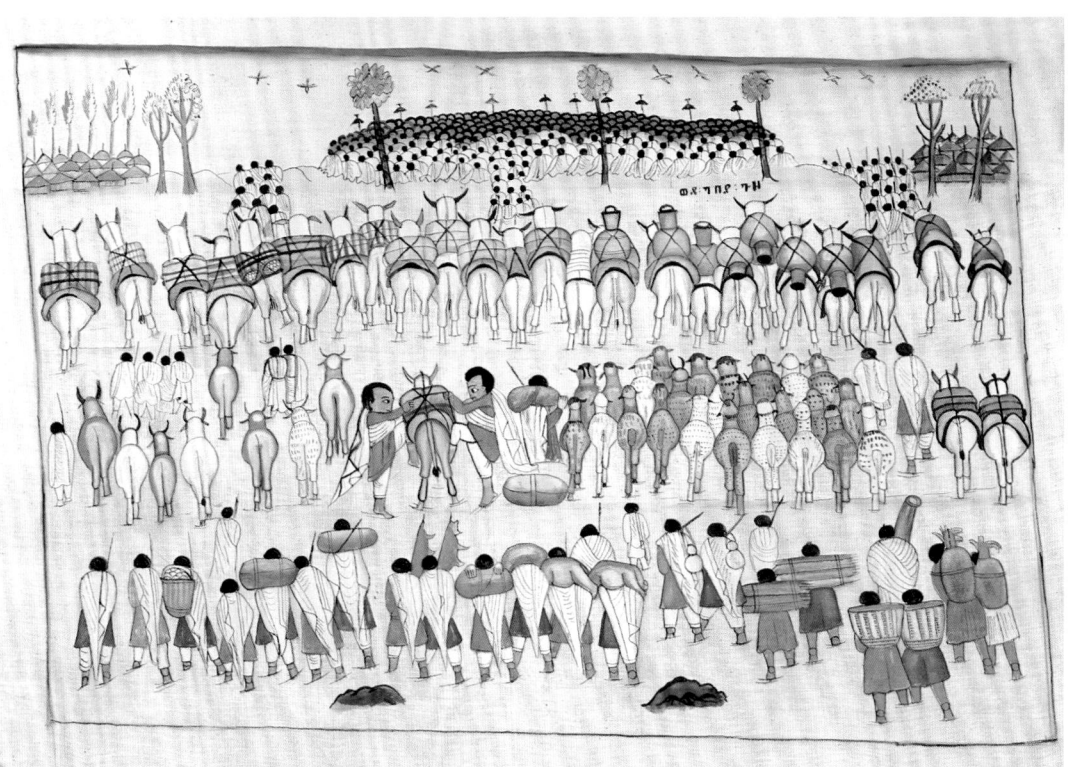

24 Qes Adamu Tesfaw. *Journey to Market,* circa 2000–2001. Paint on cloth. 78 x 113 cm. FMCH X2003.13.7; Anonymous Gift. Photograph by Don Cole.

parchment, is 38 x 26 cm. Adamu's painting on cloth is 166 x 87 cm, and in addition to creating a much larger image, he has emphasized the composition's verticality. This is in fact an excellent example of Adamu's penchant for "exaggerating the height of the figures." He also utilizes a more vibrant, almost electric, palette than was used in the original. Perhaps most significant is the life he has breathed into the composition. The original presents the kings as three distinct figures looking straight at the viewer, whereas Adamu has created a much more interesting treatment, overlapping the figures of the kings and turning the head of the one foremost so that he appears to be looking off to the right. Similarly, we can see another remarkable interpretation of an earlier work in his *Saint George Slaying the Dragon,* painted in the late 1960s or early 1970s, and loosely based on an illumination on parchment from a manuscript of the Gospels thought to have been painted in Lasta during the seventeenth century (cat. no. 7).[30]

Five years ago, Adamu produced an extraordinary image of the *Trinity* (cat. no. 5). This subject is a critical component in the pictorial programs of all Ethiopian Orthodox churches. The conventional treatment of the subject, however, involves three identical but separate figures. Adamu has dramatically conveyed the idea of the oneness of Father, Son, and Holy Spirit by fusing the three into a single entity. It is a stunning image that I originally assumed to be the product of Qes Adamu's fertile imagination. Adamu, however, indicated that Ato Yohannis had introduced him to this treatment of the subject and that he had seen it a long time ago in a religious text, although he could not remember exactly where. He noted that "the idea is not new. There were creative people in our history who created their own imaginative interpretations of reality.… I really admire the person who originally came up with the idea of melding the three aspects of God into one figure." This admiration led Adamu to "quote" the idea. He added that he has painted this theme a number of times.

In fact, one of these copies clearly demonstrates that not all of Qes Adamu's paintings are of equal quality. The Institute of Ethiopian Studies at Addis Ababa University was recently offered a painting that is very similar to the *Trinity* (cat. no. 5), but the IES painting is smaller and not as well

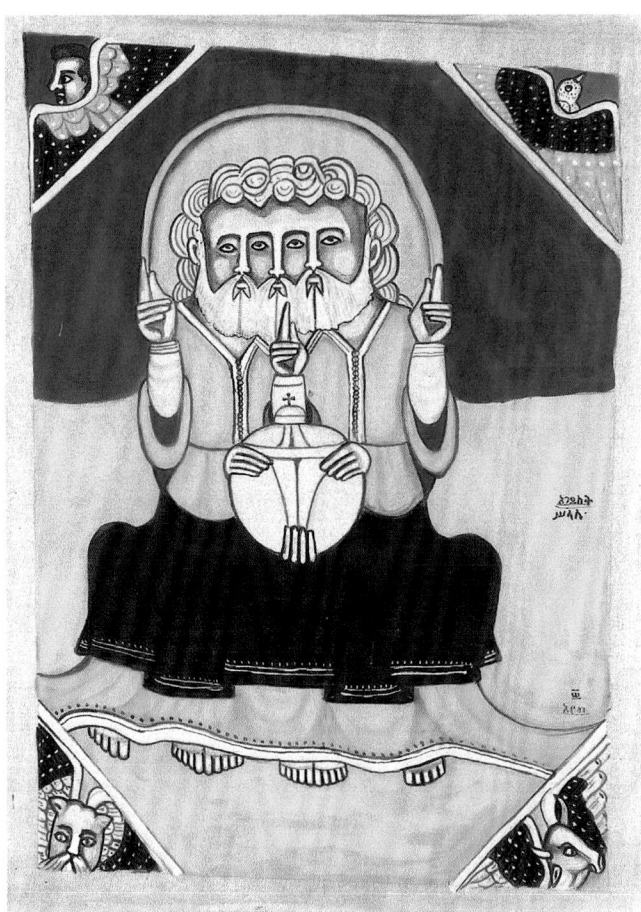

25 Qes Adamu Tesfaw. *Trinity,* circa 2000. Paint on cloth. 83 x 61 cm. Collection of the Institute of Ethiopian Studies, Addis Ababa University (non-accessioned). Photograph by Raymond Silverman. This is an example of poorly painted version of Adamu's *Trinity.*

executed (fig. 25). Though it is signed "Painter Adamu," I initially suspected that someone else may have attempted to copy the artist's work, perhaps one of his children. When asked about the painting, Qes Adamu intimated that he had probably produced it (although he wasn't positive) and admitted that it was not as good as the other painting. He explained, "sometimes I am tired or sick and I don't make a painting as full or as big as other paintings. Some days, the work is good, some days it's not good.… It's like food, some days it's nice, and some days it's not!"

Another device Qes Adamu effectively employs is truncating figures at the edge of the picture plane. These figures are only partially presented as if moving into or out of the scene. This is most effectively employed to capture the drama in Adamu's monumental compositions. His painting of *Saint Gigar Slapping King Herod* is a good example (cat. no. 9). This approach is quite unusual in Ethiopian painting, where, typically, all the action is contained within the confines of the picture's borders.

This same painting reveals another pictorial practice that is unusual in an Ethiopian context: presenting more than one aspect of the narrative in a single frame. Most often, the sequence of events in a story is presented in separate frames, each demarcated by borders. This serial treatment is used in mural paintings in Ethiopian Orthodox churches that, for instance, tell the story of the Virgin Mary (see fig. 12). This approach was taken to its limits in the extremely popular serial representations of the Story of the Queen of Sheba developed early in the twentieth century in Addis Ababa for the commercial art market and described above (see fig. 14). Adamu, however, often shows several parts of the narrative in a single composition, conflating the story. For instance, in his painting of *Saint Gigar Slapping King Herod* (cat. no. 9), the saint is depicted pursuing Herod on horseback, and in the lower right of the painting Herod is shown having fallen from his horse in the aftermath of the chase.

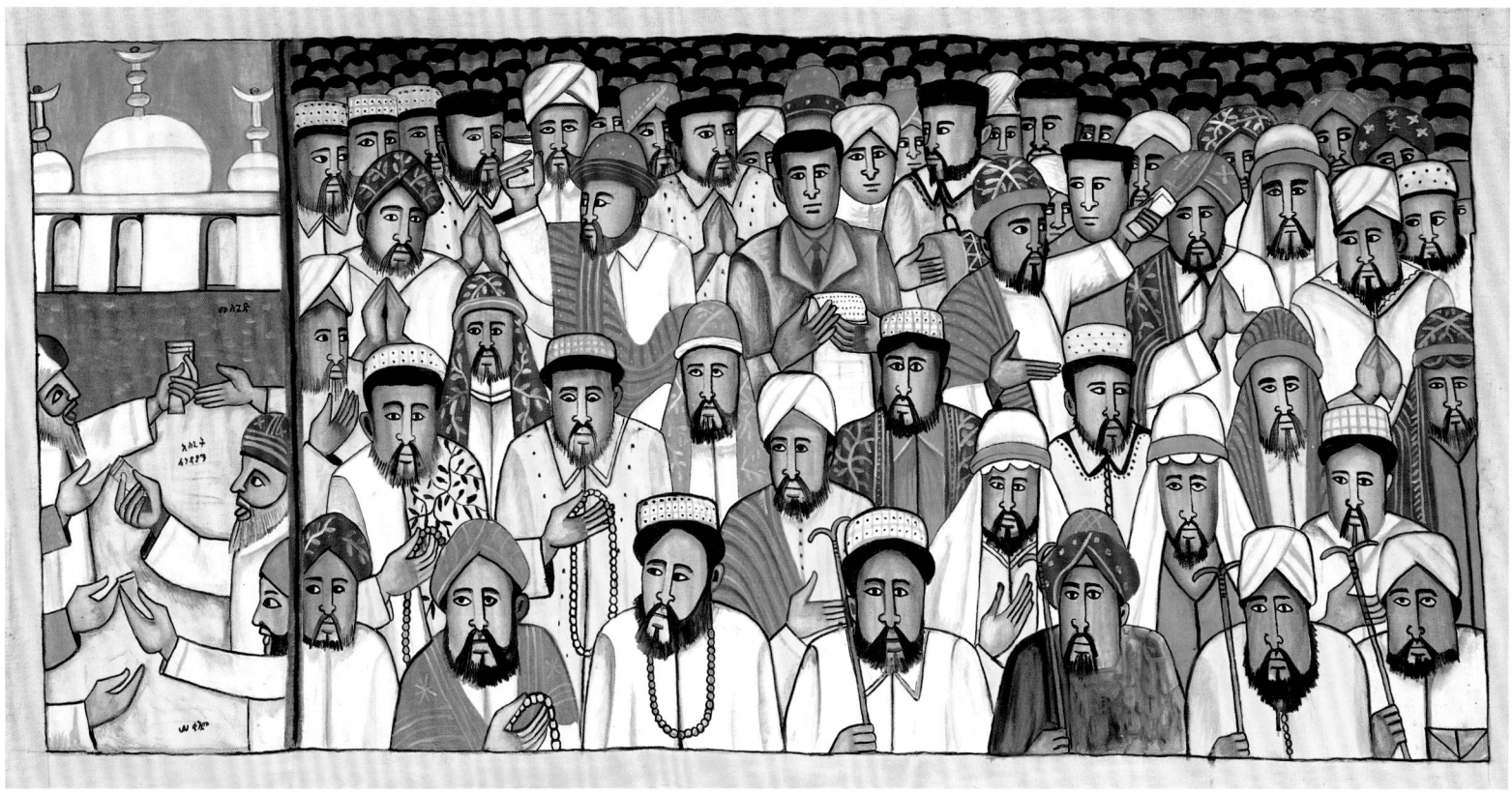

26 Qes Adamu Tesfaw. *Muslims*, circa 2000. Paint on cloth. 102 x 186 cm. Private Collection. Photograph by Don Cole.

This distinctive treatment may also be seen in *Solomon and Sheba Embrace* (cat. no. 15), wherein Adamu refers to three parts of the narrative—the spicy meal that Sheba consumes, her "stealing" water from Solomon, and Sheba and Solomon sleeping together—all in a single frame.[31]

Yet another related narrative device that Adamu has developed involves including an additional panel on one side of the painting that presents a scene separate from but related to the central story. Examples of this may be seen in *Southern Peoples' Stick Game* (cat. no. 31) or one of his recent representations of *Muslims* (fig. 26). Adamu again offers a very matter-of-fact explanation, "A painting only captures a single view of an event, it is like a window. Looking to the left and right reveals other aspects of the action." The extra panel suggests that there is another part of the story that you do not see in the central composition: "I want to give the impression that there are other things going on." Last year, Adamu painted a marvelous visual account of Haile Selassie's visit to Jamaica in 1966. In it he incorporates three different panels, each inspired by a separate documentary photograph (see figs. 16, 17).[32]

Qes Adamu's paintings reveal a level of creativity rarely encountered in a tradition so firmly grounded in the past, especially one associated with the Ethiopian Orthodox Church.[33] Indeed, in an Ethiopian context, such an expression of individuality is truly exceptional.[34] It is very likely that if Adamu had chosen to stay in Bichena he would not have become the artist he is today. Addis Ababa for the last one hundred years has been the primary locus of contact between Ethiopia and the rest of the world. It is a modern city that among other things offers people like Qes Adamu a social and cultural space for self-expression that does not exist in communities like Bichena. It is a place where new traditions, such as the art market, have evolved into institutions that afford creative spirits, like Qes Adamu, opportunities to express themselves and to be recognized, to a certain extent, for their individual creativity. Though he left the priesthood following the annulment of his first marriage, Adamu is still a devout Orthodox Christian. His involvement in a secular commercial art community has afforded him a chance to experiment, to look for new ways to represent the world around him. As Adamu has acknowledged, "I have gained a lot by coming to Addis! I've had the opportunity to learn new things. There is an energy here that has allowed me to produce more. I have excelled in my work, and for these reasons, Addis has been a much better place to live than Bichena."

Agents, Artists, and Problems of Attribution

As Adamu relates in his autobiographical statement at the beginning of this volume, he received his early artistic training in Bichena from the priest-painter Qes Gebez Anteneh Gebru,[35] who had himself been a pupil of Adamu's uncle, Aleqa Kassa Getahun. Adamu began his training as a painter at about the age of twelve, attending church school in the mornings and painting in the afternoons.[36] He briefly visited Addis Ababa with his father when he was fifteen for his ordination as a deacon. After returning to Bichena, however, he continued his religious studies and recalls "traveling with Qes Gebez Anteneh wherever he went to make paintings." When Adamu reached the age of about twenty-six, Anteneh told him that he had learned all he could teach him.

In the late 1950s, Qes Adamu decided to return to Addis Ababa to explore the painting scene there. He was fortunate in that his godfather, Yohannis Tesemma, had left Bichena for Addis Ababa in 1933. By the time Adamu arrived, Yohannis was a major commercial artist in the city, well connected with the expatriate community and the royal family.[37] Yohannis was sixteen years older than Adamu and a longtime friend of Adamu's family.[38]

Yohannis offered Adamu a place to stay in his house and was very supportive of the young painter. He especially appreciated the quality and originality of Adamu's work. Yohannis took whatever Adamu produced and sold it at the Empress Menen Handicraft School, where he himself worked during the 1950s and 1960s, or through his other contacts in Addis Ababa. In return he gave Adamu a salary of 50 *birr* a month.[39] During this period, Yohannis directed Adamu to produce "cultural" paintings. Adamu remembers painting "the history of Haile Selassie, from the time of his birth up to the present, including his daily activities." This project required that he study photographs in magazines. At roughly the same time, Yohannis asked him to produce paintings commemorating the visits of Queen Elizabeth II and President Charles de Gaulle to Ethiopia.[40] These were also produced from magazine photographs. Adamu believes that all three paintings were presented to the emperor and that the paintings of the European leaders were eventually sent to England and France, but that Yohannis had put his own signature on the paintings.[41]

The commercial relationship with Yohannis ended when Qes Adamu discovered that his godfather was selling his paintings to a souvenir shop owned by an Italian woman, Benedetta Riva. Signora Riva, as Adamu refers to her, who is now ninety years old and resides in Rome, arrived in Ethiopia with her parents in 1938. In 1961 she and her husband opened a shop that sold handicrafts, including paintings, on Churchill Road, one of the main streets in Addis Ababa. A very popular establishment, it was frequented by many dignitaries living in or visiting Addis Ababa. Signora Riva recalls visits by various members of the Ethiopian royal family and by Juliana, Queen of the Netherlands. Adamu asked Yohannes if he might approach Signora Riva directly, and his godfather gave him his blessing to do so.

Adamu and Signora Riva formed a close relationship. He relates that Signora Riva was "like a mother and a mentor.... My personality also matched hers. When she was upset with me, I would force myself to contain my emotion and let things go quietly, for I understood what was in her mind. She had high expectations for me. When she had a special need, like when her customers made special requests, she would call me to her home for a conversation. She would invite me to sit in a relaxed atmosphere and chat with her. She would then provide me with precise instructions for producing paintings. I made paintings for her based on her instructions."

Adamu remains very appreciative of this exceptional relationship and thankful for the constructive criticism that Signora Riva offered him.[42] It is significant that she never gave Adamu pictures from which to work, instead her commissions were delivered verbally. The prices Adamu received for the paintings he created for Signora Riva were based on three criteria: content, medium, and size. "Some paintings would come out very nicely, and Signora Riva would recognize the artistic quality and the effort that I had invested the moment she saw it. Based on her impression, she would offer a generous price." The income Adamu received from selling his paintings to Signora Riva made it possible for him to purchase land and build the house in which he still lives for his young family in 1970.

Life was good for the artist during the late 1960s and early 1970s. But in 1974, the emperor was overthrown in a coup d'état that marked the beginning of seventeen years of oppression by the Derg.[43] During this time Adamu and most other Ethiopians experienced hardships such as they had never known. Signora Riva and her family were forced to leave the country, and Adamu found himself without his primary patron.[44]

During this period, Qes Adamu established a relationship with another commercial painter from Bichena, Solomon Belatchew,[45] who had opened a souvenir shop next to the Empress Taitu Hotel (the oldest hotel in Addis Ababa) in 1973. It should be noted that Ethiopian "souvenir shops" carry a wide variety of locally made objects—referred to as "handicrafts" in Ethiopia—which might include baskets; silver jewelry; wooden domestic utensils, figurative sculpture, and masks; ceramic vessels; textiles and clothing; and paintings on wood panels, leather, and cloth. The patrons of such shops are typically foreign visitors or Ethiopians shopping for gifts for foreigners. The souvenir shop is the primary venue through which paintings such as those Adamu produces are sold. Solomon Belatchew's business, now known as the Belatchew Family Souvenir Shop, is currently run by his son, Gebrekristos Solomon. Qes Adamu gave Solomon hundreds of paintings to sell. Though Solomon was a friend, their relationship was sometimes strained. Solomon paid Adamu very poorly for his paintings, and at times failed to pay him at all.[46]

In fact, as was noted above, one of the first paintings by Adamu that we acquired, an image of *Saint Gigar Slapping King Herod*, was purchased from Solomon at his shop in 1993 (cat. no. 9). At the time, I remember being struck by its strong stylistic affinity with the limited number of paintings by Qes Adamu that I had studied. But Solomon was adamant that he did not know who painted it or exactly where it was from.[47] This was my initial experience with the "mystique" that has been constructed around Adamu by individuals, like Solomon, who serve as intermediaries between the artist and visitors to Ethiopia who wish to buy his work.

In the late 1990s I was alarmed to hear from colleagues in Addis Ababa that Qes Adamu had passed away. I called his home and was relieved to learn that he was very much alive and painting, as usual. This rumor, however, prompted members of the Society of Friends of the Institute of Ethiopian Studies at Addis Ababa University to raise sufficient funds to purchase roughly ninety of Qes Adamu's paintings that had been maintained at the Belatchew Family Souvenir Shop. Even today, several of Qes Adamu's paintings can be seen on the walls of the shop, displayed with paintings by a host of other artists (fig. 27). Over half the paintings illustrated in the catalog section of this volume come from the IES collection.

Ian Campbell, one of the lenders to the exhibition accompanying this publication, recently purchased several paintings from a dealer in Nairobi. Campbell was informed that the paintings had been acquired in 1971 from Bichena Giyorgis.[48] Based on this information and his knowledge of a painting in the IES collection (actually painted by Adamu but signed, "Gebez Anteneh from Bichena"), Campbell speculated that they were painted by Qes Adamu's teacher, Qes Gebez Anteneh. They are, however, unmistakably Adamu's work, and it is quite doubtful that they date from as long ago as 1970 (or earlier).[49] It is more likely the paintings were produced later, perhaps in the 1980s.

In June 1998, the Leighton House Museum in London presented an exhibition, *Adamu, Kidane, Qanna: Three Painters from Ethiopia*, which included several paintings by Qes Adamu. The brochure

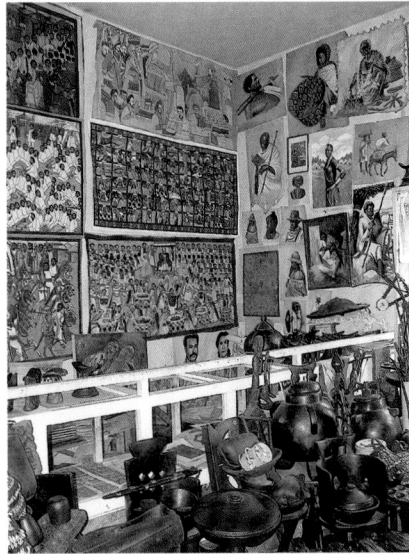

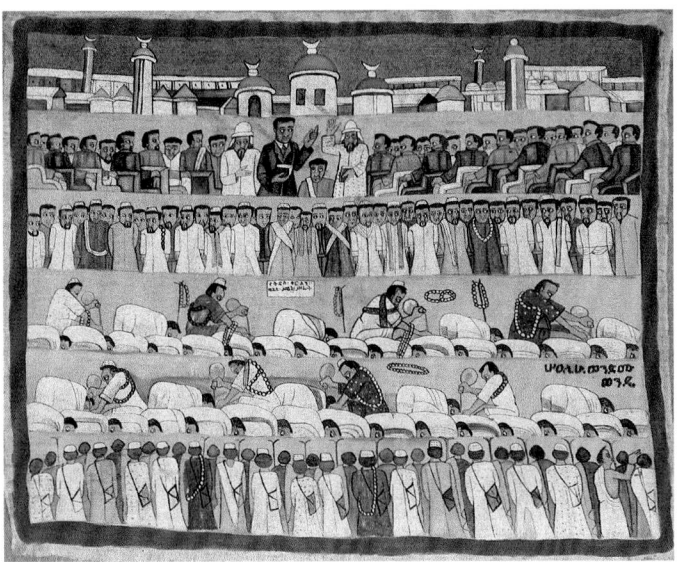

27 Interior of Belatchew Family Souvenir Shop. One of Adamu's Queen of Sheba paintings can be seen at the top of the photograph, on the left wall, near the interior corner. Photograph by Raymond Silverman, Addis Ababa, 2003.

28 Qes Adamu Tesfaw [signed Wondimu Wonde]. *Muslims*, 1998. Paint on cloth. 127 x 162 cm. Collection of the Institute of Ethiopian Studies, Addis Ababa University, no. 10252. Photograph by Raymond Silverman.

accompanying the exhibition provided the following information about the artist: "Better known as the 'Master of Gondar', Adamu's classical yet contemporary style reflects old religious mural painting, with its saints and legends. A secretive artist, little is known of his background, except that he is close to the Patriarch of Gondar and that all his work is of Christian inspiration."

Adamu is not from Gondar, in fact, he has never been to Gondar. Nor is he a "secretive" artist. His "brokers," like Solomon and Wondimu, however, purposefully kept him away from potential purchasers of his paintings. The person who collected the paintings shown at Leighton House Museum purchased them from Solomon Belatchew, and Solomon provided a "provenance" along the lines of the one he gave us in 1993.[50]

Finally, we return to Adamu's friend Wondimu Wonde, who first introduced us to Adamu. Wondimu, who passed away in 2001, was also from Bichena and, like Yohannis Tesemma, arrived in Addis Ababa in the early 1930s. As in the case of Solomon Belatchew, he seems to have had something of an ambivalent relationship with Qes Adamu, especially in his role as an intermediary between Adamu and potential purchasers of his paintings.

One specific aspect of the relationship is particularly poignant. Roughly ten years ago, Wondimu, who frequently visited the Institute of Ethiopian Studies at Addis Ababa University was asked by a member of the Institute's staff why he didn't produce paintings that included Muslims?[51] Wondimu, whose eyesight was failing, found it difficult to paint at all at this time and approached his friend Qes Adamu to produce some paintings of Muslims.[52] He also asked him not to sign the paintings. Adamu complied with the request and gave his paintings to Wondimu, who then signed them with his own name and proceeded to sell them. Though they bear Wondimu's name, the paintings are unmistakably the work of Qes Adamu, as revealed by the distinctive manner in which the figures are drawn and their placement in the compositions. One of these paintings is now on display in the Institute of Ethiopian Studies (fig. 28). In fact, I photographed the painting in Adamu's home in 1998; nearly completed, it was still in its stretcher frame (fig. 29). Wondimu Wonde also signed the painting titled *Zar*, which is reproduced as catalog number 13 of this volume.

Wondimu was not the only person to sign Adamu's work. Indeed, as mentioned just above, the IES also possesses a painting of a traditional wedding procession, undoubtedly the work of Qes Adamu, that is signed "Gebez Anteneh from Bichena."[53] Adamu knows that some of his friends have sold his work as their own. Although he is not pleased with this situation, he stoically points out, "They can steal my signature, but they can't steal my talent."

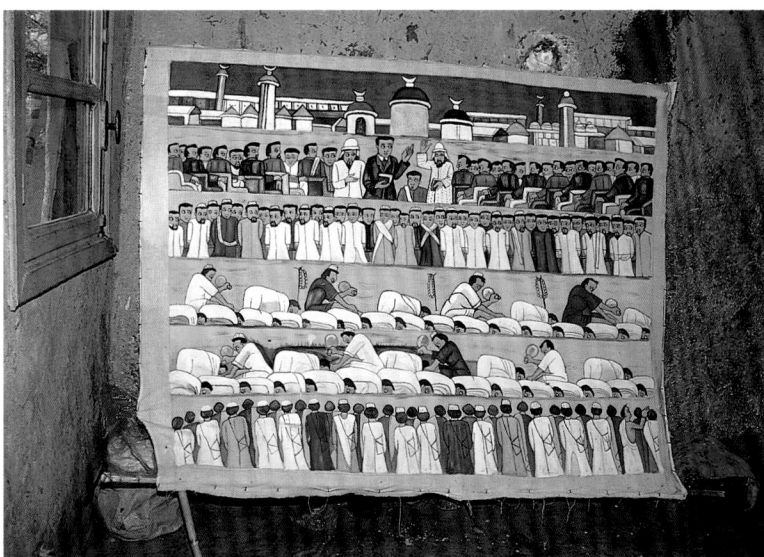 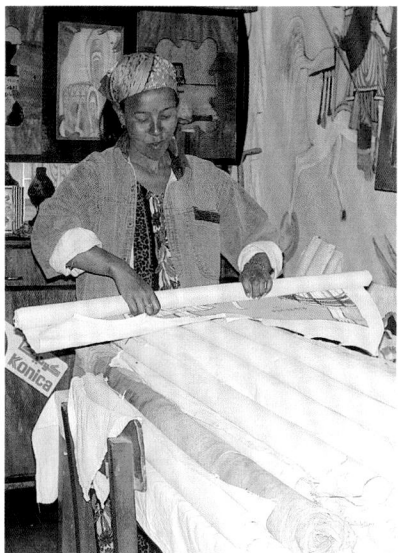

29 The painting *Muslims,* illustrated in figure 28, is shown here near completion, as it was photographed in Adamu's home in June of 1998. Photograph by Raymond Silverman, Addis Ababa.

30 Qes Adamu's daughter, Hanna, rolls up one of her father's paintings. Photograph by Raymond Silverman, Addis Ababa, 2001.

These practices reveal several interesting insights into the nature of the market for paintings in Addis Ababa. It is beyond the scope of this essay to offer a thorough analysis of this market. In the current context, however, such practices focus our attention on the relationship Qes Adamu has had with various individuals or agents. They also reveal how the marketing of his paintings has generated erroneous attributions of his work and inaccurate portrayals of his character.

Qes Adamu has a warm, genuine demeanor, and a marvelous sense of humor. He is, however, rather shy. For the first few years of our acquaintance he was a bit reticent, but he is certainly not a recluse. Adamu would be the first to admit that he is not a merchant. He has made a conscious decision not to invest much time marketing his work, time that he would rather spend painting. Instead, he has left the sale of his paintings primarily in the hands of others, and there obviously have been costs involved in so doing.

A prolific painter, Qes Adamu has not kept records of his work, but he knows that he must have produced several thousand paintings since moving to Addis Ababa. Although he paints to support himself and his family, it is his desire to express the ideas that are constantly developing in his mind's eye that forms his primary impetus. During a visit to Qes Adamu's home in November 2001, Adamu had his daughter, Hanna, pull from a cupboard roughly fifty recently completed paintings to show us (fig. 30). When I commented that he had been busy, he replied, "It is not good to sit down."

Though most of his work, since his move to Addis Ababa, has been destined for souvenir shops or on occasion sold directly to foreigners, Adamu has also produced paintings for churches. His most significant commission was in his hometown of Bichena. In 1986–1987 the priests from the church of Bichena Giyorgis asked him to paint the doors and windows of the *qine mahilet* (choir) of Bichena Giyorgis (see figs. 8, 9) Qes Adamu was not paid for the commission. He explained that, at the time, the church did not have the money to pay him anything. The priests gave him the supplies (paint, brushes, cloth) he needed, and people in the community provided him with room and board while he worked.[54] His time and expertise was thus a contribution to the church that had played such a significant part in his early life. For Adamu, it was an honor to have his work in the same church as the artists who had so inspired him as a youth.[55]

In recent years, the quality of life for Qes Adamu and his family has improved. This is due in part to the revival of tourism in Ethiopia after the fall of the Derg in 1991 and to the recognition he has received in two exhibitions. As noted earlier he was one of eleven artists represented in the 1994 exhibition *Ethiopia: Traditions of Creativity* at Michigan State University, and in 1996 he was featured in

I santi cavalieri: Arte e leggende d'Etiopia (*Saints on Horseback: Art and Legends of Ethiopia*), an exhibition of work from the collection of Benedetta Riva shown at a private gallery in Rome.[56] He was also featured recently in an episode of *Meto Haya*, a popular weekend program on Ethiopian television. Signs of prosperity may be seen in the renovations he has had made to his house: new metal windows and doors, a remodeled salon, a veranda, and a new studio space. Adamu no longer has to paint in his salon.

Last year, I asked Qes Adamu if he had any expectations about how people might respond to his paintings. Specifically, I asked, "When someone looks at one of your paintings, what is it that you would like them to see?" True to form, Adamu's response was direct and to the point. "How can I speak about what is going on in somebody's mind? Only they know why they like my work. I can't read their mind! People should form their own impressions from my work.... What I do on my part is just do my best, that is what I desire, I just try to do my best. The rest is left up to the observer." At the age of seventy-four, Adamu is still strong and still possesses the passion, the creative spirit, first experienced as a young boy, that has inspired him to produce so many remarkable works of art.[57]

Notes

1. *Qes* is the title for a priest in the Ethiopian Orthodox Church.

2. *Ethiopia: Traditions of Creativity* was installed at Michigan State University Museum in 1994. Qes Adamu was one of eleven artists featured in the exhibition and the accompanying publication. See Silverman (1999).

3. Girma Kidane (1989, 72–73) offers a brief biography for Wondimu.

4. Saint Yared, who lived in the sixth century, is remembered for introducing music into the Ethiopian Orthodox liturgy.

5. Adamu began painting the walls of his home soon after he built the house in the early 1970s.

6. People do, however, often hang religious prints and photographs on the walls of their homes.

7. Throughout this essay I have attempted, whenever possible, to present Adamu's thoughts in his own (translated) words. Since 1993, I have visited with Qes Adamu many times, often accompanied by Neal Sobania. Recently, Leah Niederstadt has been involved in our conversations with Adamu. Qes Adamu speaks only Amharic, and my Amharic is not good enough to engage in discussions concerning complex issues, such as religion or aesthetics. Over the last ten years, various field assistants have worked with Neal Sobania, Leah Niederstadt, and me, serving as interpreters and then working with me to translate and transcribe the conversations that were tape recorded—Degefa Etana Rufo in 1993, Tibebe Eshete in 1997, 2002, 2003, Daniel Berhanemeskel in 2001, and Makda TekleMichael in 2003, 2004.

8. This appears to be a fairly common trope for expressing a creative spirit. Yohannis Tesemma, Adamu's godfather, told Richard Pankhurst that "when still a child he [Yohannis] was consumed with the desire to draw and would use anything that he could find" (1966, 45). Wondimu Wonde, Adamu's friend, told Girma Kidane basically the same story about himself (1989, 73).

9. For a brief overview of this tradition, see Silverman (1999, 136–44). More in-depth studies are presented in Chojnacki (1983; 2000), Heldman (1993), Mercier (2000), and Holbert et al. (2001).

10. For example, see John Picton's essays, "On the Invention of 'Traditional' Art" (1992) and "Tradition and the 20th Century" (2002).

11. I have not seen any of his manuscript (parchment) paintings, however, and only one of his icons, a triptych (fig. 7).

12. During the twentieth century, especially after the revolution of 1974, which toppled the age-old political structure of highland Ethiopia, a new middle class, composed largely of individuals who had acquired their wealth through commerce, came to replace the nobility as major church patrons. Today, even less-affluent individuals—farmers, for example—may commission single paintings on cloth that they give to a church. See Sobania and Silverman, "Patrons and Artists in Highland Ethiopia: Contemporary Practice in the Commissioning of Religious Painting and Metalwork" (forthcoming).

13. In his recent master's thesis, Abebaw Ayalew (2002) offers insights into the political and social circumstances that created a fertile environment for the production of paintings at numerous churches and monasteries in Gojjam during the eighteenth and nineteenth centuries, especially under the patronage of Ras Hailu I and Negus Tekle Haymanot. See specifically Abebaw Ayalew (2002, 16–20). *Negus* may be translated as "king"; *ras* may be translated as "head" and signifies the highest political rank after *negus*.

14. *Aleqa* is the church title for the chief priest of a parish church. It may also be used for someone who is not a priest but is well versed in the teachings of the Ethiopian Orthodox Church.

15. The *meqdes* (lit., "sanctuary" or "temple") is the section of an Ethiopian Orthodox church where the *tabot*, an object representing the Ark of the Covenant is kept. The Ark is the symbolic core of every church. The names of the four painters are given in an inscription on the south wall of the *meqdes*. The painting of the *meqdes* is also noted in the *Chronicle of Gojjam*, written by Aleqa Teka Iyasus Waqjira, who records that it was accomplished between January and July 1910 EC. Interestingly, Aleqa Teka lists Aleqa Hailu as the chief painter, and Desta and Wudu as his assistants—he does not mention Aleqa Kassa. Personal communication, Abebaw Ayalew, August 29, 2004. Abebaw Ayalew (2002, 118) discusses the distinctive characteristics of Aleqa Hailu's paintings.

16. Information about some of these painters may be found in Girma Kidane (1989), Girma Fisseha and Silverman (1994), and Silverman and Girma Fisseha (1999).

17. Pankhurst suggests that photographs were first employed as models for painters during the first few years of the twentieth century, specifically by the painters Sahlu Lukas and Emailaf Heruy (1966, 19). The portrait of Emperor Menilek II illustrated in figure 15 in this volume—which was painted by Sahlu Lukas, the son of Aleqa Lukas—is interesting in this regard.

18. In the mid-1930s Adrien Zervos published several painted portraits of contemporary world leaders produced by a number of painters, including Belatchew. See, for example, his portrait of Japanese Emperor Hirohito (Zervos 1936, 481). This ability to move between idioms is seen in the paintings of Jembere Hailu (1913–1994), an artist from Debre Tabor in Begemdir, who before his death, was "perhaps the most versatile of

Ethiopia's old-style artists" (Pankhurst 1989, 98). See Silverman and Girma Fisseha (1999) for a discussion of Jembere's life and work, particularly the discussion of his portrait of Emperor Haile Selassie (1999, 165–66, fig. 8.4). The same can be said of Gebrekristos Solomon, Belatchew Yimer's grandson. Carrying on the family tradition, he is a consummate copyist who works in many different idioms.

19. The two Amharic terms also do not present the same problems posed by the Western terms. Much has been written about the cultural biases, as well as the ambiguities and contradictions, associated with "traditional" and "modern," especially when they are used to describe African (and other non-Western) societies. See for example, Comaroff (2002, 130n).

20. The paintings selected for the exhibition include works produced at various stages in Adamu's career, thus representing a range of styles and subject matter. Several paintings included in the exhibition were commissioned in 2003 and hence had not yet been produced at the time of this request.

21. The seven paintings were *Saint Longinus* (cat. no. 3), *Trinity* (cat. no. 5), *Saint George Slaying the Dragon* (cat. no. 6), *Menilek and Taitu at Adwa* (cat. no. 23), *Haile Selassie Receiving Queen Elizabeth* (cat. no. 24), *Court of Justice* (cat. no. 29), *Buying and Selling Sheep* (cat. no. 30).

22. One of the paintings, *Saint Gigar Slapping King Herod*, is included in the exhibition (cat. no. 9).

23. See Levine (1965, 238–86) for an interesting discussion of individuality in Amhara society. See also note 34, below.

24. This is the primary reason why most paintings associated with the Ethiopian Orthodox Church produced prior to the nineteenth century are anonymous. There are, however, a few exceptions, particularly in manuscripts, where the painter is identified.

25. Emperor Menilek II and his consort, Empress Taitu, led the Ethiopian forces in the battle of 1896 that thwarted Italy's attempt to colonize Ethiopia. Menilek and Taitu are always depicted in the "miniature" versions of the subject, usually on the left side of the composition.

26. Formerly, painters prepared their own pigments from natural mineral and plant materials, but since the twentieth century, factory-produced oil paints and tempera have been imported, and artists have stopped producing their own pigments. Prior to the revolution of 1974, good-quality paints were readily available, but during the ensuing period of the Derg (see n. 43, below), there was a shortage of art pigments. As a result, many painters, like Adamu, were forced to use oil-based, enamel house paint. Things are better now, higher-quality paint is available in the markets, but still, tempera or artists' oil pigments and good brushes are the best gifts that one can bring Adamu.

27. There has been a good deal written on this practice in Africa. One of the best recent studies is Christopher Steiner's *African Art in Transit* (1994).

28. *Ato* is an Amharic word meaning "Mr."

29. The original painting is reproduced as plate XI in *Ethiopia: Illuminated Manuscripts* (Leroy et al. 1961). It is also illustrated in the catalog for the exhibition *African Zion* (Heldman 1993, 149). For a description of the Kebran Gospels see Heldman (1993, 178–79).

30. The manuscript is maintained in the British Library. The illumination is reproduced in Heldman (1993, 216).

31. For a full account of the story, see the caption accompanying cat. no. 15.

32. Interestingly, this painting as well as several other works that Adamu completed at roughly the same time were inspired by my commissioning him to produce a portrait of George W. Bush. He thought that he should produce some paintings of Ethiopia's leaders.

33. The church is one of the most conservative institutions in Ethiopia, a powerful social and cultural force that has often stood in opposition to the changes that the twentieth century brought to the country. This situation, of course, is not unique to Ethiopia. Members of the clergy associated with religions throughout the world have been resistant to changes that threaten the authority of the church and the institutions it controls.

34. A few authors have written about the notion of individuality and creativity in highland Ethiopian culture. One of the best discussions is Donald Levine's (1965, 273–86) consideration of individualism as it relates to the notion of modernity among the Amhara peoples in mid-twentieth-century Ethiopia. (The Amhara, one of the two largest ethnic groups of Ethiopia, live in central and western Ethiopia, including Gojjam, where Adamu spent the first part of his life.) Levine observes that in a traditional context, self-expression, as a cultural value, is discouraged. He writes, "with the limited exception of oral literature, they [Amhara] do not cherish originality or creativity" (Levine 1965, 275). Levine's observation is perhaps overstated, but it does point to the fact that, relative to other

societies, Amhara culture is not known for celebrating these traits.

35. Qes Gebez Anteneh was roughly the age of Adamu's father. He died in the early 1990s at approximately age eighty. *Gebez* is the title for a chief priest in the Ethiopian Orthodox Church.

36. For an overview of the curriculum of a typical church education see Haile Gabriel Dagne (1970).

37. Yohannis was an important source of information for Pankhurst's article of 1966 on the history of secular painting in Ethiopia, which still stands as the best overview of the tradition.

38. Yohannis was born in 1914 (Björnesjö 1980, 54). Adamu has indicated that Yohannis also studied with Qes Gebez Anteneh.

39. Based on the standard of living in Ethiopia in the 1960s, this was an average income. In 1960 the annual per capita income was US $260, or roughly US $22 a month. Adamu was earning roughly US $20 a month.

40. Queen Elizabeth II visited Ethiopia with her husband, Prince Philip, in February 1965. President Charles de Gaulle visited the country in 1966; He had also visited in 1953, however, before being elected president of France.

41. Yohannis Tesemma, as well as several other artists, sold Adamu's paintings as their own, as will be discussed in greater detail below.

42. Adamu's wife and children have also played a key role in critiquing his work. Like Signora Riva, they have provided him with critical comments that have allowed him to improve his painting. In an Ethiopian context, seeking such feedback from one's family is extremely unusual.

43. "Derg" was the popular name given the Provisional Military Administrative Council, the Marxist regime that ruled Ethiopia from 1974 to 1991.

44. Signora Riva and her husband, despite having lived in Ethiopia for all of their adult lives and having raised a family there, were perceived as European expatriates and harassed by the new government. The Riva family fled the country soon after the Revolution in 1974, returned again a year or so later, but finding it impossible to live under the Derg, left permanently in 1977.

45. Solomon was the son of one of the pioneers of the commercial painting tradition in Addis Ababa, Belatchew Yimer, mentioned above. Earlier, around 1948, Solomon had established a shop at Merkato (the large central market in Addis Ababa), which he later closed when he began to work at the Empress Menen Handicraft School. Solomon Belatchew died on October 21, 1998.

46. An expression of their friendship is seen in the small portrait of Adamu's deceased son, Yidras, which hangs on a wall in Adamu's home. Though it is signed "Solomon Belatchew," it was painted by an artist named Mamo who worked for Solomon.

47. Solomon suggested that perhaps the painting came from a church in Gondar, but maintained that he didn't know for certain.

48. It is not known how they ended up in Nairobi. Personal communication, Ian Campbell, April 15, 2003.

49. If one compares the paintings in the Campbell collection to works produced for Signora Riva in the 1960s and early 1970s, there is a noticeable difference in the manner in which Adamu renders the physiognomy of the figures depicted in the paintings.

50. Personal communication, Remy Audouin, August 19, 2003.

51. Personal communication, Ahmed Zekeria, June 4, 2003.

52. Ian Campbell owns another of Adamu's paintings of "Muslims" that is signed by Wondimu.

53. The signature is in a different hand and in a different color pigment than the other inscriptions found on the painting.

54. Qes Adamu's paintings were produced on cloth that was pasted on the wood doors and windows that opened into the *qeddest* (the area in which communion is administered) of the church.

55. In addition to Bichena Giyorgis, he donated two paintings of *Saint George Slaying the Dragon* to a church near his house in Addis Ababa, Debre Yedras, and he recalls producing panel paintings that he knows were donated to other churches as presents.

56. A book titled *Santi guerrieri a cavallo: Tele di Qes Adamu Tesfaw. Warrior Saints on Horseback: Paintings by Qes Adamu Tesfaw* (Raineri 1996), accompanied the Rome exhibition.

57. Several years ago an eye infection left scar tissue on his left eye that impaired his vision, but a new pair of glasses has helped to restore his sight.

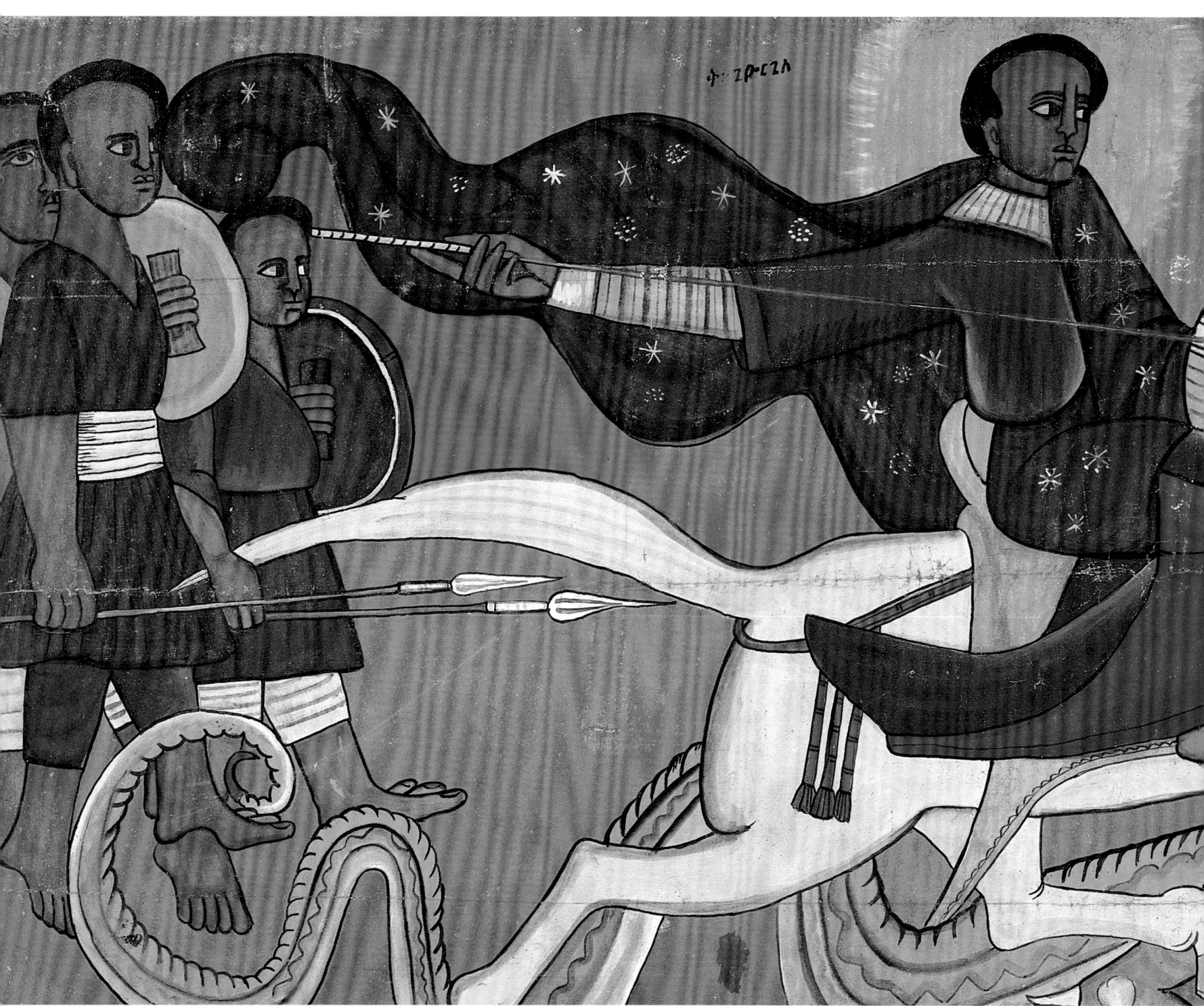

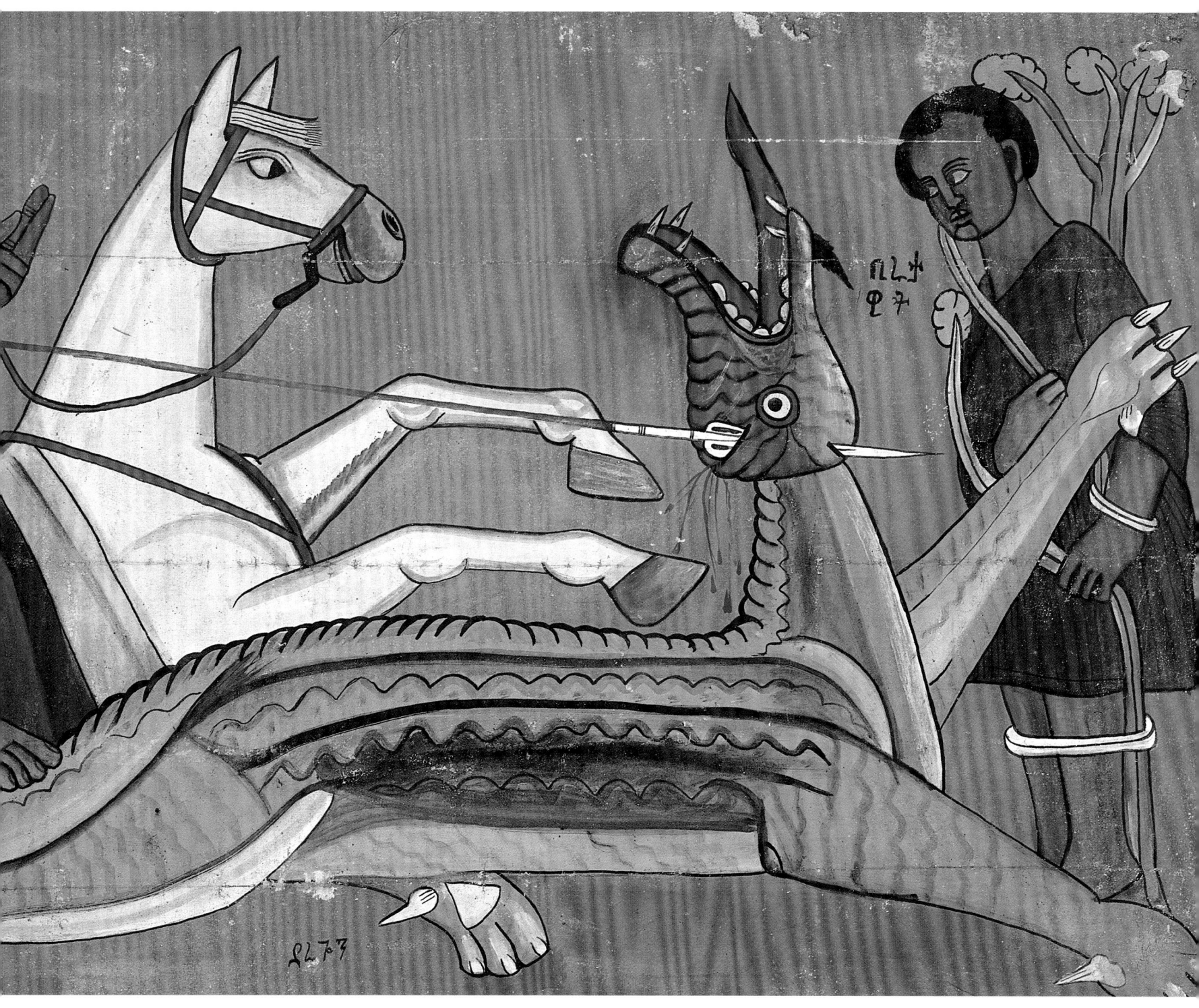

Catalog

NEAL SOBANIA, LEAH NIEDERSTADT, RAYMOND A. SILVERMAN

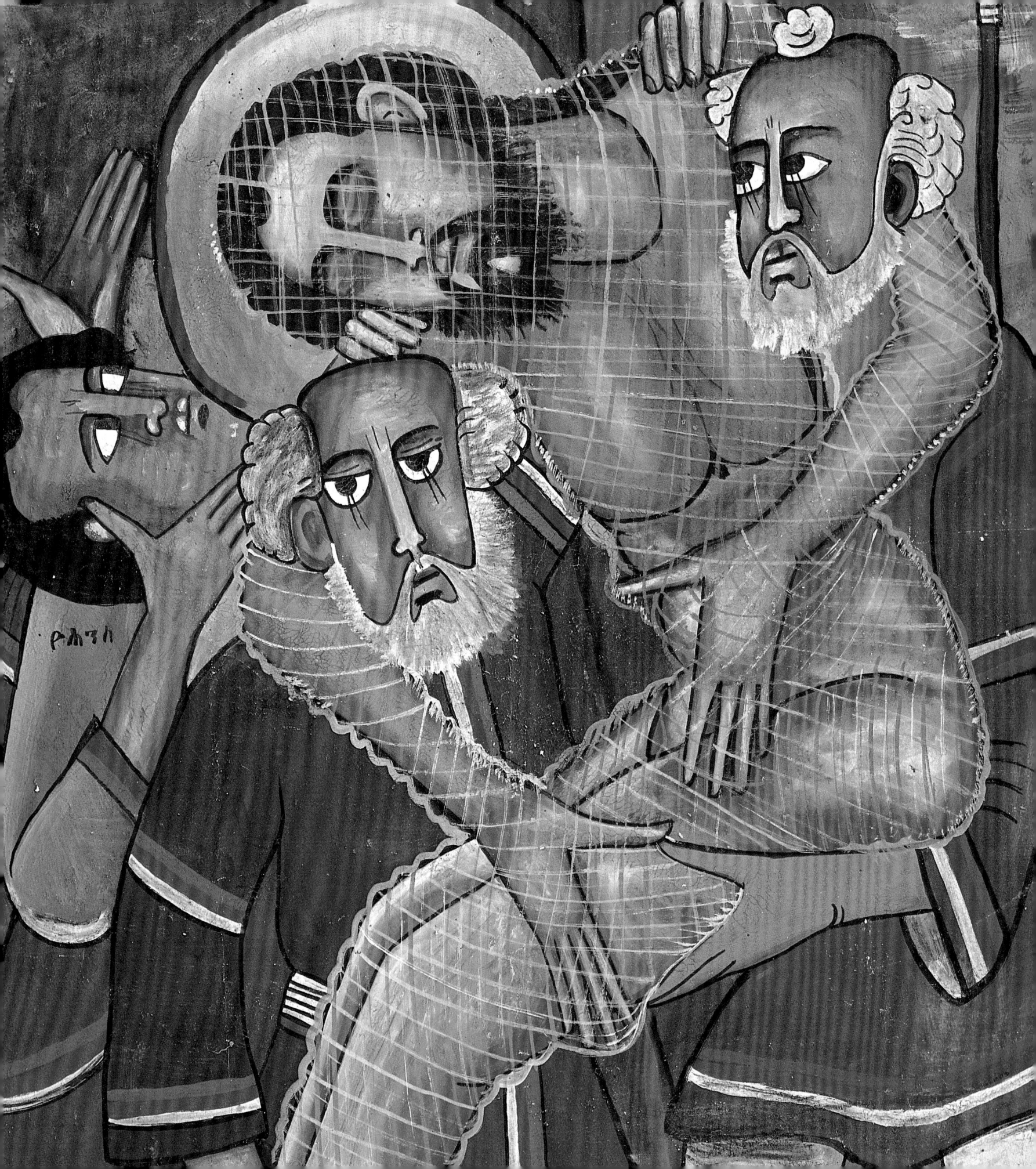

Expressions of Faith

Adamu Tesfaw asserts that subjects drawn from Ethiopian Christianity are the most important themes he paints. They are also the most difficult. A painter, especially one who is closely affiliated with the Ethiopian Orthodox Church, must adhere to a prescribed set of cultural expectations in the representation of religious episodes. Adamu notes that a painter can get in trouble if he strays too far from accepted traditions. This is what makes working with religious imagery so challenging: there simply "is not much room for creativity."

Qes Adamu has, however, been quite successful in incorporating the required iconographic elements in fresh and innovative ways. Sometimes he "quotes" imagery that he has encountered in specific pictorial settings, especially the mural paintings, illuminated manuscripts, and icons of Ethiopia's Orthodox churches. These quotations, however, are seldom direct as Adamu often creatively manipulates this imagery.

Having spent much of his early life studying for the priesthood, Adamu is very familiar with the texts that have guided religious practice in Ethiopia for over fifteen hundred years. This knowledge has informed his visual thinking about stories from the Bible, the Gospels, and hagiographies (texts dedicated to the lives of the Christian saints). It is his interpretation of these themes that sets him apart from many other church-trained painters. He draws inspiration from his own deeply felt religious convictions for his paintings of Christian subjects, and he regards his talent, his passion for painting, as something that God has bestowed upon him. This spirituality is strikingly revealed in the manner in which he depicts certain subjects, for instance, the grief and torment he so effectively conveys in his portrayal of the *Descent from the Cross* (cat. no. 1) or the drama that is apparent in *Herod Falling from His Horse* (cat. no. 10)

Adamu is very much aware of the important role that visual imagery has played in teaching and sustaining the faith of Orthodox Christians in Ethiopia. He knows that many Ethiopians do not read and that the narrative paintings that people encounter on the walls of Orthodox churches relate what Adamu refers to as the "history" of Christianity. For this reason he sees himself as a teacher. Adamu is also aware that images representing the saints, especially those depicted in murals or as icons on portable wood panels, provide a tangible means for the faithful to venerate and petition these holy figures.

Most of the imagery that appears in Orthodox churches and that Qes Adamu paints is drawn from the New Testament, especially the stories of the lives of Christ, Mary, and Saint George. Indeed, imagery of equestrian saints—Saint George being the most famous—is a favorite subject, and one that is encountered in many churches, as well as for sale in the urban art market. Adamu has painted literally hundreds of versions of Saint George Slaying the Dragon, and nearly all are different. He also paints narratives from the Old Testament, the most popular of these being the story of the Queen of Sheba.

Though most of Adamu's religious paintings draw upon his own faith, he also produces compositions that represent other spiritual traditions. He has, for example, represented the local institution known as *Zar* (cat. no. 13), which deals with exorcising malevolent spirits, and he has recently begun depicting the religious activities of Muslims (cat. no. 14). Adamu approaches these subjects as an observer rather than a participant. This has a definite impact on his work, and his non-Christian religious compositions often do not possess the dynamism, the energy, seen in many of his Christian paintings. Nevertheless, they are marvelous vignettes of religious life and effectively convey the diversity of spiritual traditions in Ethiopia.

CAT. NO. 1

Descent from the Cross
circa 1980–1995

Paint on cloth
223 x 90 cm
Collection of the Institute of Ethiopian Studies,
Addis Ababa University, no. 10303

In this dramatic painting Nicodemus and Joseph of Arimathea lower the body of Jesus Christ from the cross. Christ is wrapped in a white gossamer fabric similar to the *netela* used for men's and women's clothing in many parts of Ethiopia. The ground is stony, reflecting Adamu's notion of the starkness and desolation of Golgotha. The sky is red because, as Adamu notes, "When he was crucified, the sun went dark and the sky looked blood red." As in most Ethiopian church mural painting, the major figures in the narrative are identified with a brief inscription written in Geez, the ancient ecclesiastical language of the Orthodox Church. Kneeling at the base of the cross, Maryam (Mary), with tears streaming down her face, gazes up at her son. Yohannis (John) stands on a ladder at the left. The inscription beneath Nicodemus's foot, on the right side of the painting, reads, "Joseph and Nicodemus pulled him from the cross." An inscription at the top of the cross reads, "The Jews crucified Jesus," and below this, wrapped around the cross itself, is the blood-soaked cloth removed from Christ's body. Above the right arm of the cross are nails representing the five wounds of Christ, and to the right, behind Nicodemus, is the spear used by Saint Longinus to pierce the side of Christ (see cat. no. 3).

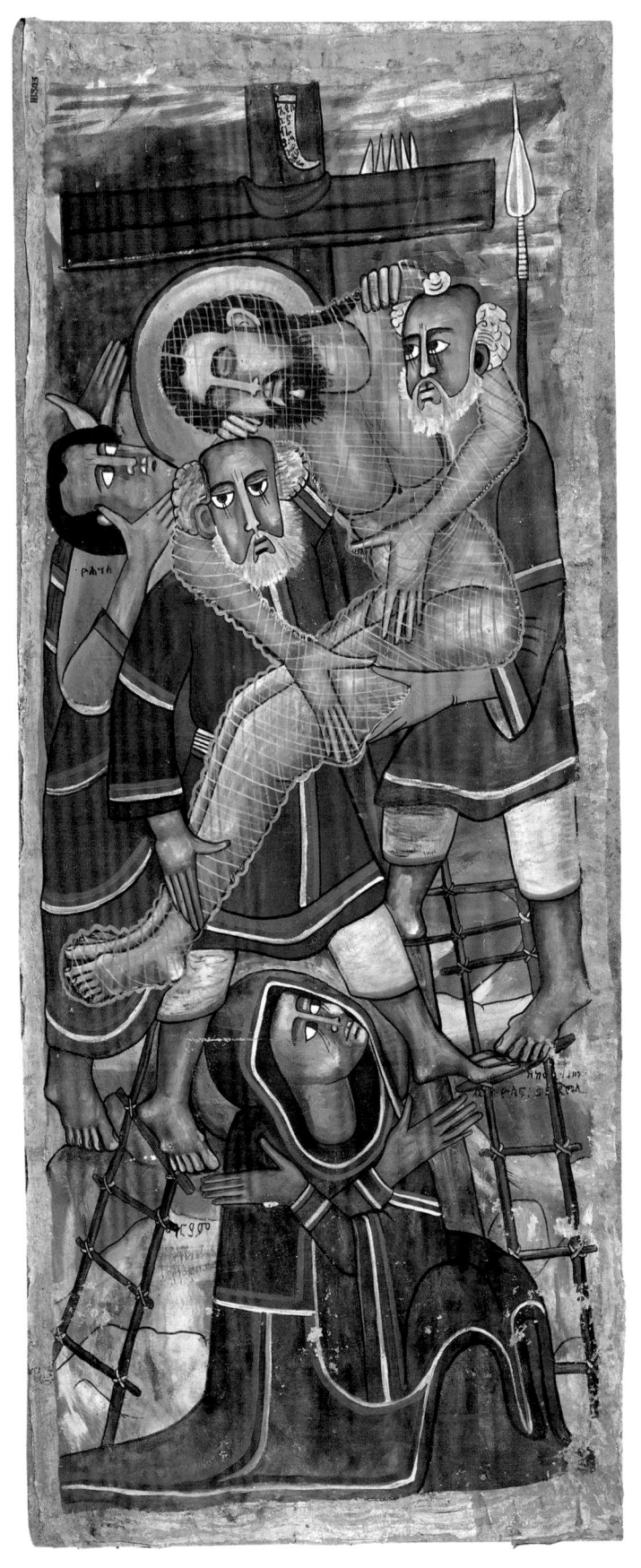

CAT. NO. 2

Nailing of Christ to the Cross
circa 1980–1995

Paint on cloth
75 x 192 cm
Collection of the Institute of Ethiopian Studies,
Addis Ababa University, no. 10306

Adamu identifies the three individuals at the top left of this painting as "the Jewish leaders who supported the Crucifixion" (i.e., members of the Sanhedrin, the supreme council of the Jews), including Annas (known as Hanna in Ethiopia), the father-in-law of the high priest, Caiaphas. After the ruling was made against Jesus by the Sanhedrin, he was taken to Pontius Pilate for sentencing. Below the three Jewish leaders, a blacksmith is shown forging the nails for the Crucifixion, while another works traditional Ethiopian goatskin bellows. Interestingly, Adamu identifies the blacksmiths as Jewish. Blacksmithing in the highlands of central and northern Ethiopia is historically associated with the country's Jewish population, the Beta Israel. The semicircular form above Christ's head represents a halo, or *igir tsehai* (lit., "legs of the sun"). At the top of the cross is a blank space where Adamu explains that the workers will write "Jesus of Nazareth, King of the Jews." The other figures in the painting are busy nailing Jesus to the cross. Bunches of nails are scattered about to underscore the inhumanity of the act. Adamu indicates that the scriptures say that "they laid him down [on the ground] and nailed him," but that he chose to show the cross being held up so that "everyone can nail at the same time." He also elected to manipulate the story, so that the viewer could see more of what was going on, "If I laid him flat and showed people nailing him, it would cover Christ and you wouldn't see him clearly."

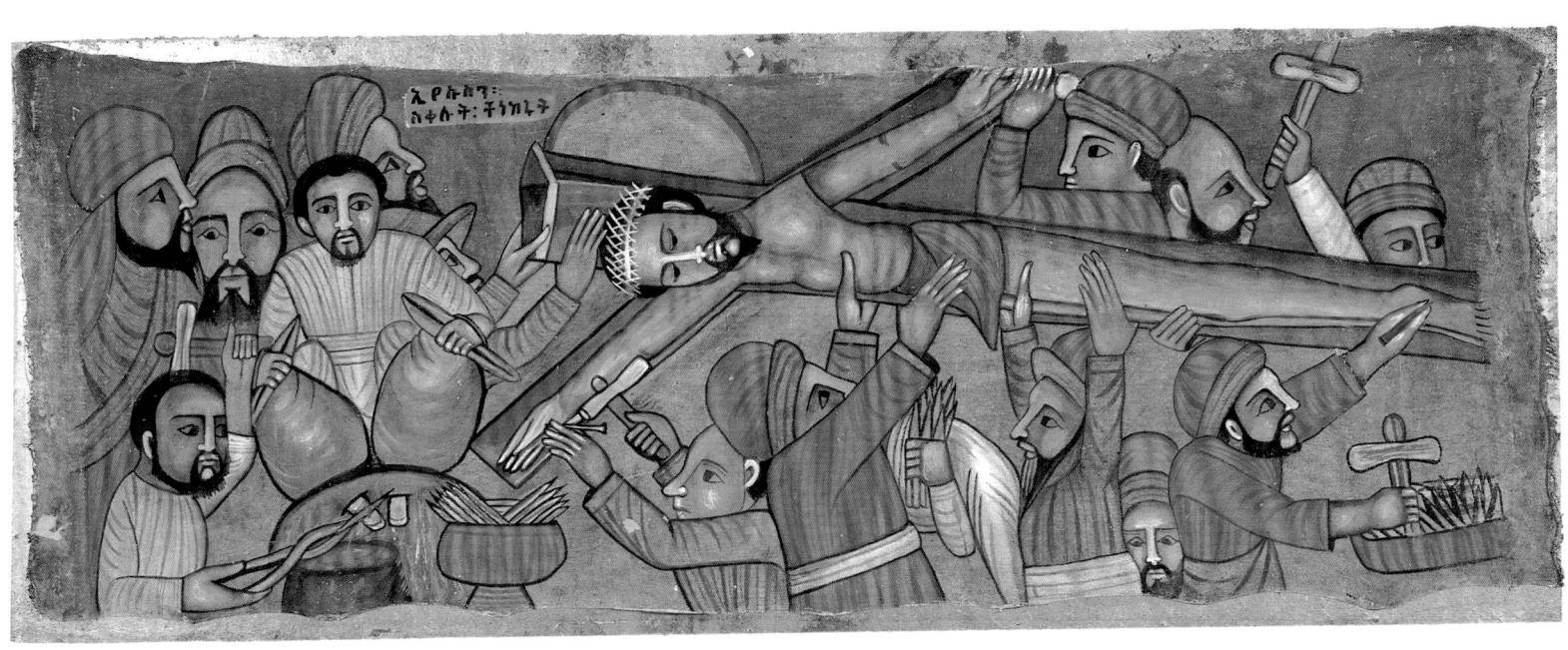

CAT. NO. 3

Saint Longinus
circa 1980–1995

Paint on cloth
187 x 104 cm
Collection of the Institute of Ethiopian Studies,
Addis Ababa University, no. 10316

Saint Longinus was a Roman soldier. As Adamu relates his story, "Longinus believed in Jesus and said, 'I won't be there when they crucify him.'" Later, however, Longinus's wife told him that his fellow soldiers had come looking for him, and so he went to Golgotha where Christ was being crucified. Seeing Jesus on the cross, Longinus began to fear for his own life and pierced Christ in the side with his lance. A drop of blood from the wound fell into Longinus's eye, and Longinus, who was nearly blind, regained his sight. Thereupon he gave up the military, converted to Christianity, and later died a martyr.

Longinus sometimes appears in pictorial representations of the Passion at the scene of the Crucifixion, usually accompanied by the Virgin Mary and Saint John, but in this very unusual interpretation, Adamu shows him alone, looking back toward Golgotha. He is so far away that the cross appears empty. The blood of Christ still drips from his lance. Adamu remarks, "John, Longinus, the sun, the moon, and Mary…you always find him [and the others] in paintings of the Crucifixion, but I am the only one who shows [Longinus] alone; for the market because perhaps some people might be interested."

Adamu presents Longinus as an Ethiopian soldier, carrying a traditional animal hide shield and sitting astride a beautifully outfitted horse, complete with decorative bridle, saddle blanket, and other trappings—evidence of the artist's attempt to "Ethiopianize" this biblical narrative. Critiquing his painting, Adamu remarks, "It would have been better if his clothes were those [of Longinus's time]…long, flowing clothes—it would be more beautiful."

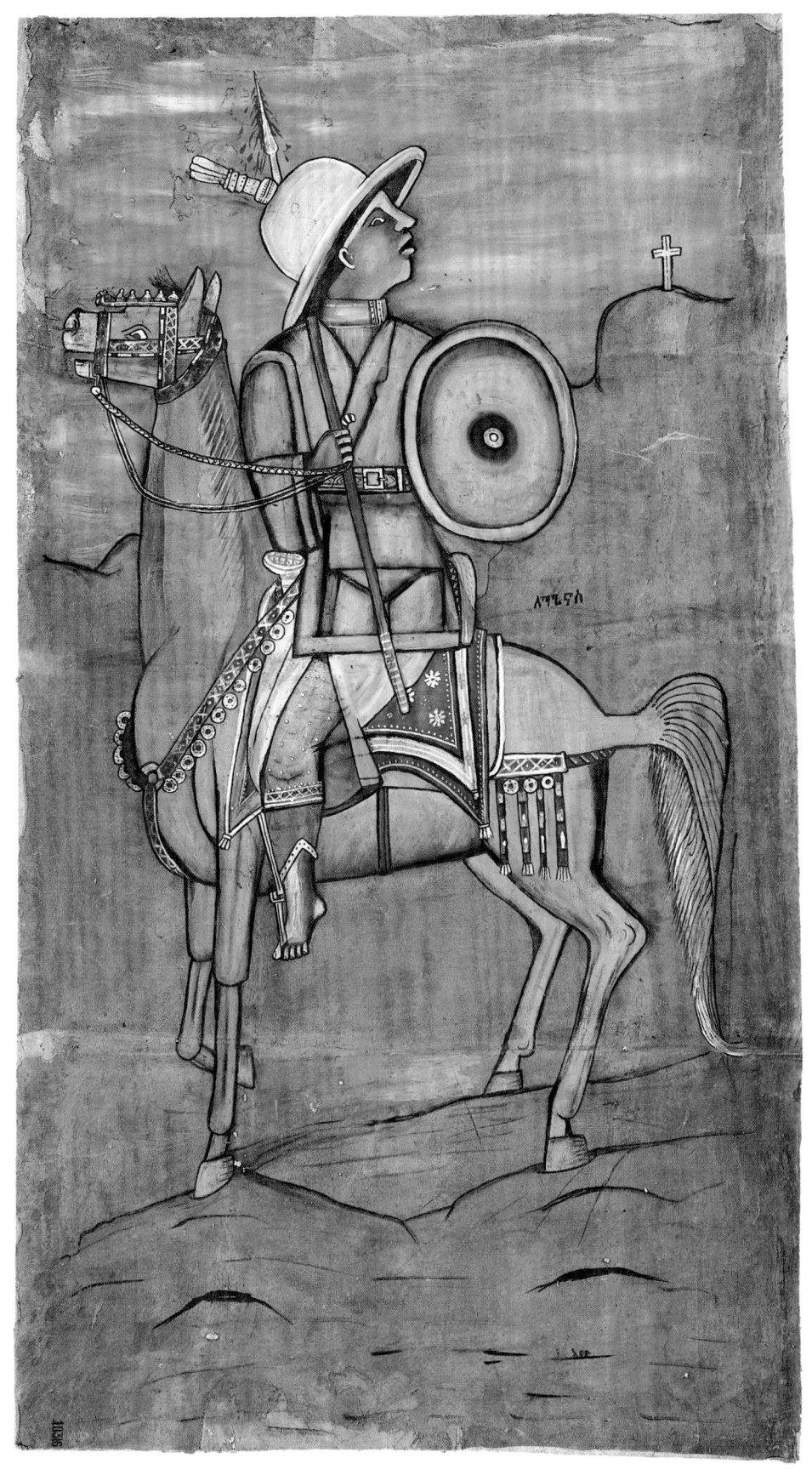

CAT. NO. 4

Adoration of the Magi
circa 1980–1995

Paint on cloth
160 x 80 cm
Collection of the Institute of Ethiopian Studies,
Addis Ababa University, no. 10331

This painting departs from Qes Adamu's characteristic style because he was asked to copy a late-fourteenth- or early-fifteenth-century manuscript illumination reproduced in a book that was widely circulated within the art community of Addis Ababa. Adamu explains, "[It was] not my idea. It is an old-style church painting." He notes that "old-style paintings are more valuable, so I copied it.... I painted this for the market because a lot of people like it, especially foreigners; they prefer that it looks old, so I painted it on old cloth with light colors...but if it was my own, I could make improvements. I could add new things, but when I copy, I just copy." Adamu, however, did not simply copy the photographic reproduction of the original painting on parchment. The scale of the painting is an obvious difference, as the original is only 38 x 26 cm. He has also drawn out the composition vertically, one of the distinguishing features of his paintings, and has used much brighter colors.

Though Adamu prefers not to produce what he refers to as "photocopies," he has great respect for religious paintings from earlier times and refers to them as "heaven paintings." He comments, "You see [the painter's] imagination.... Nowadays you don't see this kind of imagination.... I admire these old paintings...but nowadays, they make [paintings] look like photographs." Adamu has also spoken disparagingly about the modern practice of displaying mass-produced prints of religious imagery in Orthodox churches instead of paintings. As he notes, "they even take out old paintings and replace them with photographs.... I try to tell the church people to protect the old paintings, but they don't listen; they prefer the new ones."

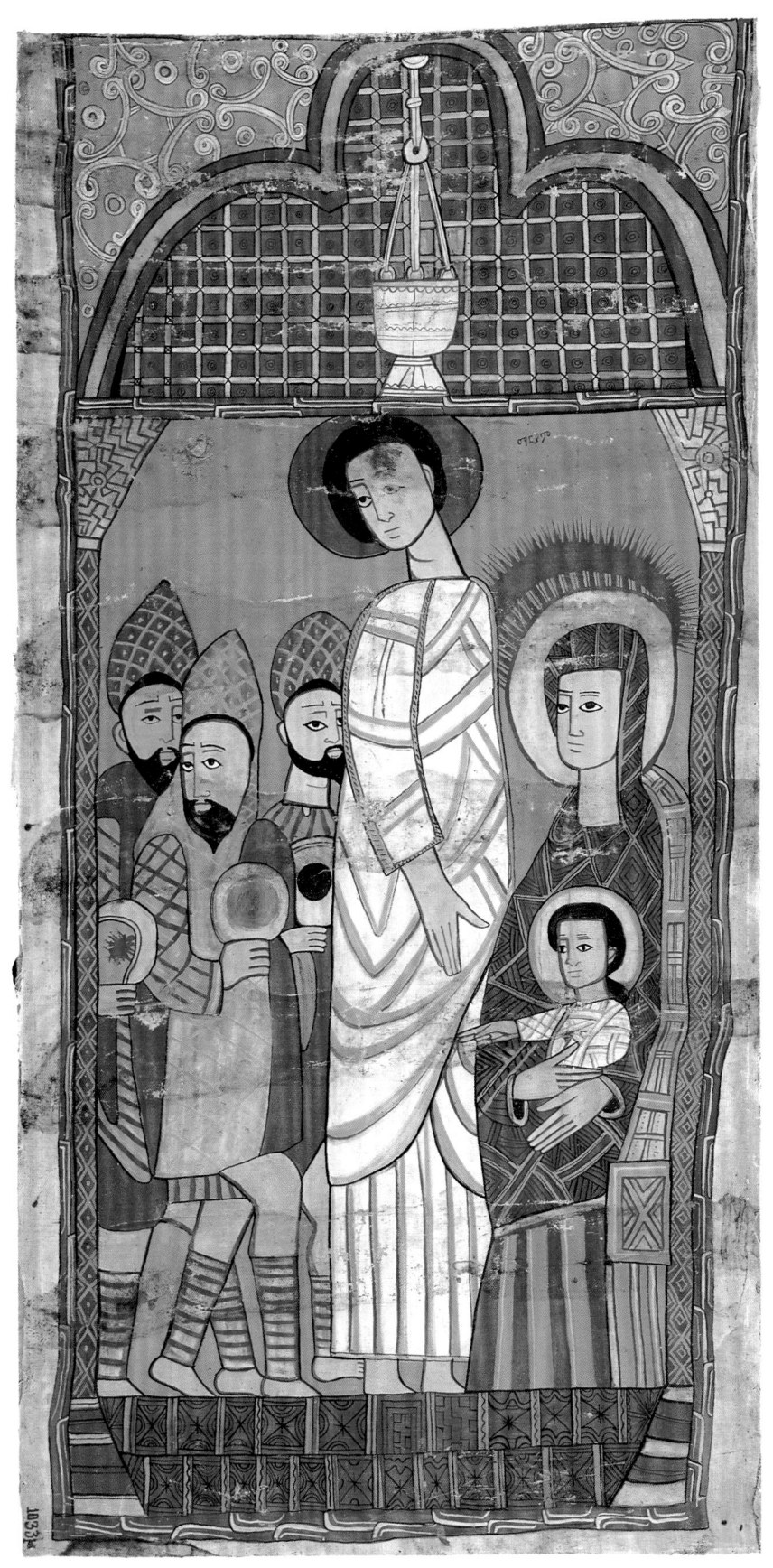

CAT. NO. 5

Trinity
circa 2000

Paint on cloth
144 x 100 cm
Private Collection

In this ingenious interpretation of the Trinity, Adamu presents the Father, Son, and Holy Spirit fused into a single being. Typically, three identical, white-bearded men are portrayed, and each holds an orb representing the world in his left hand and makes a sign of blessing with his right. In this painting, Adamu indicates that the single orb signifies that "Everything is in their hands. God created the world, and it's all in his hands.... They are all touching it.... They created the world, and everything in it and they can destroy it." An image of one of "the four heavenly animals" is presented in each corner of the painting. As Adamu explains, "They are the keepers of the throne of God. They are guards. They don't have flesh, but they have wings." Each is associated with one of the four evangelists, clockwise from the top left, a man (Matthew), an eagle (John), an ox (Luke), and a lion (Mark).

Adamu has indicated that he did not originate this interpretation. He learned about it from his godfather, the well-known urban painter, Yohannis Tesemma, who in turn had learned of it "from his elders." Thus, the precise source of this distinctive treatment of a very important theme—one that forms part of the pictorial program of all Orthodox churches in Ethiopia—is unknown. Adamu recalls seeing it in illuminated religious manuscripts, but he does not remember the specific texts. Though he generally prefers not to copy paintings, he refers to this as a "photocopy." He has produced paintings of the Trinity similar to this one a number of times in response to the demands of the market.

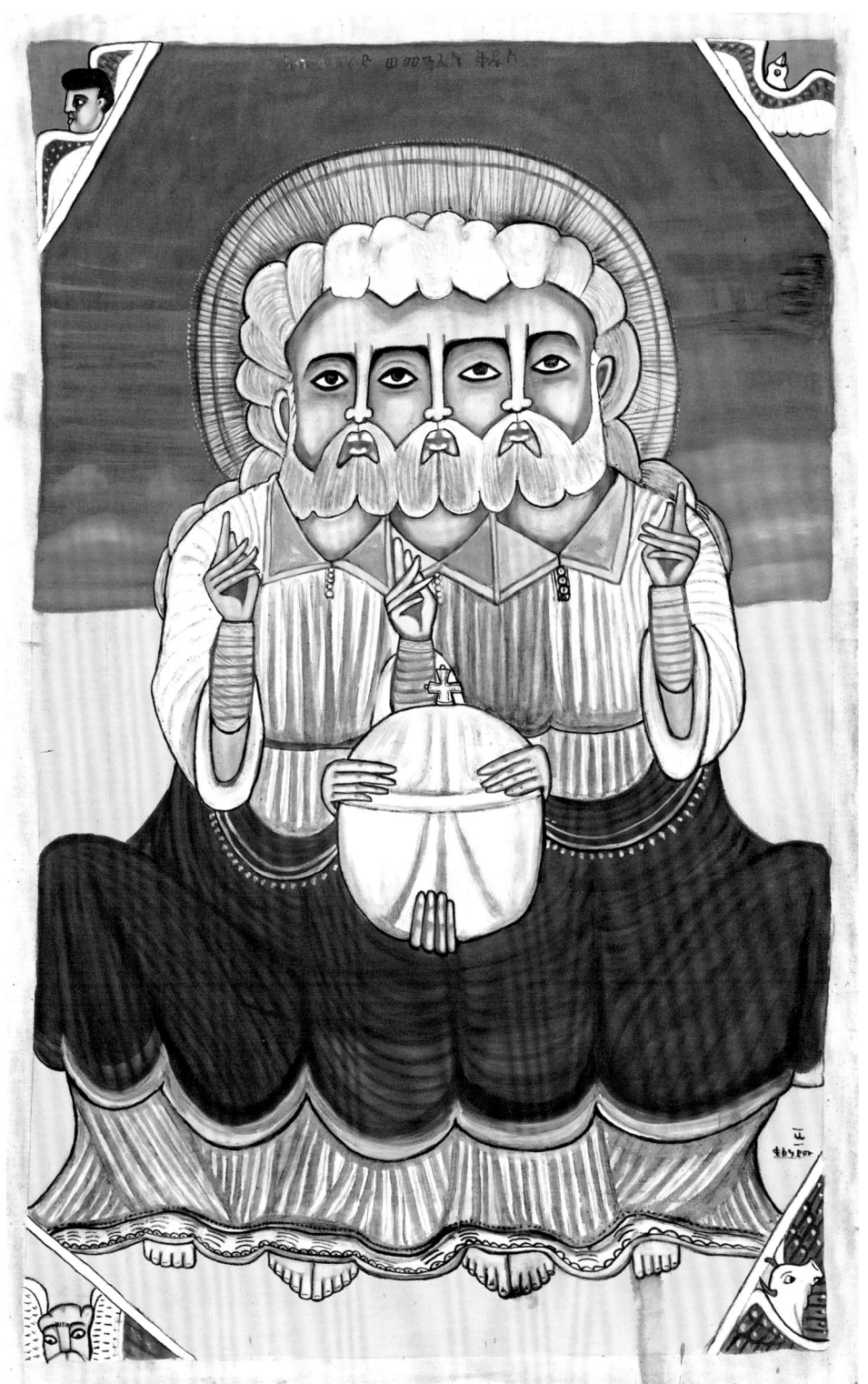

CAT. NO. 6

Saint George Slaying the Dragon
circa 1980–1995

Paint on cloth
90 x 219 cm
Collection of the Institute of Ethiopian Studies,
Addis Ababa University, no. 10343

Saints fill the world of the Ethiopian Orthodox Church, and warrior saints riding horses and slaying dragons or enemies are especially popular. Among the most widely reproduced is Saint George (Giyorgis), who is given a place of honor as the protector of Saint Mary. Little is actually known about the life of Saint George. He is believed to have died a martyr in the third or fourth century and is generally associated with Cappadocia, an ancient state in eastern Asian Minor. From there his story was carried to other parts of Christendom. Although he is linked with many legends and miracles, foremost among them is his slaying of a dragon and rescue of Princess Birutawit. As the story is generally told, a dragon held an entire city at bay, and many soldiers had been lost trying to slay it. The king was thus on the point of appeasing the beast by agreeing to present it with a new maiden every day, beginning with his own daughter, Birutawit. As a last resort, however, he offered a great reward to anyone who would save her. As Adamu relates the story, when Saint George arrived on the scene, he "saw this girl and she told him she was a sacrifice, and he said, 'I will protect you.' She said, 'Go because he'll eat you,' and he said, 'No' and killed the dragon with the power of God." Saint George then tied up the dragon and took it to the city where, it is said, thousands of people became believers and were baptized by him. Adamu explains, "I have painted this subject many times, and this [particular painting] has some of the improvements I have made over time.... The horse has power and is moving fast. The dragon has to cause fear and horror, so I have painted it big." Indeed, Qes Adamu has probably painted Saint George Slaying the Dragon more than any other theme, but unless he is specifically asked to copy an earlier work, no two of his paintings of the saint are alike.

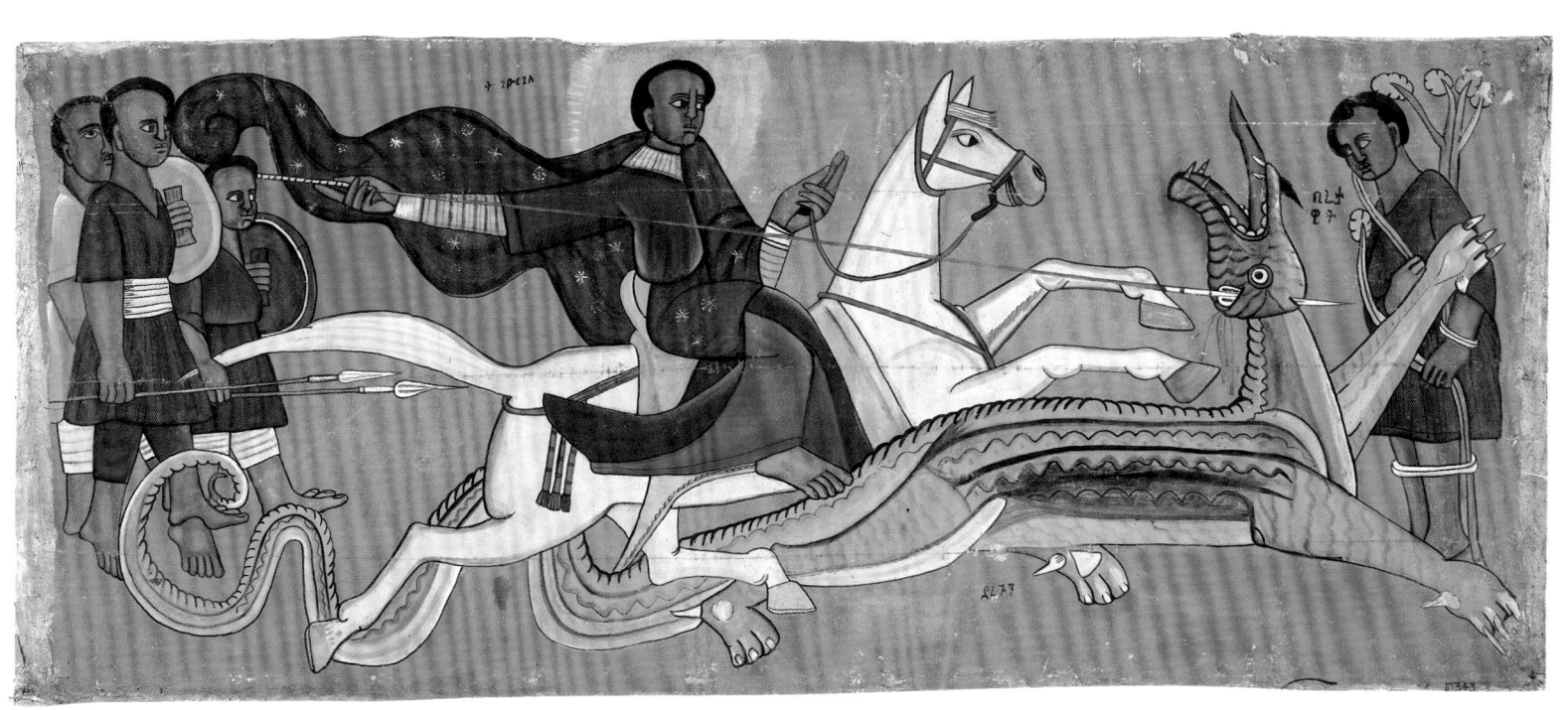

CAT. NO. 7

Saint George Slaying the Dragon
circa 1970

Paint on cloth
90 x 70 cm
Collection of Mrs. Benedetta Riva

This depiction of Saint George forms part of a collection of roughly one hundred paintings of equestrian saints commissioned from Adamu during the 1960s and early 1970s by Benedetta Riva. Most of the paintings in the Riva collection are of more-or-less uniform size, significantly smaller than many of his other works included in this volume. Many of them, like Adamu's *Adoration of the Magi* (cat. no. 4), are modeled after religious imagery dating from earlier eras.

The striking geometric patterning and palette of this painting—inspired by fifteenth- through seventeenth-century Gospel and Psalter illuminations—stand out from his other works illustrated here. Adamu's reducing the figures of Saint George, his horse, Birutawit, and the snake-like dragon to basic cylindrical and circular shapes further accentuates the geometry of the composition. Interestingly, Saint George and Birutawit are both depicted with halos. Adamu indicates that he normally paints a halo on only one woman, Saint Mary. In this instance, however, he felt it important to depict Birutawit in a similar fashion. "The halo is normally on Saint Mary, not on Birutawit. [But] I did this to give her grace and respect."

Looking at other paintings in the Riva collection, one is struck by how similar this work is to a number of Adamu's images of equestrian saints. Adamu points out that "there is no reason for the different color scheme. It's based on my mood or feeling, [or] if I am tired; also on what [paint] I have." He recalls that he "used to paint these a lot, they sold out due to high demand for this design. If you ask me to paint this painting with another color, it is not a problem for me because it doesn't change the history. The important thing is that the design [the iconography] is the same."

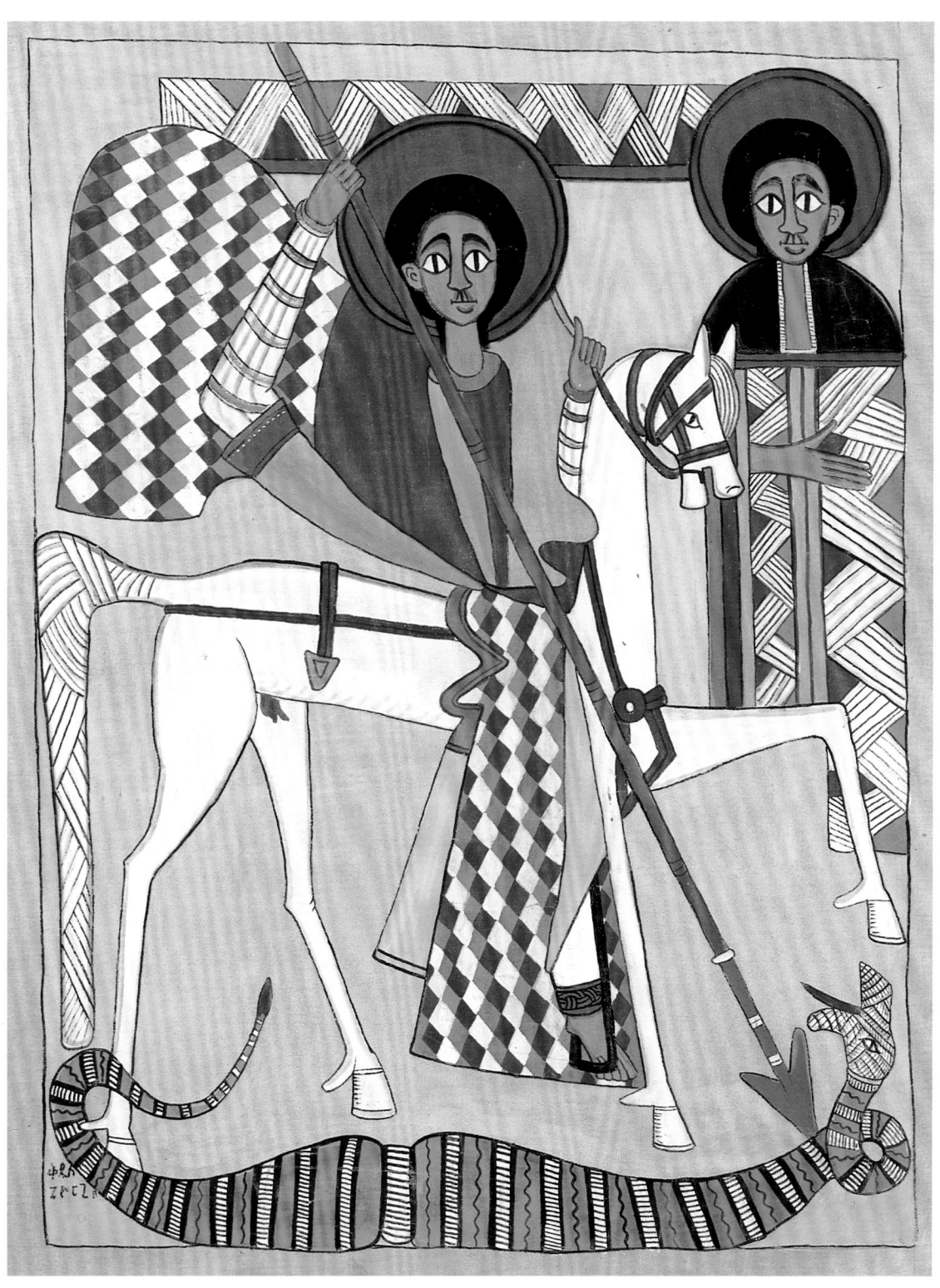

CAT. NO. 8

Saint George Slaying the Dragon
circa 1980–1995

Paint on cloth
187 x 100 cm
Collection of the Institute of Ethiopian Studies,
Addis Ababa University, no. 10313

Saint George (Giyorgis) is a popular and widely venerated saint in Ethiopia. His image appears in most churches, usually painted in the panel to the left of Saint Mary with the infant Jesus. Many Orthodox churches in Ethiopia are dedicated to Saint George, including Bichena Giyorgis, where Qes Adamu was first introduced to painting. One of Ethiopia's best-known churches, Bet Giyorgis (Saint George's Church) in Addis Ababa, was built at the end of the nineteenth century to commemorate Ethiopia's victory over the Italians at Adwa. Adamu and many other artists, usually include the image of Saint George, hovering over the battlefield, in renderings of the Battle of Adwa.

Typically paintings of Saint George show him killing the dragon, but Adamu clarifies that "It is not because of the power of the spear but because of the power of God [that the dragon was killed]." In this composition the saint stabs the dragon in the mouth. "Sometimes he stabs [the dragon] with both hands; sometimes with one hand. It depends on the painter…and because [the dragon] roars, [Saint George] usually stabs it through the tongue or mouth." Adamu alters other elements in the painting and understands that he has a certain degree of artistic license, as long as the basic "history" is there.

Like a number of paintings in the exhibition, this work was purposefully painted to look old; and like the *Descent from the Cross* (cat. no. 1), it reveals Adamu's ability to create a monumental composition by manipulating the figures in a scene so they completely fill the picture plane. Though Birutawit appears to be standing under Saint George's rearing horse, upon closer scrutiny one sees that she is actually tied to a tree that Adamu situates in the background.

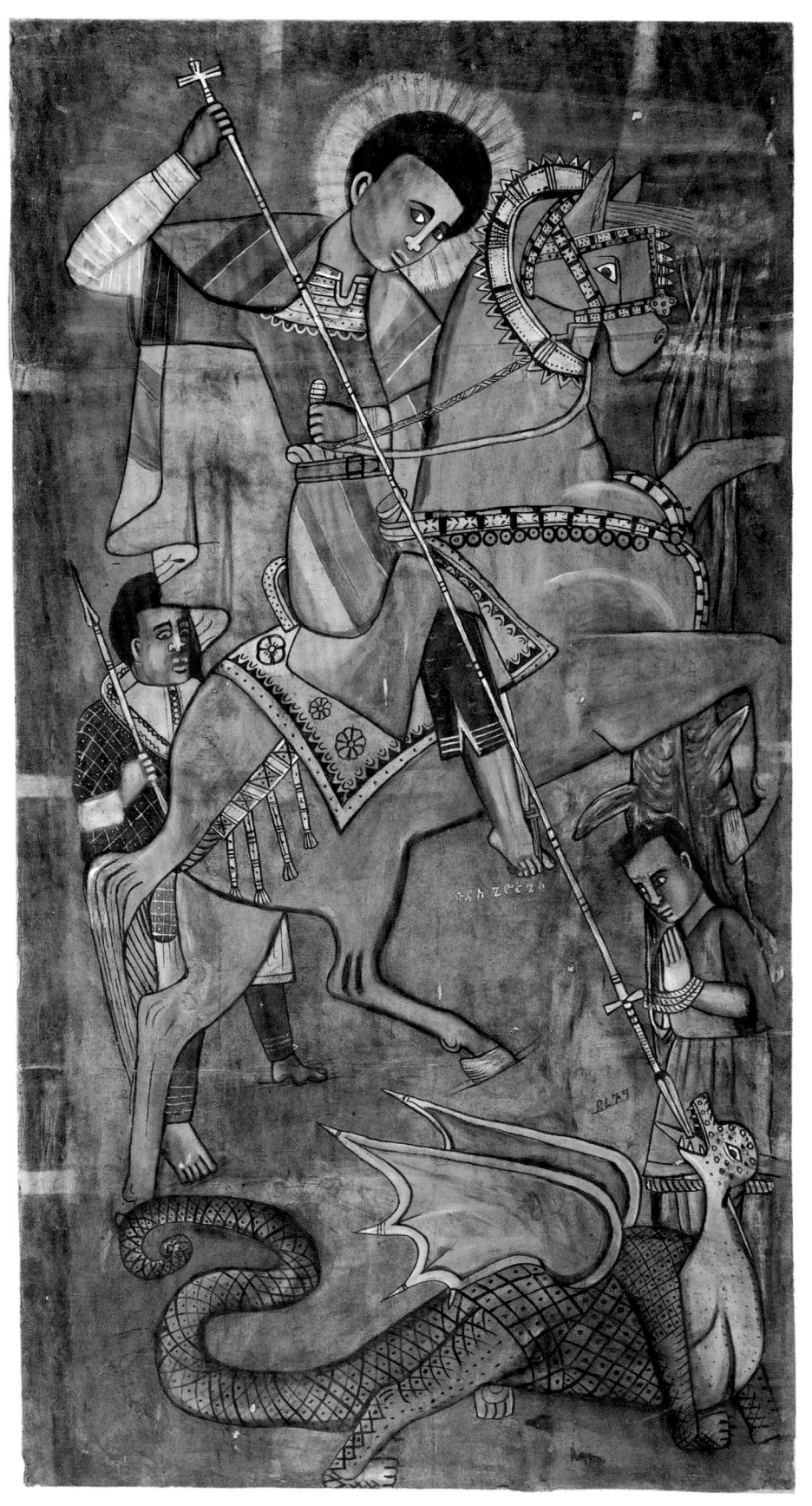

CAT. NO. 9

Saint Gigar Slapping King Herod
circa 1990

Paint on cloth
79 x 175 cm
Collection of Michigan State University Museum,
no. 7557.42

Saint Gigar, like a number of saints associated with Orthodox Christianity in Ethiopia, is not especially well known in the West. His story is a long and involved one. Adamu declares that, "If you take this painting and ask older people about the story, they will not stop [recounting it] for three days!" During the flight to Egypt, the Holy Family took refuge in the Lebanese desert where Gigar, a magistrate, helped hide them from King Herod. Upon discovering this, the furious Herod had Gigar jailed, tortured, and ultimately beheaded. A spring burst forth from the place where Gigar's head fell, and when Herod went to see the miraculous site, he was greeted by Saint Gigar riding a horse of white fire. Gigar grabbed Herod, struck him on the head, knocked him from his horse, and then disappeared. Following this, the Angel Gabriel went to Saint Mary, and she, Joseph, and the Christ child continued their journey to Egypt.

Adamu notes that as with other saints' legends, he focuses on the most important part of the story, showing the fearful Herod clinging to his horse as Saint Gigar grabs his scarf and prepares to "slap" him. Adamu conflates events by depicting Herod on the ground as well, after having been knocked off his horse. The artist explains, "Though [Herod] was a king, he was a human being, so he was afraid." God and belief in God were more powerful than the earthly king. "Gigar believed in the coming of Christ, and he saw what Herod was doing and was courageous enough to stop him."

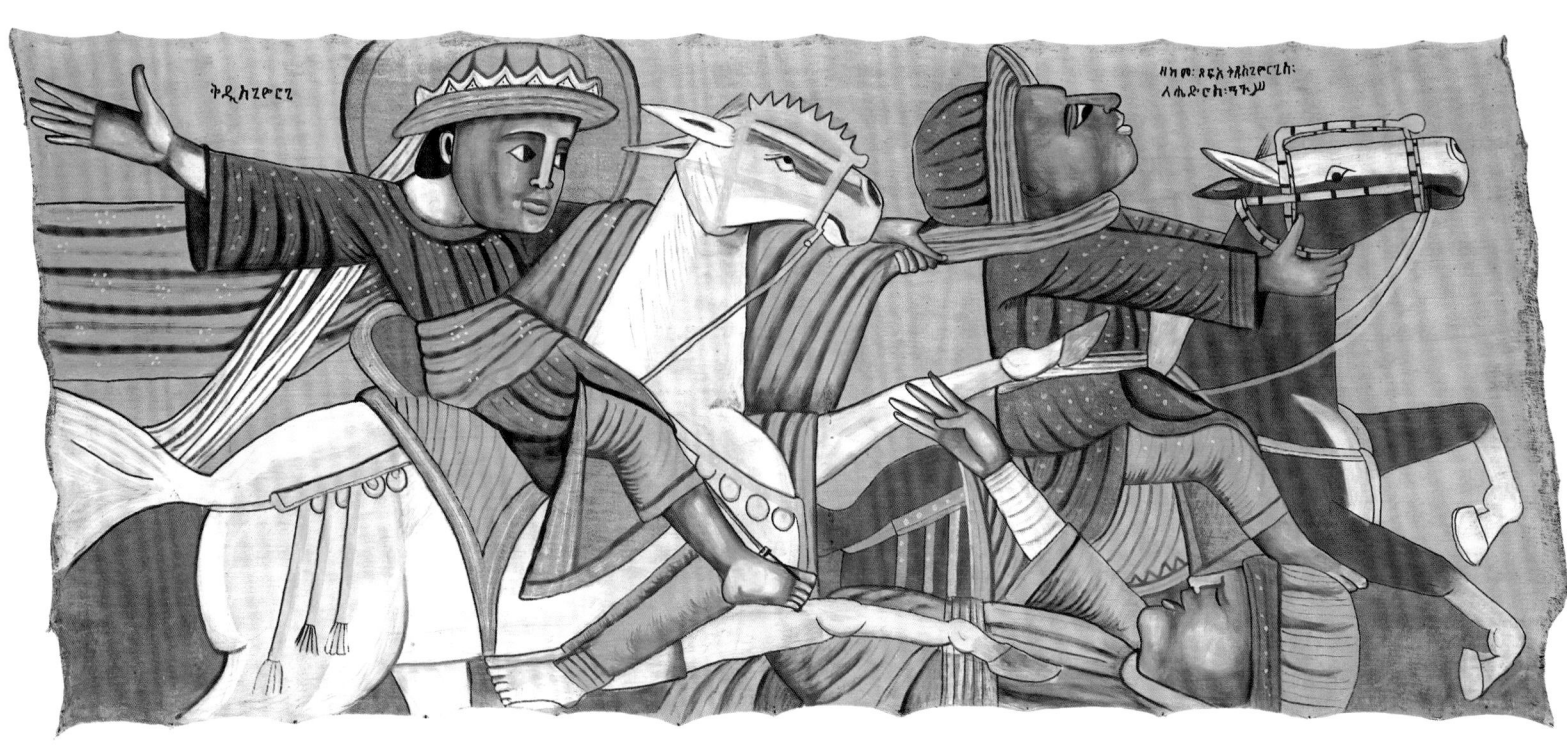

CAT. NO. 10

Herod Falling from His Horse
circa 1970

Paint on cloth
92 x 65 cm
Collection of Mrs. Benedetta Riva

Ethiopian Christians believe that during the Holy Family's flight to Egypt to escape the wrath of King Herod, they made a stop in Ethiopia. Paintings and icons of the family fleeing Herod's soldiers are legion, and the best-known Ethiopian image shows the family hiding behind a tree and their donkey peering out from it. Some Ethiopian paintings also depict the slaughter of the innocents, Herod's ordering the killing of every boy child under the age of two in and around Bethlehem. Here, however, Adamu presents a less-sinister image of Herod. Drawing upon the story presented in the *Negere Maryam* (*History and Miracles of Our Lady Mary*), Adamu presents the intervention of Saint Michael in assisting the Holy Family to make their escape.

Adamu describes Saint Michael as coming "out of nowhere" to put the cross in front of Herod to turn him away. Then Saint Michael "cursed Herod and he fell off his horse." This painting was titled *Herod's Horse Prostrating before the Cross* in an exhibition of 1996. Adamu is emphatic, however, that Herod's horse is not prostrating; it has fallen because of God, as signified by the cross. Adamu calls the ornately carved wooden hand-cross carried by Saint Michael, "the Apostles' cross." It is of the type carried by priests and bishops. In describing further how he came to depict this subject in this fashion, Adamu points out that he did not know what sort of clothing Romans or Jews wore in those days, so he studied how they were represented in older paintings. As a result, Herod is clothed in regal garments such as were once worn by Ethiopia's highland nobility. Armed with a traditional sword and spear, he rides a richly caparisoned horse whose trappings are similar to those that could be seen on royal occasions well into the twentieth century.

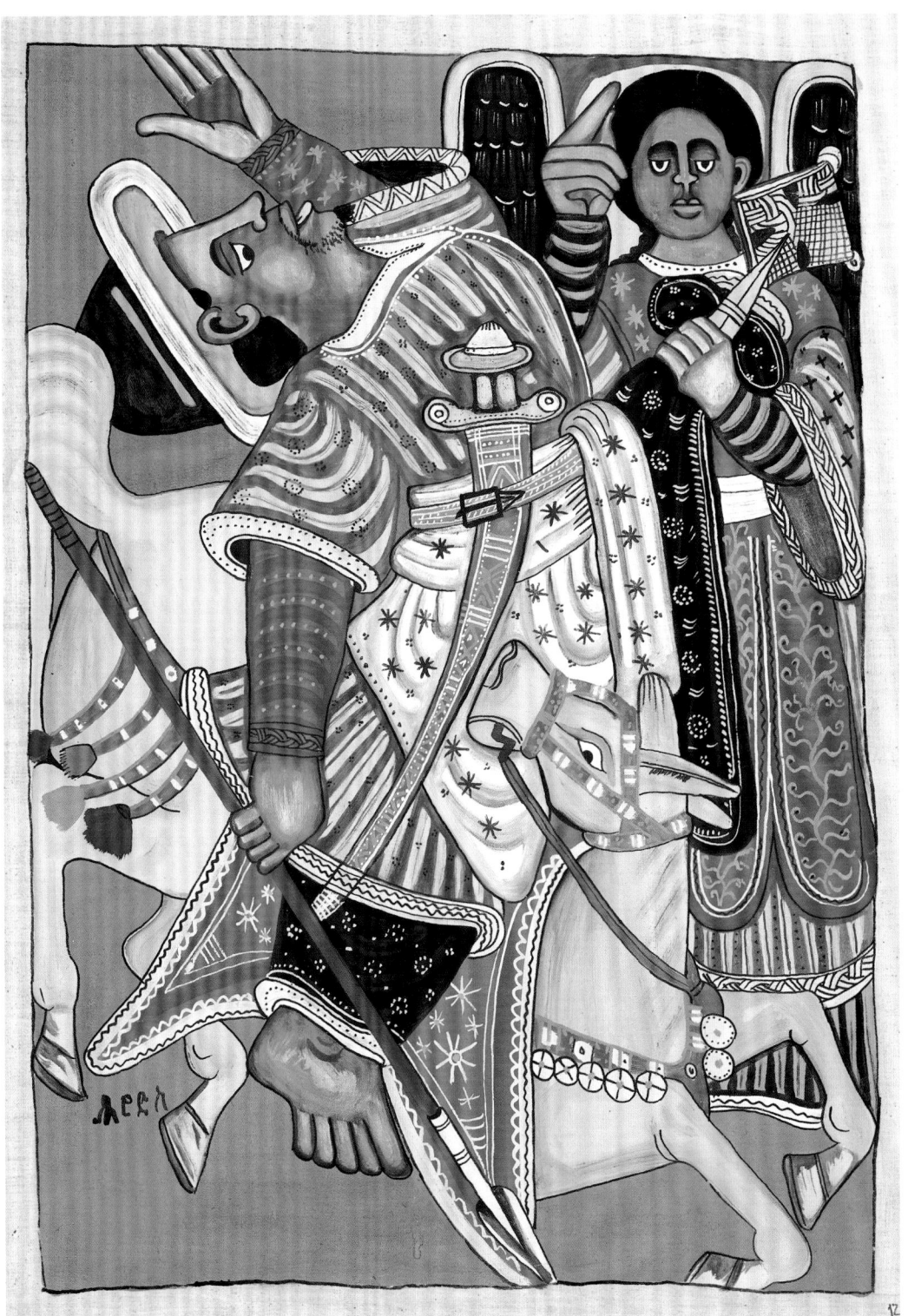

CAT. NO. 11

Clergymen
circa 1980–1995

Paint on cloth
74 x 192 cm
Collection of the Institute of Ethiopian Studies,
Addis Ababa University, no. 10285

This painting presents the hierarchy of the clergy in the Ethiopian Orthodox Church. In the front row are archbishops (*pappas*), each holds a hand-cross, which all priests carry and offer to anyone who approaches them for a blessing. Adamu explains, "You kiss the cross because you believe that the cross on which Jesus Christ was crucified will heal you, and when the priest blesses you, it shows that you are blessed with the cross of Jesus Christ." Those in the second row are bishops (*ippisqoppos*). To achieve the rank of archbishop or bishop in the church hierarchy requires considerable religious study in one of the many monasteries dotting Ethiopia's highlands, as well as a high degree of discipline and piety. Historically, appointment as a bishop was also based on experience in the church, but Adamu observes that today, there is an element of politics involved. Behind the bishops, Adamu has painted the priests (*kahin*) and, finally, at the back, the congregation.

One of the features of paintings that derive from Ethiopian Orthodox Church tradition is an emphasis given to eyes. This painting is a marvelous example of how Adamu elaborates on this convention by including figures who gaze out of the picture space, effectively pulling the viewer into the story. In this work, the archbishops and bishops are all depicted facing in one direction, but the pupils of their eyes suggest they are not looking at the same thing.

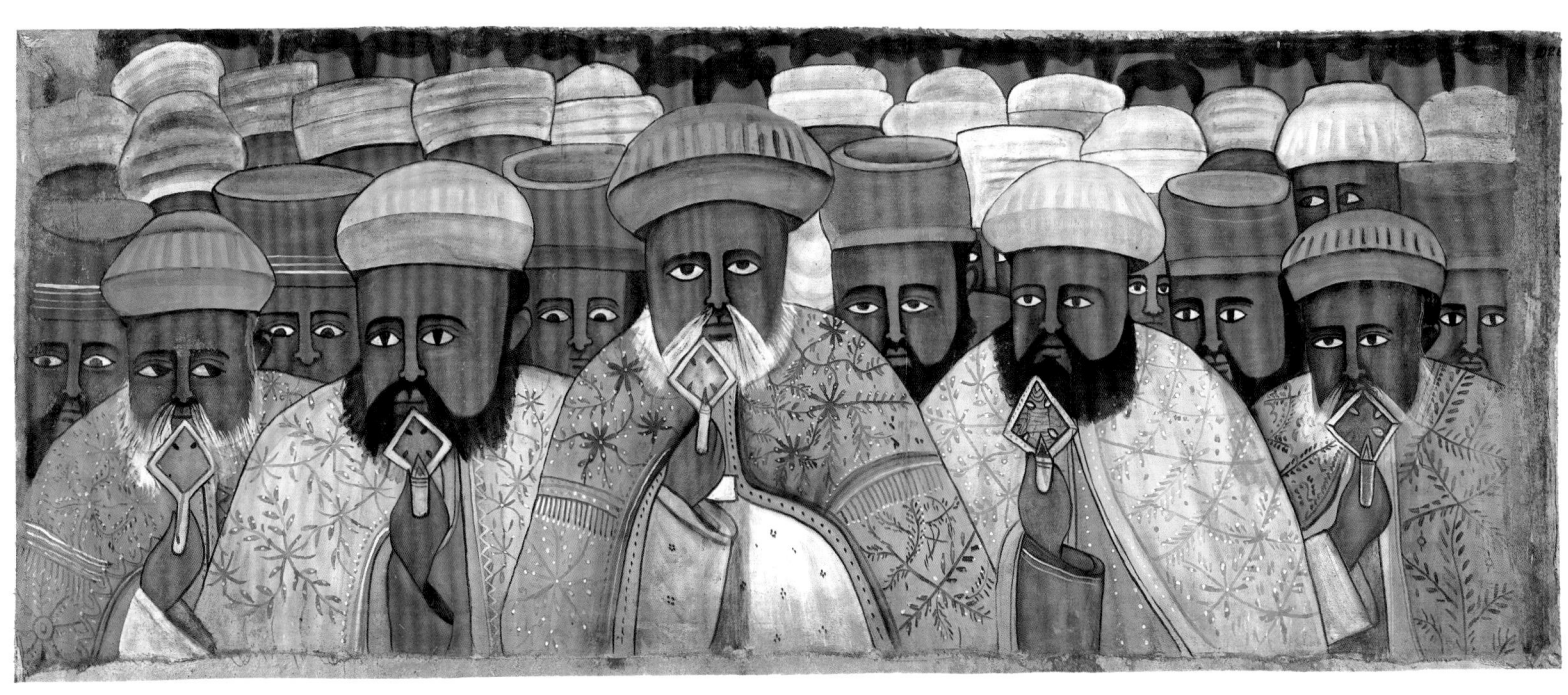

CAT. NO. 12

Returning to the Church
1998

Paint on cloth
100 x 55 cm
Collection of Neal and Elizabeth Sobania

Typically, the church is the most prominent building in rural Christian communities in highland Ethiopia. It is often set in a grove of trees at the village's highest point with houses grouped below it. Most churches are not large enough to accommodate all of a community's congregants, however, and as a result, services are often conducted outdoors on the church grounds. For the celebration of Timqet (Epiphany), the *tabot*—a tablet representing the Ark of the Covenant and serving as the symbolic core of every church—is taken from the *meqdes*, or the sanctuary, inside the church to an open field. Although this is a solemn religious occasion, throngs of people accompany the *tabot* with singing and dancing. The celebration culminates with the sprinkling of holy water in commemoration of Christ's baptism in the Jordan River. At the conclusion of the service, the *tabot* is returned to the church, carried under a decorative cloth atop the head of a priest. In the center of this painting, at the base of the hill, two priests are depicted carrying *tabots* under red cloths. Leading the procession to the church are children singing the glory of the *tabot*. To the left of the procession are the *mezmuran* (members of the choir) who sing and chant to the beat of a large drum, accompanied by dancing and the rhythmic movement of prayer sticks. These are carried by the turbaned priests at the end of the procession. Once the *tabot* has been returned to the church, people bring bread to the priests to be blessed, and it is then given to the congregants. In the foreground, a priest is shown blessing bread, which a nun, on the right, then offers to the assembled congregation.

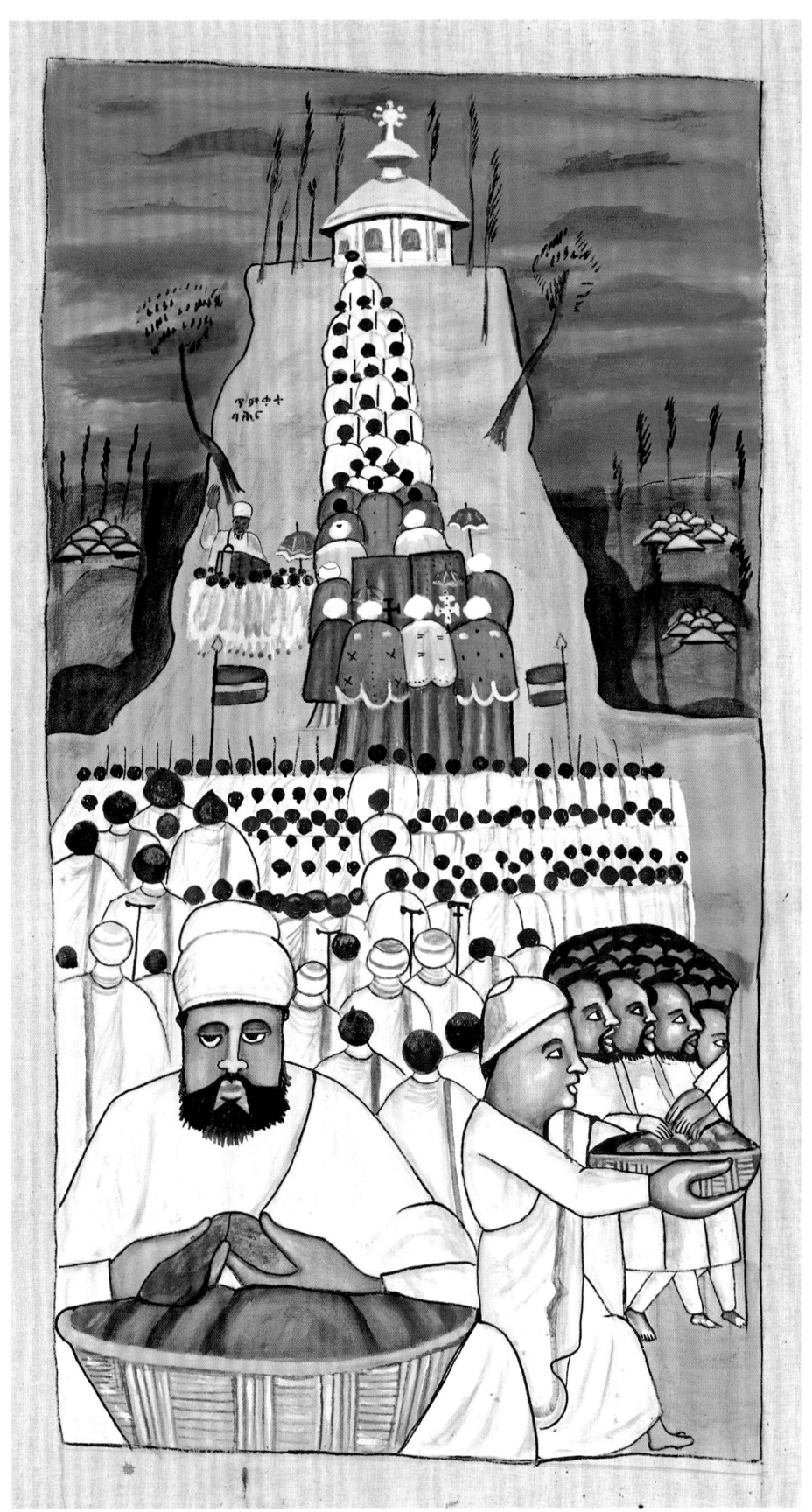

CAT. NO. 13

Zar (Adbar Coffee Ceremony)
circa 1990

Paint on cloth
96 x 178 cm
Collection of the Institute of Ethiopian Studies,
Addis Ababa University, no. 9641

In Ethiopia, everyday life can be full of difficulties, and these are sometimes attributed to the presence of malevolent spirits. *Zar* spirits, recognized in Ethiopia and other parts of northeast Africa, are understood to be the cause of many physical and mental illnesses. The central figure in this painting is a female medium who, according to believers, is able to identify the spirit tormenting an individual, as well as to predict the future. The sheep in the lower-right corner is a payment for the medium's services. When a spirit demands coffee, the medium must drink it quickly to satisfy the spirit. This is referred to as the Adbar Coffee Ceremony. The veiled medium holds a *sini*, or cup, of coffee. Her bodyguards sit beside her. To the right, her assistant prepares additional cups of coffee for later consultations.

A popular medium will attract many people, as shown in this painting. At the center right, the man with his back turned and hand outstretched controls the flow of people seeking to visit the medium. Often while people wait their turn to approach her, they join together to summon the *zar* spirit through singing and beating drums. The people in the upper-right quadrant of the painting clap their hands over their mouths in surprise or amazement as they witness the medium's performance. The man on the left smoking a water pipe—a sinful act according to Adamu—has his head wrapped in a cloth, signifying that he is possessed by a spirit. Significantly, Adamu does not condone this cultural practice. As he points out, "I paint this subject to show the reality, but not to show that it is right [accepted behavior]—what they [mediums] do is against God. People still do this around here—for money. If you go [to visit a medium] you have to pay."

This painting is signed by Qes Adamu's friend Wondimu Wonde (1918–2001). As mentioned earlier (see p. 36), Wondimu, at times, wrote his own name on paintings that Adamu had given him to sell. It is easy to see that the signature and the inscription describing the subject of the painting were produced by two different hands.

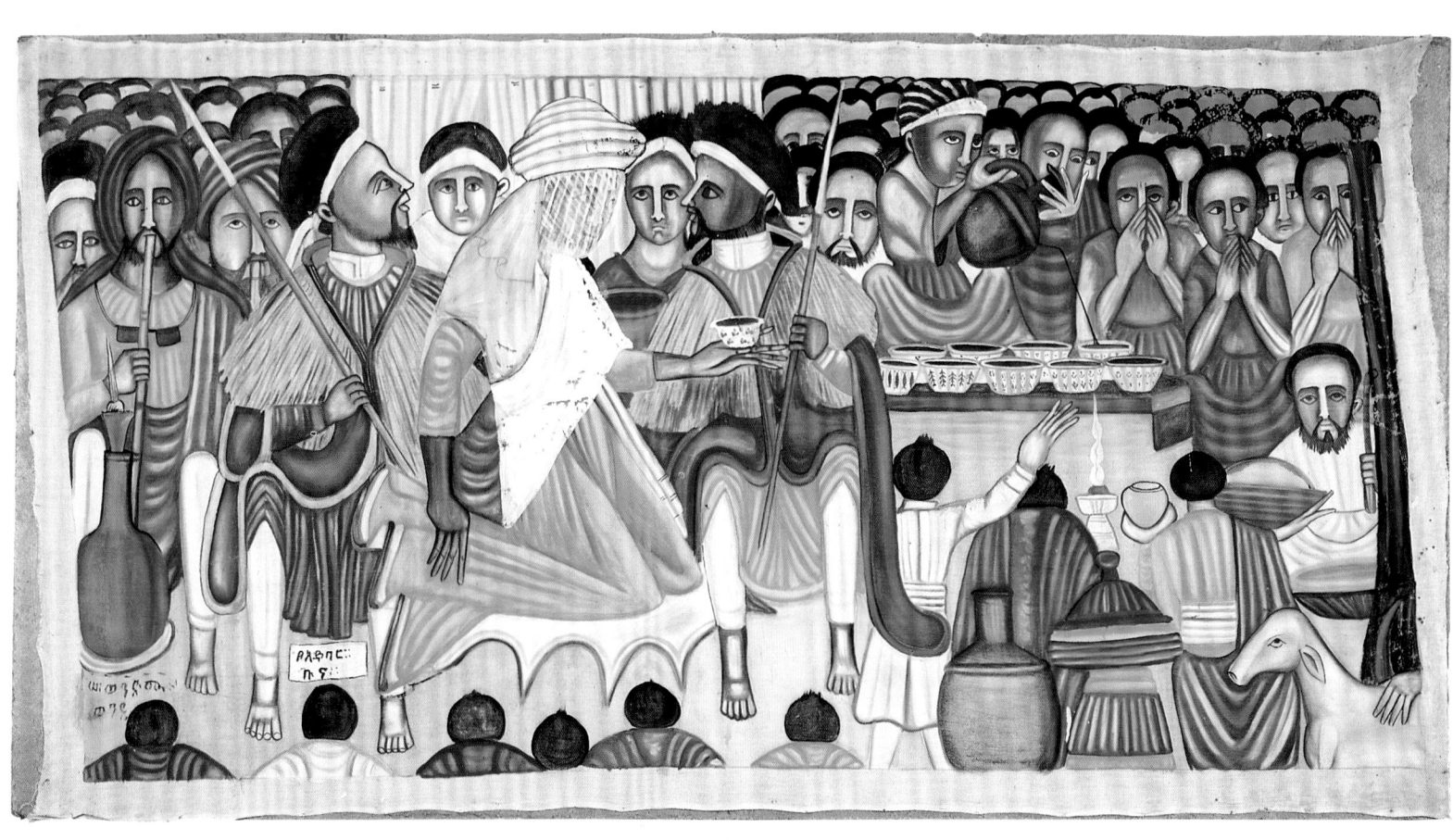

CAT. NO. 14

Muslims in Their Mosques
circa 2000

Paint on cloth
99 x 150 cm
FMCH X2003.13.10; Anonymous Gift

Over the past few years, Adamu has begun to include Muslims, who currently make up nearly half of the population of Ethiopia, in his paintings. He portrays various aspects of their lives and the important role they play in the country. Adamu credits the original impetus for approaching this subject to his friend Wondimu Wonde. Roughly ten years ago, Wondimu was asked by a member of the staff of the Institute of Ethiopian Studies at Addis Ababa University why he and his fellow artists never painted scenes of Muslim life. Adamu recalls that Wondimu, not knowing how he might approach this subject, was advised to "paint almsgiving," as this practice is shared by Islam and the Ethiopian Orthodox Church. Wondimu, whose eyesight was failing at the time, passed this advice on to Adamu, who began painting scenes drawn from firsthand experience and what he saw on television, including depictions of Ramadan at the Grand Mosque in the Merkato neighborhood of Addis Ababa. As to why he took up the challenge to paint something so very different, Adamu explains, "I just want to paint history. The Muslims don't like painting but they are a part of our history."

Using the conventional approach of painting scenes in registers, Adamu has captured an array of activities that take place in and around a mosque. In the lower register are men from the countryside arriving at the mosque. Adamu portrays them as pilgrims—identified by the distinctive forked wooden staffs they carry—who are stopping en route to the shrine of Sheikh Hussein in the Bale Mountains of south central Ethiopia. The central figure, who is seen from the back entering the mosque, carries a gourd of water suspended from his staff for use in performing ablutions. Adamu identifies the people praying in the second register as women, while the fourth register depicts men praying. In the third, men perform their ritual ablutions before prayer, and the fifth register presents sheikhs, whom Adamu portrays "like priests to show they are important." Behind them, the archways, like the one at the center of the bottom register, indicate that these activities are taking place within the mosque.

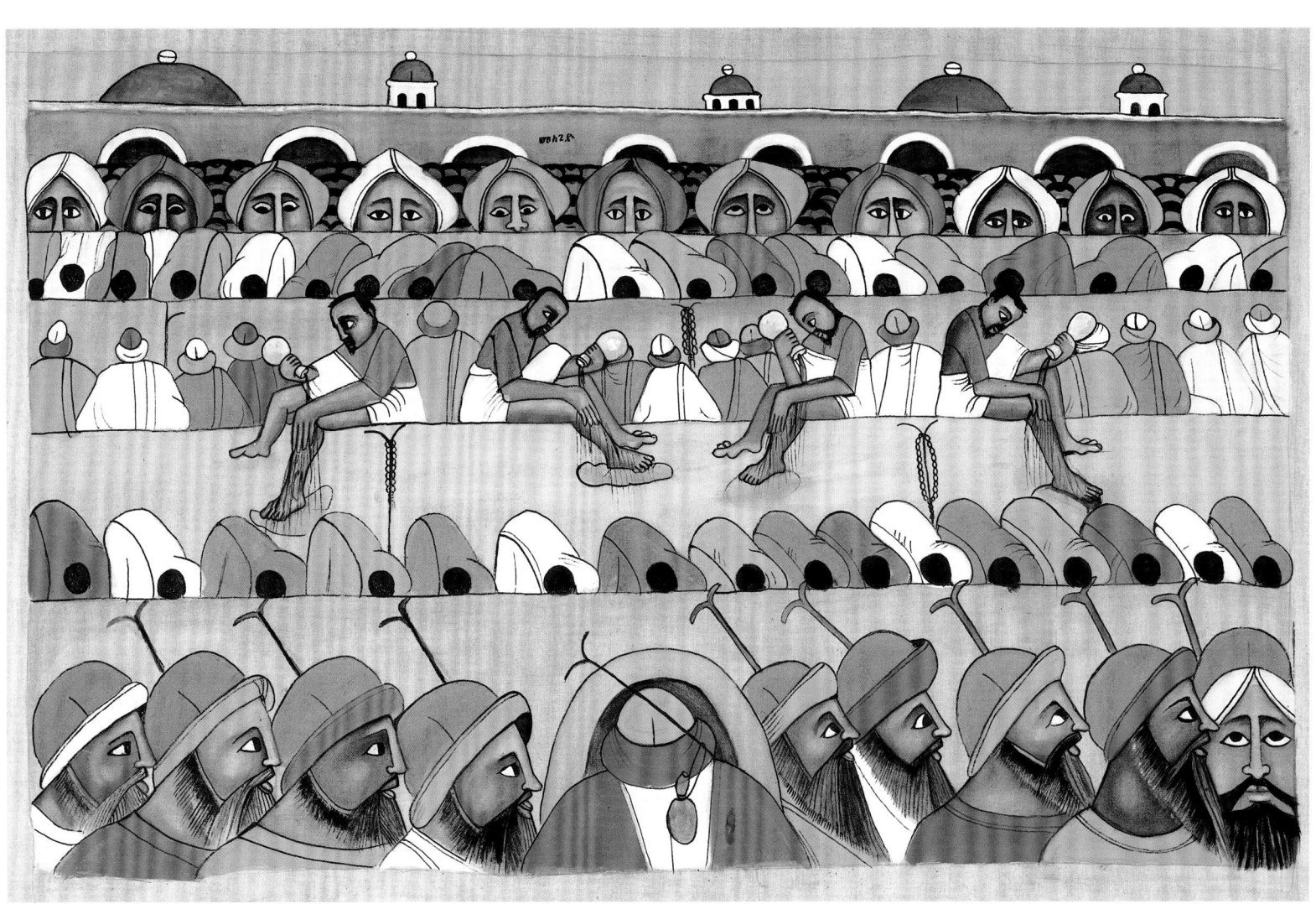

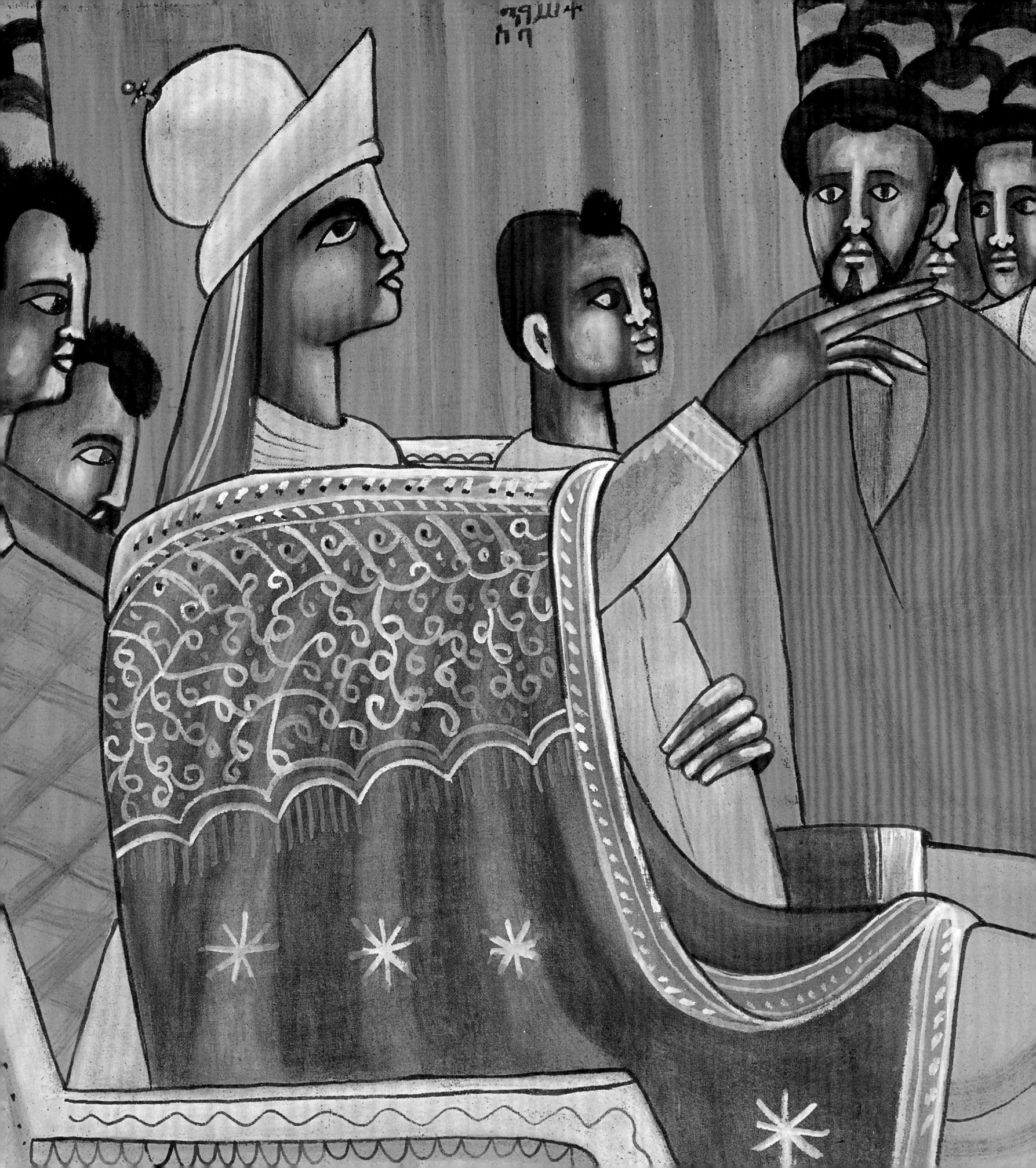

Recalling the Past

Like his paintings of religious subjects, Qes Adamu's history paintings are a mix of tradition and his own creative thinking. This is perhaps nowhere more evident than in his treatment of the legend of the Queen of Sheba (known as Makida, Saba, or Azeb in Ethiopia) and King Solomon. In addition to having religious significance for Ethiopian Orthodox Christians, this legend has acquired tremendous historical importance. Menilek, the son supposedly born from the union of the Ethiopian queen and King Solomon, became the first king in Ethiopia's Solomonic dynasty. The last Ethiopian ruler to trace his ancestry to King Solomon was Haile Selassie I (r. 1930–1974).

Since the beginning of the twentieth century, thousands of visitors to Ethiopia have purchased paintings of the story of Sheba and Solomon. These usually take the form of a serial narrative presented in a rectangular grid of frames (see fig. 14)—each dedicated to one episode. Adamu, however, avoids this convention, choosing instead to depict only a few parts or even a single event in the story. His paintings frequently celebrate the majesty of the two monarchs (cat. nos. 15–17). It is inconsequential to most Ethiopians that the Queen of Sheba is a historical enigma generally associated with the ancient south Arabian kingdom of Saba. Similarly, it does not matter that King Solomon lived during the tenth century BCE and the Aksumite Empire, with which Sheba has been associated by Ethiopians (see cat. no. 16), dates from first century BCE to the eighth century CE. The national epic of Solomon and Sheba is to many highland Ethiopians, their one true history.

Aside from the story of Solomon and Sheba, most of the historical events that Qes Adamu and other urban painters focus on are drawn from the last 150 years, beginning with the exploits of Emperor Tewodros II, who ruled from 1855 to 1868. To this day, Tewodros is remembered as the quintessential Ethiopian ruler, a great military leader and politician who ultimately sacrificed himself for his country. He attempted to unify a politically fractured Abyssinia (the region corresponding to present-day central and northern Ethiopia and Eritrea) and to establish diplomatic and cultural relations with the world's great states. His strong rebellious character set him apart from the great leaders who succeeded him, specifically Yohannis IV (r. 1872–1889) and Menilek II (r. 1889–1913). It was Menilek II, however, who realized Tewodros's dream of a unified Abyssinia. Menilek led a series of successful military campaigns against the peoples living to the south of Abyssinia, and during his reign, the new nation of Ethiopia grew to the limits currently defined by the borders of Ethiopia and Eritrea. Menilek also managed to thwart Italy's attempt to colonize Ethiopia at the famous Battle of Adwa in 1896, another extremely popular theme of paintings, second only to depictions of the story of the Queen of Sheba. Under Menilek Addis Ababa was established as the new capital of the nation and Ethiopia's first modern city. The emperor also negotiated diplomatic relations with most of the then-powerful nations of the world. Adamu's portrayals of Tewodros with Tewabetch (cat. nos. 18, 19) and Menilek with Taitu (cat. no. 23) successfully bring the dynamism and monumentality seen in many of his religious works to the interpretation of historical events and figures.

Qes Adamu often draws upon his firsthand experiences and observations in rendering historical events. A very interesting example of this may be seen in his representation of the Italians retreating after their defeat at Adwa (cat. no. 22). Adamu has depicted the Italian forces, not in the military garb of the late nineteenth century, but in the uniforms that he saw them wear as a young boy in the 1930s and early 1940s, during the Italian Occupation. Similarly, he combines visual references taken from media coverage of Queen Elizabeth II's celebrated visit to Ethiopia in 1965 with his own recollections of the event, which he witnessed just a few years after moving to Addis Ababa.

Qes Adamu deliberately avoids painting politically charged subjects. Obviously, all his history paintings have political significance, but time often lessens their impact. In particular Adamu was reticent about accepting a commission for a painting depicting the entry of rebel forces into Addis Ababa in 1991, an event that ended Ethiopia's former Marxist regime and marked the beginning of the country's current government (cat. no. 25). His painting, as well as his explanation of it, make it clear that the composition is not a political statement but rather a historical document, based on the artist's own observations, what he heard from friends, and what he read in the media and saw on television.

CAT. NO. 15

Solomon and Sheba Embrace
circa 1980–1995

Paint on cloth
100 x 192 cm
Collection of the Institute of Ethiopian Studies,
Addis Ababa University, no. 10317

Of all the episodes that make up the story of the Queen of Sheba (known as Makida in Ethiopia), Qes Adamu is most taken with the queen's initial meeting with Solomon. The events Adamu portrays in this painting are arguably the most significant in the narrative of their first encounter. Solomon, clearly enamored with Makida, fetes her with a banquet of spicy and salty food. He expresses his desire for her, but she refuses him. Solomon then has Makida promise that she will not take anything that belongs to him without first asking permission, and the Ethiopian queen agrees that if she breaks this promise, she will give herself to her host. Awakening during the night, consumed with thirst after the spicy meal, Sheba takes a drink of water without asking. Solomon confronts her with her transgression, and, as agreed, they sleep together. Upon her return to Ethiopia, Makida gives birth to a son, whom she names Menilek. When he is old enough to assume the throne, she abdicates, and Menilek, according to the legend, becomes the first king of Ethiopia's Solomonic dynasty.

In this painting Adamu depicts Solomon and Sheba as having eaten dinner, the cloth-covered table (*mesob*) is situated in the central foreground. The royal pair sit on a bed, embracing. Adamu comments that Makida "is happy and raises her arm with happiness." He indicates the late hour by portraying the two monarchs in nightclothes, and the queen's hair, which is worn in a Tigrean style in reference to her northern Ethiopian origins, is shown uncovered. In the foreground, in front of the *mesob*, Adamu presents the queen's hand filling a gold cup with water from a spigot. The color palette and surface of this painting are very similar to Adamu's *Tewabetch Assisting Tewodros to Prepare for Battle* (cat. no. 18). Both were made to look old, in a manner suggesting that they were produced at roughly the same time.

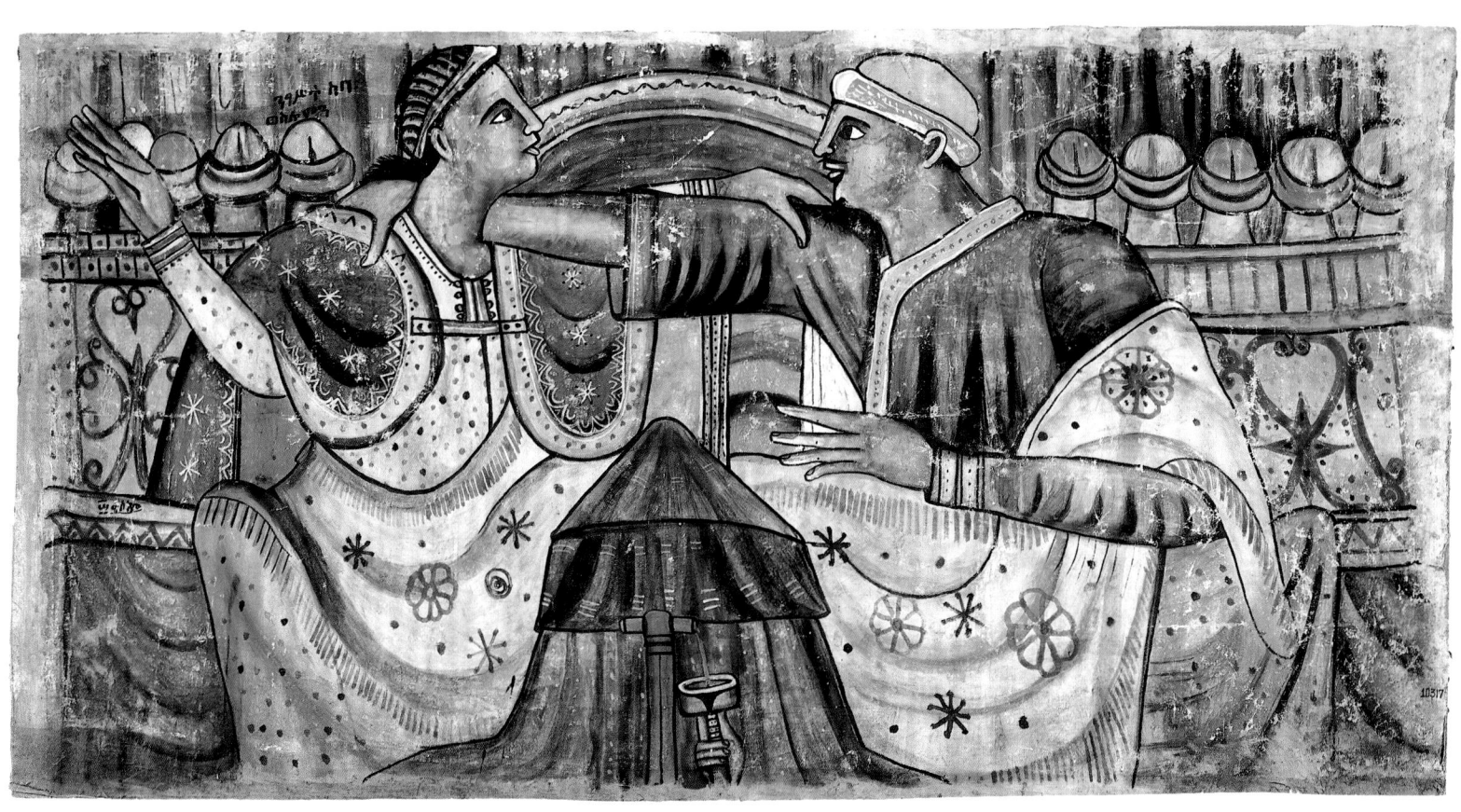

CAT. NO. 16

*Sheba Shows Menilek
a Photograph of His Father*
circa 1970–1980

Paint on cloth
71 x 198 cm
Ian Campbell Collection

In this episode from the story of the Queen of Sheba (Makida), courtiers in the palace surround Makida and her young son, Menilek, who sits in her lap. Menilek is depicted with a traditional Ethiopian boy's hairstyle. This is the eve of his departure for Jerusalem to meet his father. Qes Adamu portrays Makida showing her son an image of his father, a gift given to her by Solomon for this very purpose. Interestingly, the inscription in Adamu's painting identifies the portrait as "Solomon photograph." When asked, however, Adamu is very much aware that "they didn't have photography back then." The painting is not the only means by which Menilek is believed to have been taught to recognize his father. According to Adamu, and the early-fourteenth-century chronicle known as the *Kebra Negast* (*Glory of the Kings*), the queen also used a mirror to show her son his resemblance to the great king. In addition Menilek is often said to have taken with him a gold ring that Solomon had given to Makida. Adamu attributes the incorporation of the painting of Solomon to his godfather, the painter Yohannis Tesemma.

Menilek is supposed to have returned from his journey with the eldest sons of Israel and the Ark of the Covenant, which he presented to his mother. Makida then abdicated and Menilek became king. Later, Menilek erected a monument in her honor, which over time came to be identified with one of the great stele in the town of Axum. In addition, a large reservoir in Axum is, today, popularly referred to as the Queen of Sheba's Bath; and the ruins of an ancient royal palace situated on the modern town's southern outskirts are called the Queen of Sheba's Palace. Thus the Queen of Sheba's kingdom is understood to be the Aksumite Empire, and her visit to Solomon is associated with the coming of Christianity to Ethiopia.

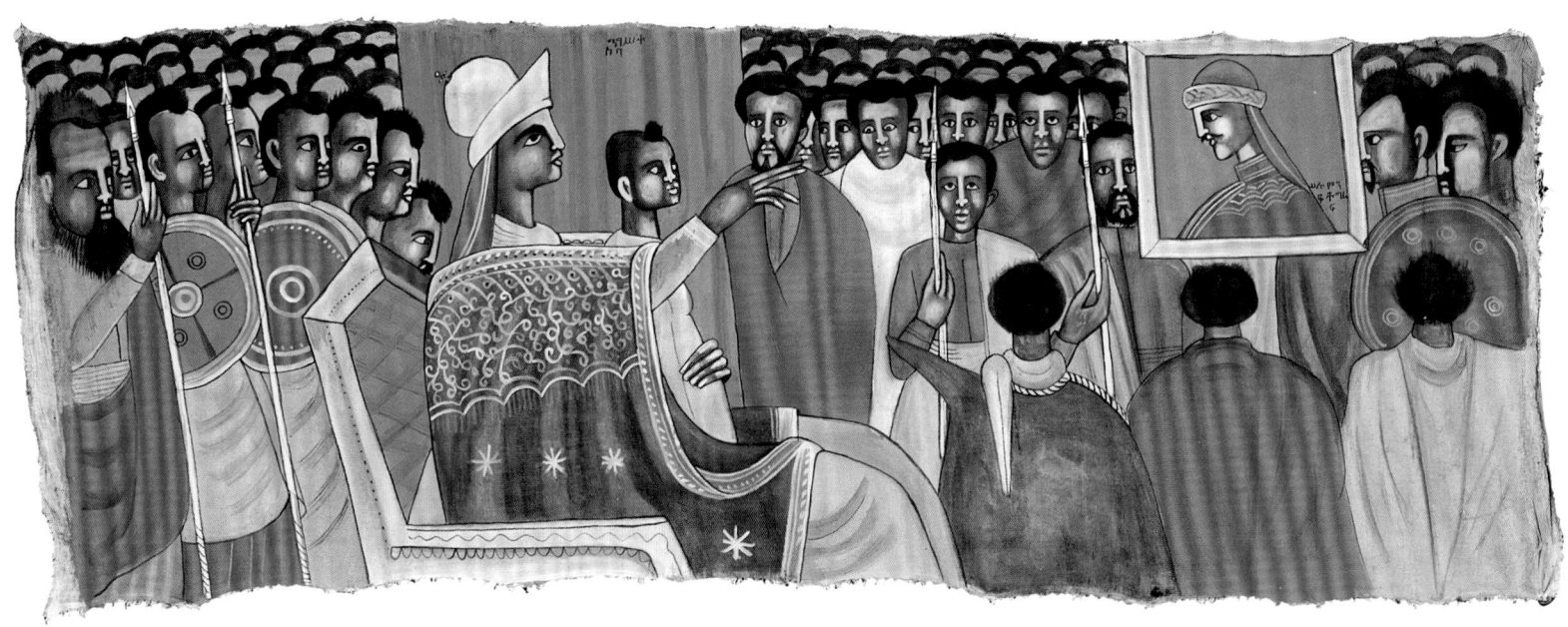

CAT. NO. 17

Solomon Shows Sheba His Servants
circa 1980–1995

Paint on cloth
76 x 195 cm
Collection of the Institute of Ethiopian Studies,
Addis Ababa University, no. 9901

The story of the Queen of Sheba and King Solomon is arguably the most common theme in Ethiopian popular painting today. Recounted in the sacred books of Judaism, Christianity, and Islam, the dynastic story, as presented in the *Kebra Negast* (*Glory of the Kings*), has become an integral part of Ethiopia's national and religious identity. When, in the Ethiopian telling, the Queen of Sheba learns of Solomon's wisdom and the glories of his kingdom, she travels to Jerusalem to meet him, bearing gifts of spices, incense, ivory, and gold.

The story of Solomon and Sheba is also one of Qes Adamu's favorites. His interpretations of the epic, however, are not the typical serialized "comic strip" narratives that are so common among Ethiopia's urban painters. Instead, he focuses upon individual segments of the story, of which he says there are seventy-two. In recounting this particular episode, Adamu explains that it is part of the queen's history but that it is not found in the Bible. "The story is not from the *Kebra Negast* or the Bible. You cannot find it in the 'big' books; you find it in *gedil* [hagiographies], books about the lives of saints and martyrs."

According to the story, after receiving her gifts, Solomon shows Makida his three demon servants, whom Adamu sees as representing Satan. The queen is, of course, awestruck upon witnessing Solomon's power over Satan's minions. Importantly, Adamu portrays these servants carrying water, which later figures prominently in the story of her visit (see cat. no. 15), and chopping wood. Makida's maidservant, who is always with her and who also plays an important role later in the story, is portrayed with a recognizably northern Ethiopian hairstyle, standing among the retinue immediately behind the queen.

Adamu divides this painting into two sections. On the right, where Solomon and Makida stand, he has represented the interior of the palace. Adamu points out that he used his imagination here, since he didn't know what the palace looked like. Outside of the palace walls, the queen's other advisors and servants wait. Demonstrating once again his interest in representing what the eye actually sees, Adamu depicts only the tops of their heads because "when you see many people in the distance, you just see their heads."

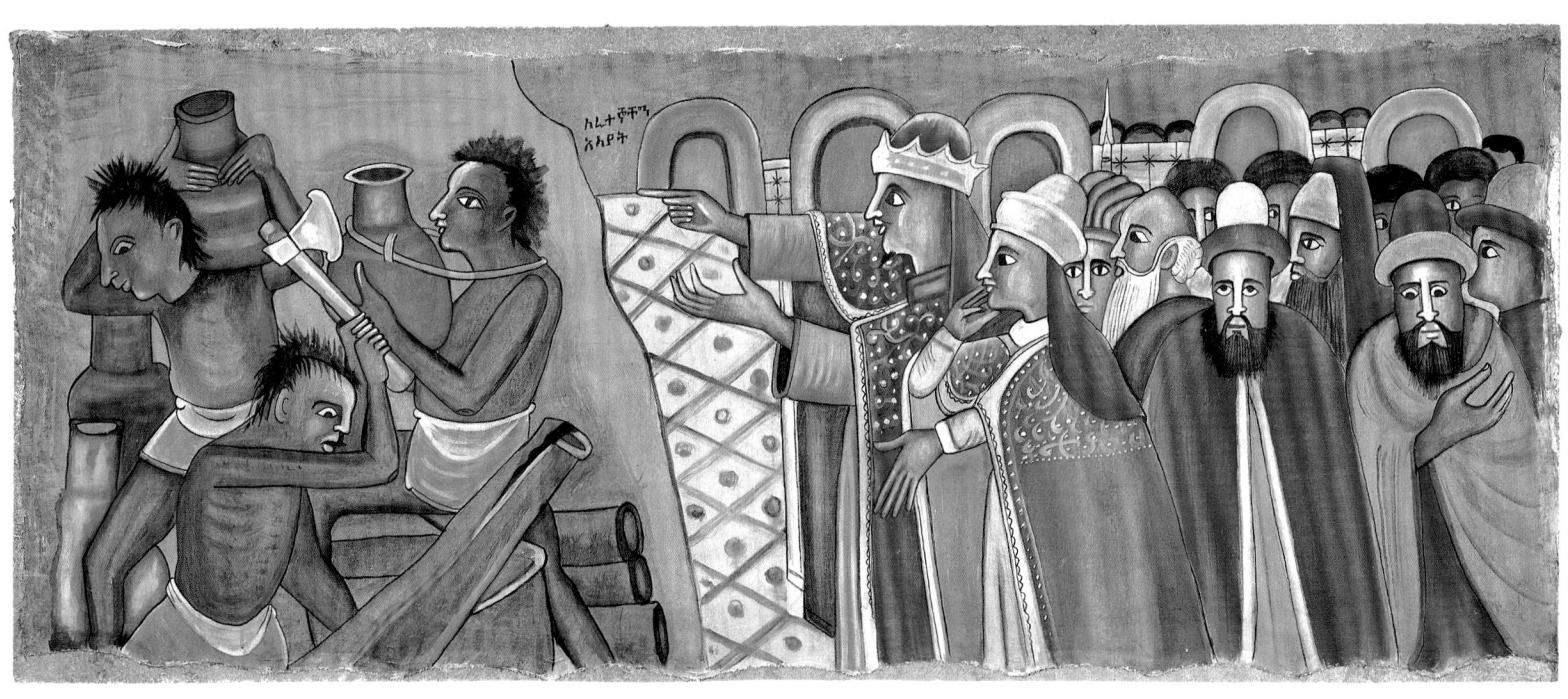

CAT. NO. 18

*Tewabetch Assisting Tewodros
to Prepare for Battle*
circa 1980–1995

Paint on cloth
102 x 190 cm
Collection of the Institute of Ethiopian Studies,
Addis Ababa University, no. 10318

Emperor Tewodros II (r. 1855–1868) was an ambitious and energetic monarch who sought not only to unite the many kingdoms that made up the country but also to modernize Ethiopia. In the end, despite his administrative reforms, he was unable to overcome local rulers—including members of his wife's family—who had a vested interest in sustaining political fragmentation. The military forces he mustered were in large part responsible for his being crowned emperor. He created a new command structure, forming regiments that drew together soldiers from various regions of the country. Later, as his reforms began to unravel, Tewodros grew increasingly violent and erratic in his conduct and actions. When he failed to secure the foreign assistance he needed for his projects, he took a group of European missionaries hostage in frustration. On the eve of being overwhelmed by a British military expedition sent to rescue the hostages, Tewodros committed suicide.

To this day, however, Tewodros is regarded as one of Ethiopia's great national heroes. Adamu, like the vast majority of Ethiopians, admires the emperor. But the painter holds in especially high regard the support Tewodros received from his wife, Tewabetch, and notes, "They are one." He elaborates, "Some women are like this, some are not [so] strong and do not support their husbands.… This painting shows that [Tewabetch and Tewodros] had the same aim, their purpose was one even though her family were his rivals." Tewabetch was the daughter of a regional king, and her marriage to Tewodros was part of his efforts to centralize the monarchy. Adamu has not just painted her assisting her husband to dress for war but actually giving him bullets. He relates, "It is a sign of respect" for her to do this, and Tewabetch told Tewodros, "Be awake in battle." Tewodros is pictured wrapping a *dig*, a type of cloth belt worn by warriors, around his waist. Qes Adamu explains, "Everyone wore one [in battle], not just royalty.… It supports one's back, provides a place to hang swords, and keeps your stomach pulled in if you are hungry." In the background we see Tewodros's sword, spear, and large hide shield, as well as a handsomely decorated wooden chair. For Adamu, however, "the painting shows an example of how people should treat each other, especially husbands and wives."

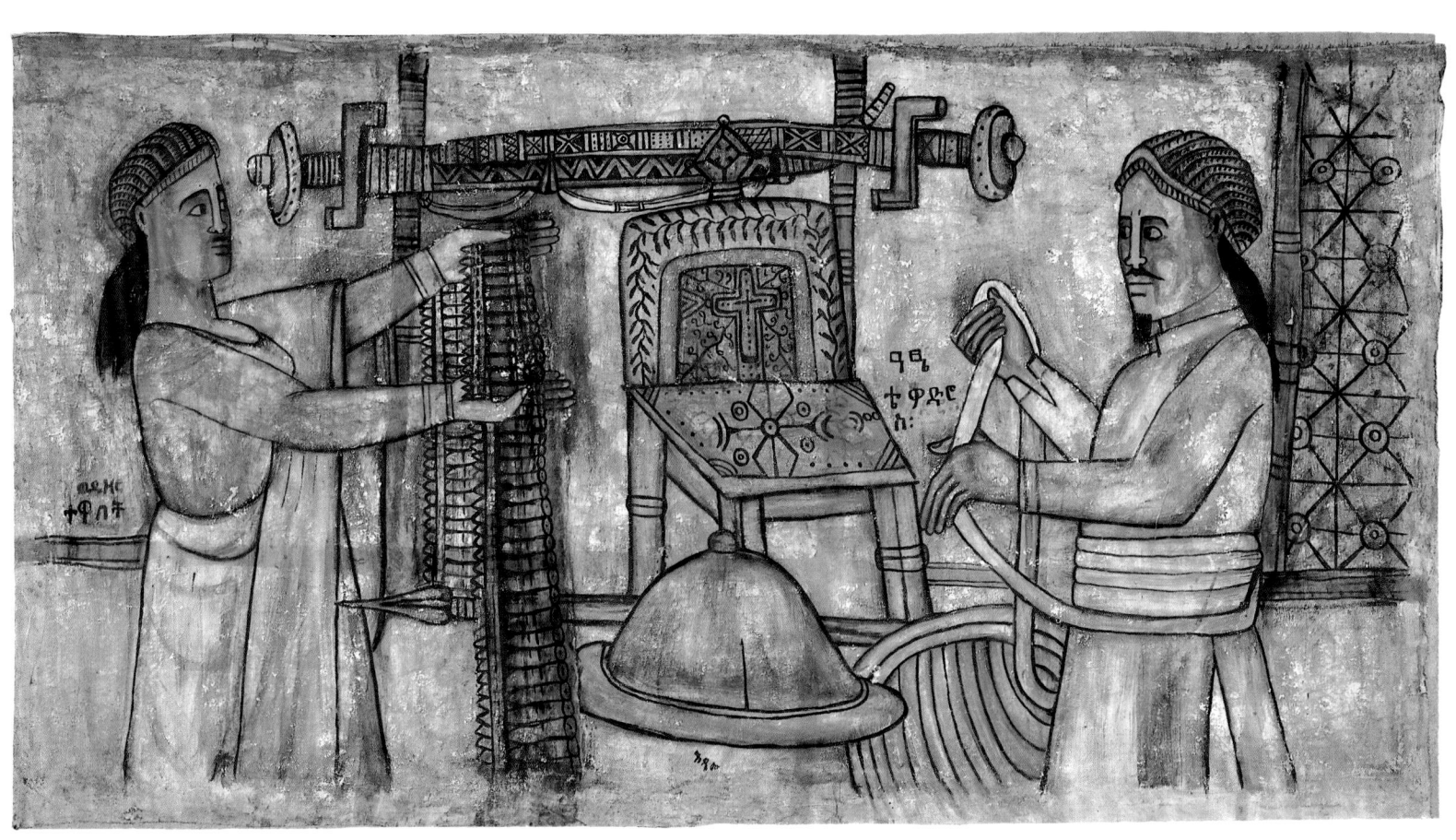

CAT. NO. 19

*Tewodros and Tewabetch
on an Official Visit*
circa 1980–1995

Paint on cloth
78 x 216 cm
Collection of the Institute of Ethiopian Studies,
Addis Ababa University, no. 9898

In this painting, Qes Adamu returns to one of his favorite subjects, Tewodros and Tewabetch, who are shown "on horses going together for a visit…their journey to the country," but no place in particular. Adamu remarks that "the horse is like the rider, strong and looking forward." When asked how he learned to paint horses, Adamu indicates that it is "like a gift…. I always watch them in action—[being ridden,] eating, walking—and I paint them all the time because I like them."

In the painting, Tewodros's status is indicated by the fine border on the cloak draped over his left shoulder, and the couple wear their hair in the traditional plaited fashion that is always used to portray the emperor. It "shows their grace [style], and the plaiting protects them when the sun comes out, at least I heard from people it does this…. Emperor Yohannis and *shifta* [rebels, renegades, or bandits] do this too…. It makes others afraid…. Young men now wear this [hairstyle], not because they are warriors, but because it's the fashion."

The royal couple is surrounded by soldiers carrying spears and shields. Qes Adamu comments that their retainers would also have carried guns but that he doesn't like to include guns in every painting. He has depicted the extent of the royal retinue using the device of painting only the heads of those in the background. Adamu points out that these "were young men, so many of them don't have beards." When "the men go to fight, the women wait [behind]…. The king and queen are always together [and] stay behind the battle. Their presence is very important but they stay back for their safety." Adamu explains that Tewabetch rides in front of her husband because Tewodros is showing her proper respect. It is also quite possible, however, that Adamu is referring to the emperor's interest in keeping a watchful eye on his wife, something that concerned many Ethiopian rulers intent on maintaining the integrity of their lineage.

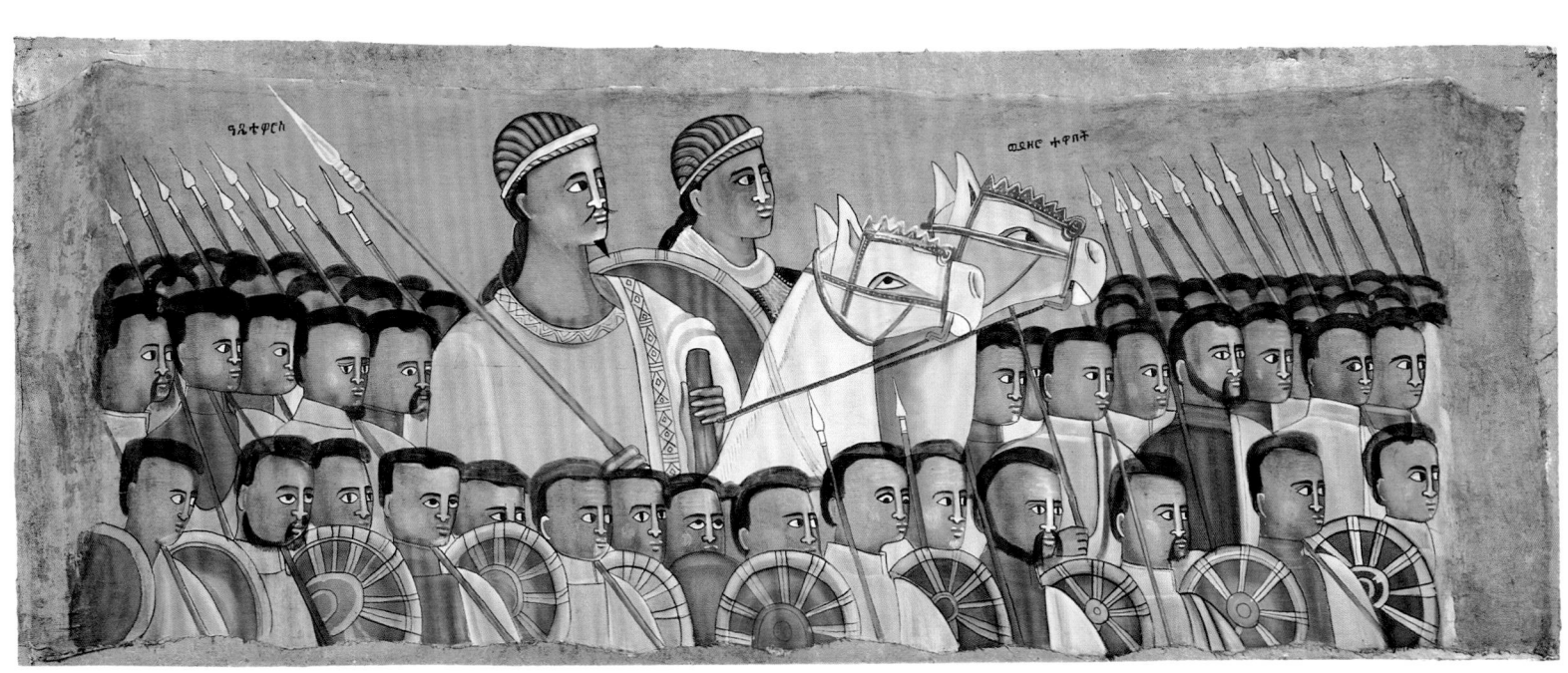

CAT. NO. 20

Battle of Adwa
circa 1980–1995

Paint on cloth
75 x 189 cm
Collection of the Institute of Ethiopian Studies,
Addis Ababa University, no. 9904

In this most unusual painting of the Battle of Adwa, Adamu has preserved all the features associated with conventional representations of this genre—the most salient characteristic being the schematic treatment of the famous battle with the Ethiopians on the left and Italians on the right. But he has ingeniously employed brown lines, representing stone walls, in a diamond-shape configuration to focus the viewer's attention on a few individuals in the center of the sprawl of battle. Within the diamond, soldiers of both armies fight hand-to-hand with swords and bayonets. Figures with closed eyes and splayed arms represent those killed in battle. All of this occurs under the watchful eye of Saint George—representing the providential hand of God—whose intervention is believed by Ethiopians to have assured their victory. Below Saint George are the flags of both countries, and in the top left are Emperor Menilek II (r. 1889–1913) wearing his signature hat, Empress Taitu with braided hair and gun, and priests carrying cloth-covered altar tablets (*tabot*) on their heads (see cat. no. 12). At the bottom right are the retreating Italians, and at the top right is their general who watches the battle with his binoculars. As Adamu notes, "My paintings are never identical," yet they have everything that is expected to appear in these Adwa paintings. As he explains it, "For Adwa paintings there is no need for description. You just say, 'It's Adwa.'"

For Adamu, the overall theme is the Ethiopian victory, and "I always show [the Italians] defeated and retreating." "People often ask who this [Ethiopian officer] is, who this [Ethiopian general] is, but those who died fighting are the poor and no one cares." Adamu's strong feelings about the inattention given to the role of the poor in times of war may in part be explained by the conscription of his eldest son who died on the battlefield in the 1980s. He remarks that "the poor can die while the children of the rich go to school and abroad." Along the same lines, Qes Adamu comments that people seldom care about the animals that are killed and the houses and trees that are destroyed during times of war.

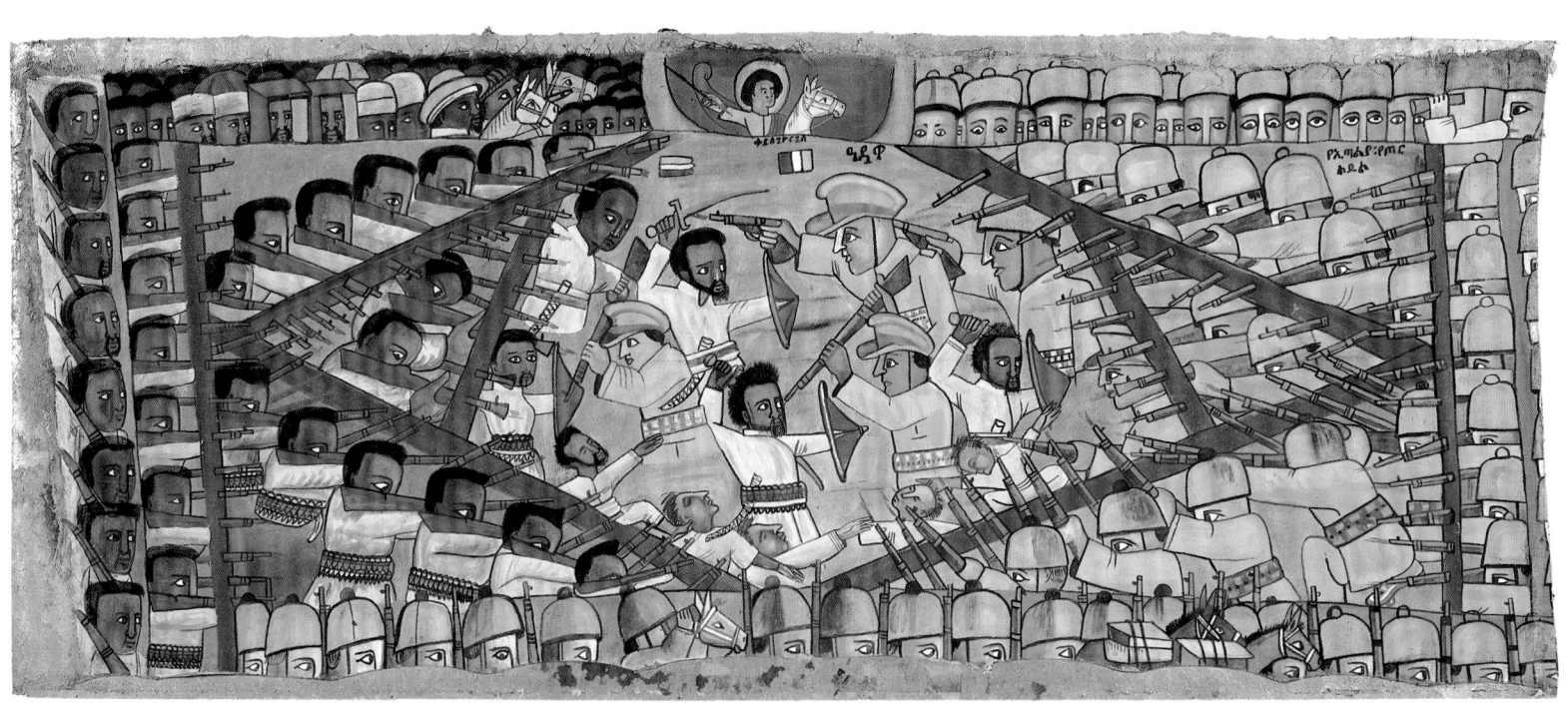

CAT. NO. 21

Battle of Adwa
circa 2000

Paint on cloth
102 x 152 cm
Collection of Neal and Elizabeth Sobania

In 1896 an army led by Emperor Menilek II thwarted Italy's attempt to colonize Ethiopia. It was one of the most significant events in modern history, not only for Ethiopia but for colonized peoples worldwide. Artists began creating paintings of the famous battle soon after the event, and the subject quickly gained an audience. Indeed, the Battle of Adwa has been one of the most popular themes since the end of the nineteenth century when paintings were first produced for sale in Addis Ababa. Menilek himself commissioned and presented Adwa paintings as gifts for visiting foreign dignitaries. Today, Adamu continues to create "a lot of paintings of Adwa because people still like to buy them."

In this particular interpretation, an undulating brown line, representing a stone wall, bisects the composition. Adamu follows the standard convention for depicting the battle, presenting the Ethiopians on the left and the Italian army on the right (note their flags). The stone walls of the battlefield are arranged in a series of inverted "V's" that draw the viewer's attention to an image of Saint George at the top of the painting. It is believed that the saint's intervention insured the Ethiopian victory. In the center of the composition, heads that seem to float between the guns of the Ethiopians and Italians represent the dead. A horizontal band in the upper third of the composition shows Ethiopians and Italians engaged in hand-to-hand combat. At the upper-left edge, Adamu depicts Emperor Menilek and above him Empress Taitu, with her ubiquitous pistol; both are mounted on horseback. Above the empress, are priests. In the lower-left corner, Adamu depicts the numerous servants, male and female, who carried the supplies and provided the labor needed to support the massive army. To the right of the two groups of servants, the emperor and the empress are again represented: Menilek dictating to a scribe and Taitu consulting a priest. In the upper-right corner, the commanding Italian general holds an announcement prepared by the clerks who are at work in the scene immediately below. In the same vertical register, an Italian soldier sleeps in his tent, his compatriots gather, and the Italian armory is depicted full of rifles and pistols. Across the bottom, among retreating Italian soldiers, another general peers through a pair of field glasses to see how the battle ended. Directly above him is an Italian field hospital, while to the left, victorious Ethiopian soldiers escort prisoners, whose "hair is light to identify them as *ferenji* [foreigners], because *ferenji* hair is light."

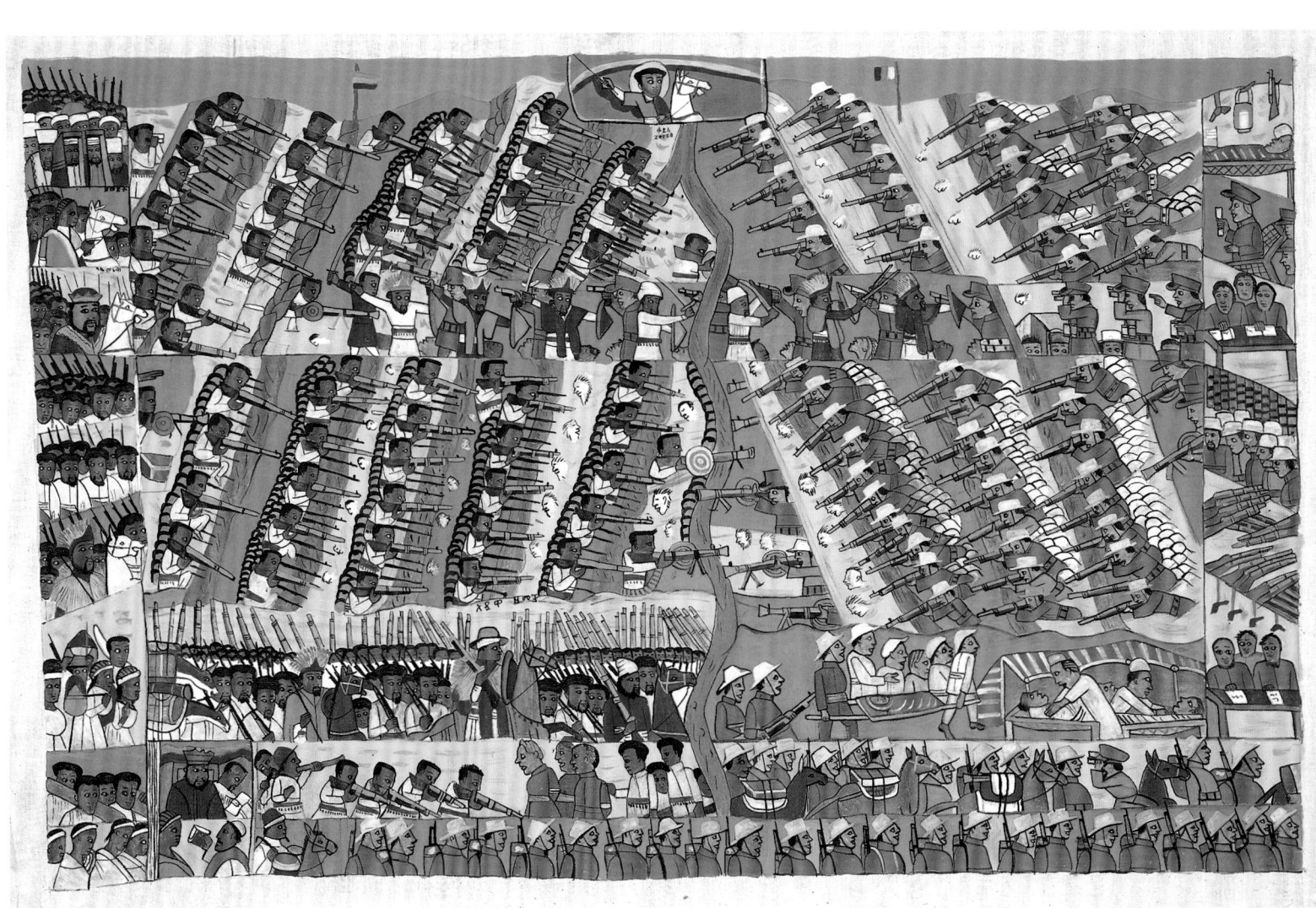

CAT. NO. 22

Retreat of the Italians from Adwa
circa 1980–1995

Paint on cloth
74 x 197 cm
Collection of the Institute of Ethiopian Studies,
Addis Ababa University, no. 10277

This painting is unusual in that it focuses on a single aspect of the famous Battle of Adwa, the retreat of the Italians. Adamu explains that "the Italians are returning from the war front…retreating back to their country through Eritrea." Qes Adamu depicts the Italian troops not in the nineteenth-century military garb they would have worn, however, but in the uniforms he observed at firsthand as a youth during the Italian Occupation of Ethiopia (1936–1941). Indeed, without Adamu's explanation, one might assume that this painting depicted the occupation.

Forty years after the humiliating defeat at Adwa in 1896, Italy, continuing its hegemonic designs on the Horn of Africa, again invaded Ethiopia. Although it managed to occupy Ethiopia until 1941, it faced fierce resistance from the very beginning. As a young boy, Adamu lived through this period, and he remembers a company of Italians stationed in his home province of Gojjam.

In this painting mounted officers carrying pistols appear among the troops. Adamu made a conscious decision to space the walking soldiers so that the pistols would be visible since "only generals had this type of gun." The generals are also depicted looking through field glasses for the Ethiopians. The depicting of enemies or evil people in profile is a pictorial convention associated with Ethiopian painting. When asked if he was consciously employing this device, Adamu indicated that he no longer uses the technique and added, "I feel more freedom to do what I want with my ideas." According to Adamu, "These soldiers are simply marching forward and you only see them from the side."

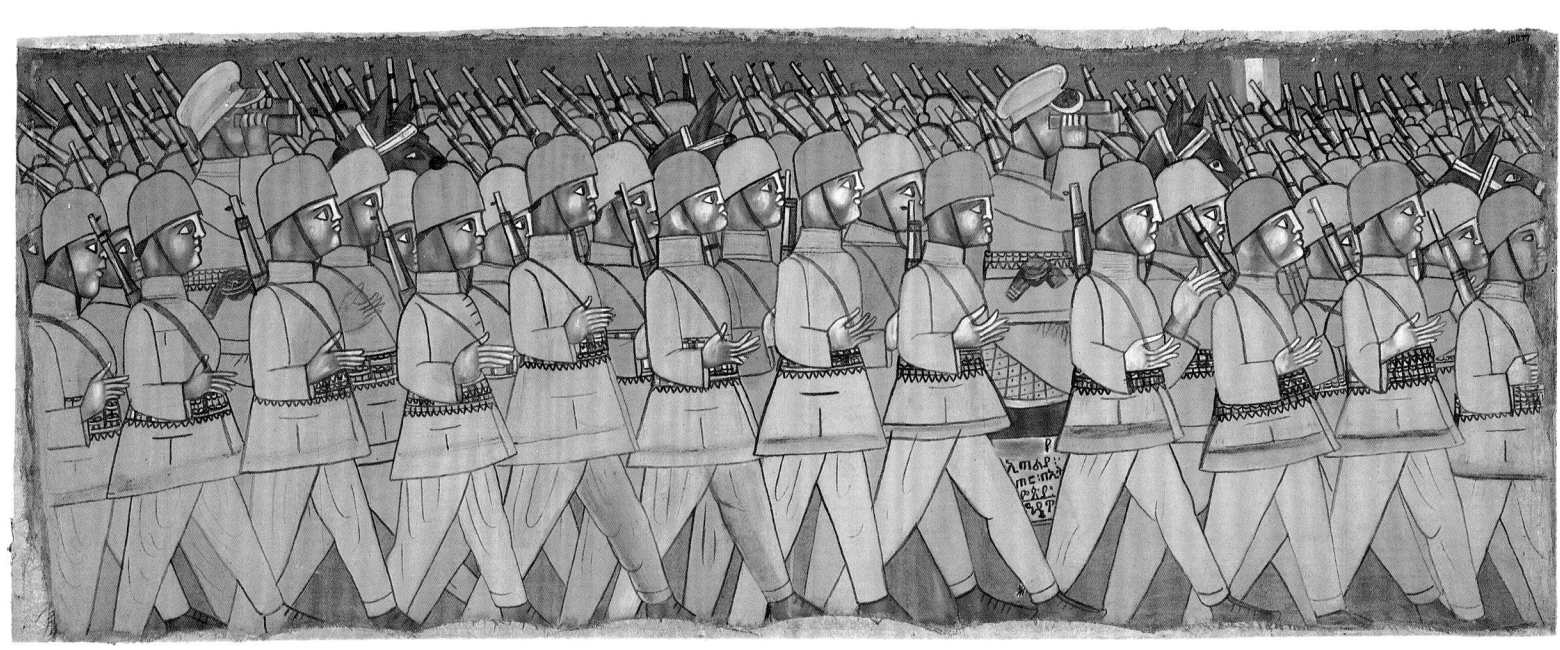

CAT. NO. 23

Menilek and Taitu at Adwa
circa 1980–1995

Paint on cloth
104 x 184 cm
Collection of the Institute of Ethiopian Studies,
Addis Ababa University, no. 10315

Empress Taitu, the consort of Emperor Menilek II, was a commanding personality in her own right and played significant a role in internal politics and foreign affairs. She is understood to have personally intervened in the negotiations between Menilek and the Italian government envoy who presented the claim that Ethiopia was a protectorate of Italy and would have to conduct its foreign affairs through Rome. It was ultimately this claim that led to the Battle of Adwa in 1896. Here Adamu shows Taitu and Menilek on their way north to confront the invading Italian army.

Taitu led her own army in that great battle, and Adamu signals her important role in this warfare and at court by painting her riding in front of Menilek. Adamu explains that he is representing Menilek's respect for Taitu and his partnership with her, as well as her contribution to the Battle of Adwa. This is basically the same idea that is expressed in Adamu's painting of *Tewodros and Tewabetch on an Official Visit* (cat. no. 19). Regally dressed, Emperor Menilek II and Empress Taitu ride on richly caparisoned horses. Neither of them would actually have been in the front lines, but Qes Adamu points out that like other women who assisted in the battle carrying food, water, and guns, Taitu "took care of the wounded and dead." She is portrayed with a modern revolver because "it shows that women can be heroes." He further explains, "I don't know the types of guns [that were used at that time] so I just painted one," and Taitu must be shown holding it because "if the gun was in her pocket, you couldn't see it!" In fact, Empress Taitu's position at court was so strong that when Menilek's health began to decline in 1907, she effectively became the country's ruler for the next few years.

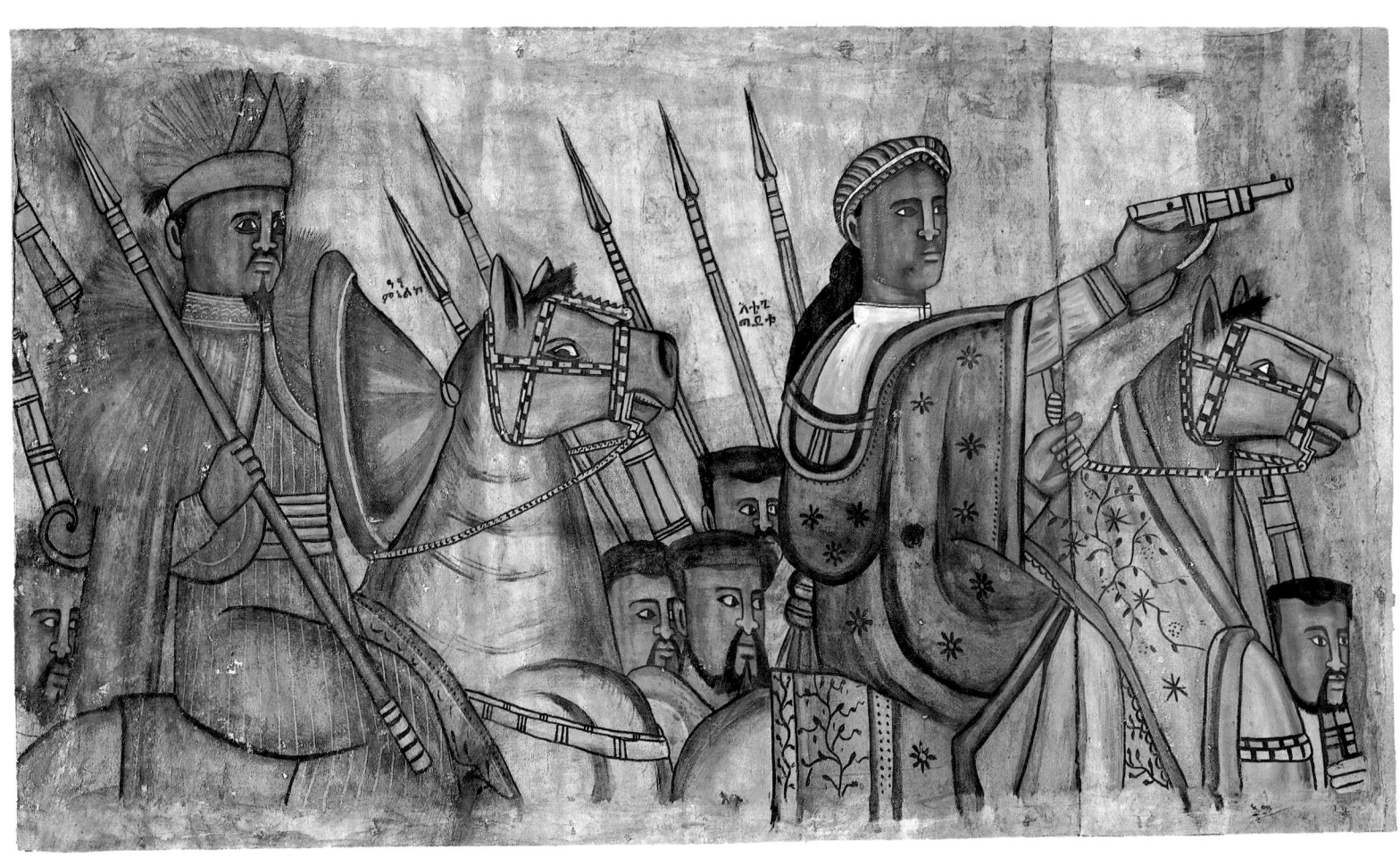

CAT. NO. 24

Haile Selassie Receiving Queen Elizabeth

2001

Paint on cloth
100 x 151 cm
Collection of Neal and Elizabeth Sobania

Emperor Haile Selassie I (r. 1930–1974) was a considerable presence among world leaders in the 1950s and 1960s. At this time, Ethiopia maintained strong diplomatic relations with a number of the most powerful nations in the world. Those who remember President Kennedy's funeral in 1963 may recall the diminutive Ethiopian leader walking next to President Charles de Gaulle of France at the head of the funeral cortege. On numerous occasions heads of state, especially royalty, visited Ethiopia. The first state visit that clearly put Ethiopia on the map for many Western governments came in February 1965, when Queen Elizabeth II of Great Britain, accompanied by Prince Philip, honored Ethiopia and the emperor with a visit. Adamu witnessed this historic event at the age of thirty-five and was very taken with the grand spectacle, as were most of the residents of Addis Ababa. On the occasion of state visits by royalty, the emperor abandoned his silver Rolls Royce limousine for a gold state carriage pulled by horses from the royal stables.

Almost forty years later, Adamu still enjoys painting this theme. Haile Selassie and Elizabeth are depicted riding in the emperor's sumptuous horse-drawn carriage. Members of his imperial bodyguard process at the bottom of the painting. Ever impressive in their dress uniforms of red pants, green tunics, gold epaulets, and white pith helmets decorated with lions' manes, the imperial bodyguards were a source of pride not only for the emperor but also for the nation. Their helmets and the tops of spectators' heads in the background suggest the multitudes that assembled to witness the royal procession. Adamu noted that Queen Elizabeth came to Ethiopia with her husband, but that Prince Philip rode in another carriage with Ethiopian Crown Prince Asfa Wossen. He also explained that he included churches and mosques in the background, to "show that they were passing through the city."

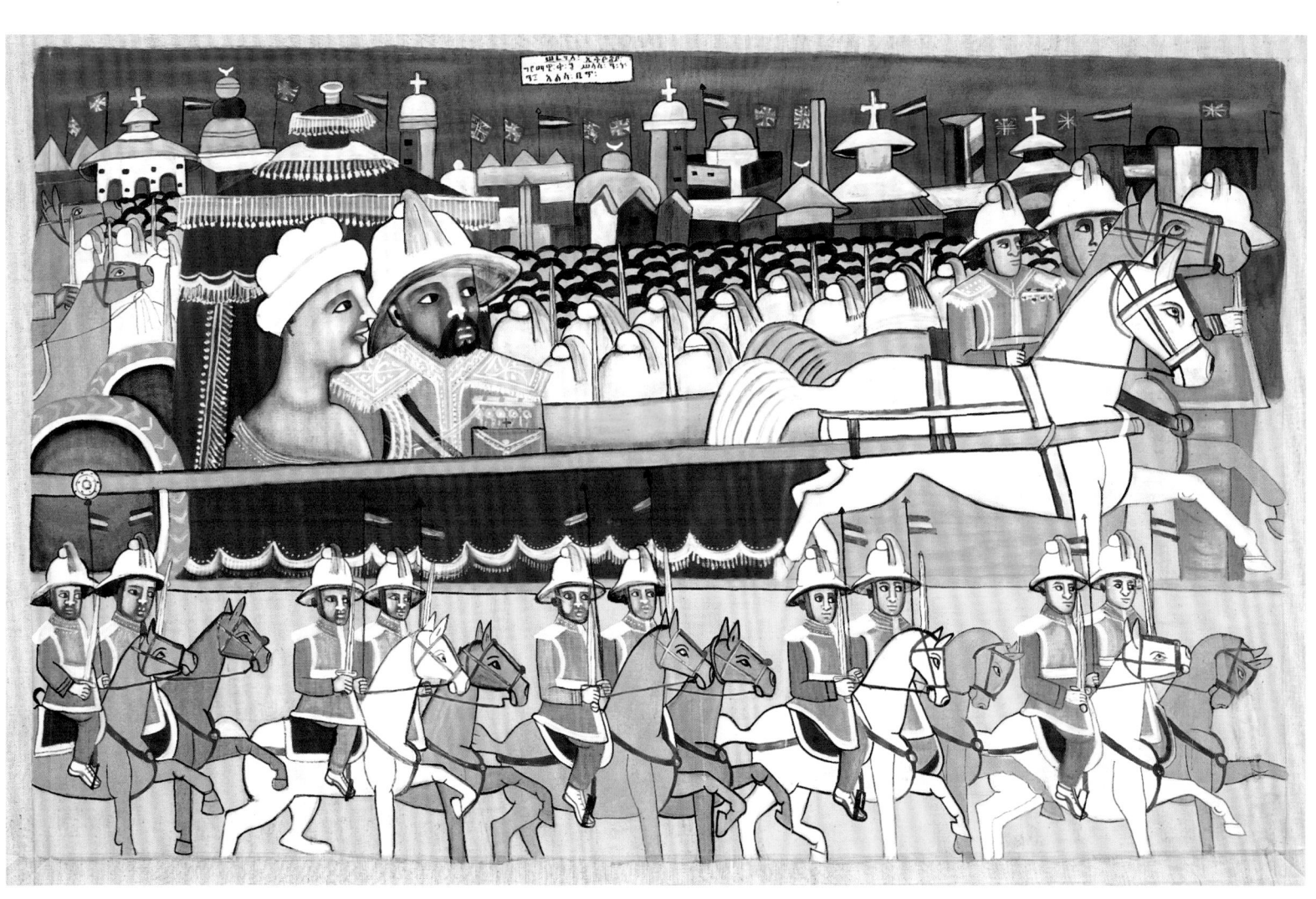

CAT. NO. 25

Entering Addis Ababa
2003

Paint on cloth
97 x 149 cm
FMCH X2004.4.3; Anonymous Gift

When famine struck Ethiopia in the early 1970s and massive numbers of people were starving, students, teachers, and workers, ignored by the government of Haile Selassie, agitated for change. In 1974 the military joined them and overthrew the emperor. The Derg—as the military committee that took over the government was known—plunged the country into a state of terror and adopted a Soviet-style economic system that insured it would remain one of the poorest nations in the world. This intolerable situation lasted until a loose coalition of rebel forces—starting from Eritrea in the north—pushed south, attacking and defeating government troops. Miraculously, they entered the capital of Addis Ababa in May 1991 without the loss of life or destruction of the city.

In 2003 Raymond Silverman asked Qes Adamu to create a painting of the moment when the rebel forces entered Addis Ababa, effectively bringing to an end the seventeen years of rule by the Derg. Adamu, who is not politically inclined and actually avoids painting recent political events, accepted the commission but made it clear that "I never would have done it if [Silverman] had not asked me to." He is explicit in stating that this is not a political painting but merely the recording of a historic event, like Queen Elizabeth II's visit to Ethiopia. Interestingly, Adamu pointed out that he probably would not have begun producing paintings of the British queen's visit to Ethiopia if he had not been asked to do so by his godfather, Yohannis Tesemma.

Adamu draws upon his own observations, what he learned from the press, and what he heard on the streets for his interpretation of this important moment in Ethiopia's recent history. "I heard the fighters were told their final goal was Arat Kilo [a major traffic circle in Addis Ababa], and when they reached there they stopped...so I showed them there" by the parliament building, clearly depicted in the upper center of the painting and identified by the clock tower. The soldiers with their long braided hair and their distinctive short pants and rubber sandals (usually made from used automobile tires), entered the city from many directions. Their followers were numerous and are shown at the bottom center marching toward the palace. At the top left are the people of the city, who are happy. Among them are women dancing on each side of parliament. At the top right, members of the Derg government are depicted with their hands over their mouths in a gesture of disbelief or surprise.

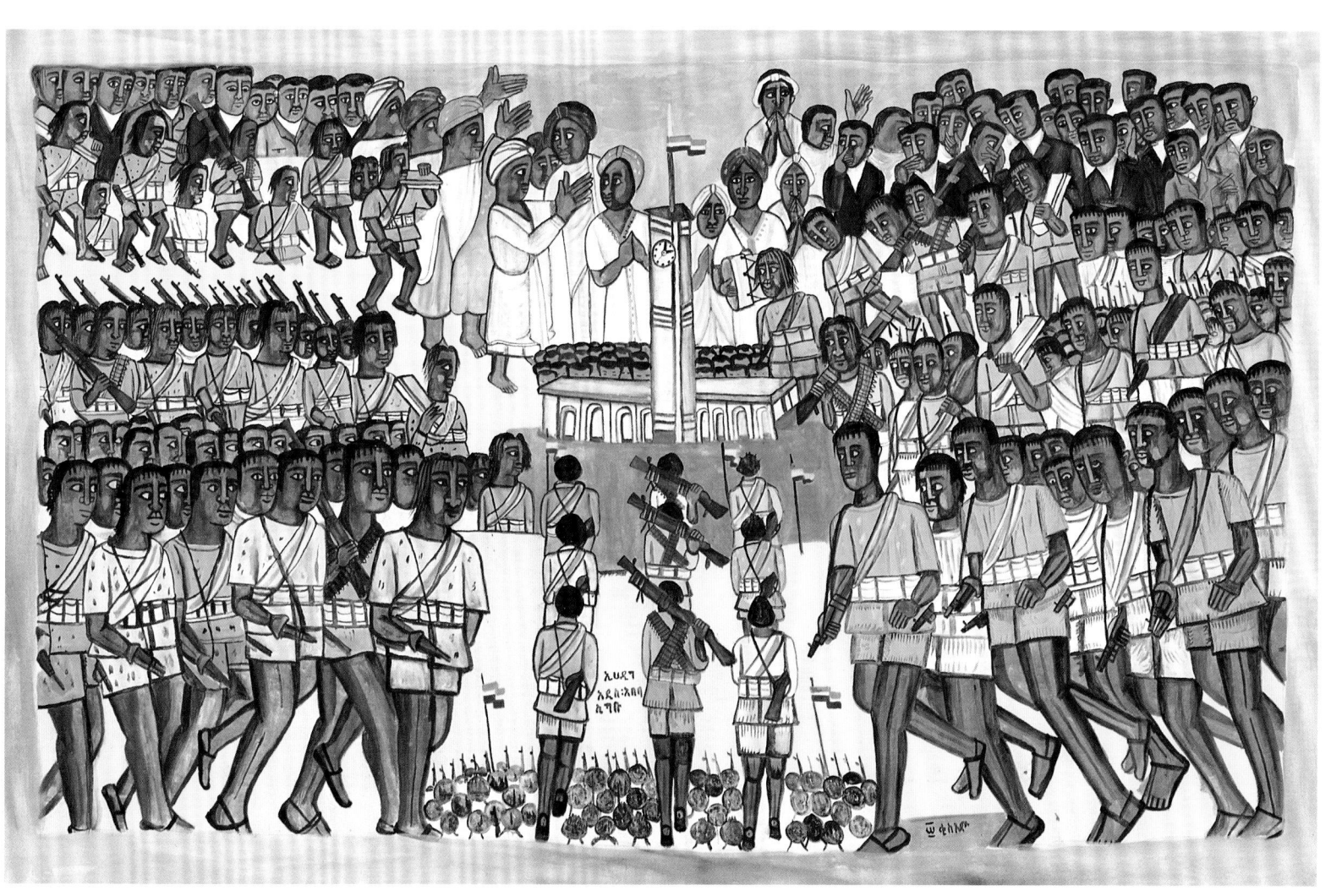

CAT. NO. 26

Fight between Lions and Hyenas
circa 2000

Paint on cloth
83 x 186 cm
FMCH X2003.13.12; Anonymous Gift

Adamu listens to the radio and recently has begun to watch television. Thus he is aware of events in other parts of Ethiopia. Those that he finds particularly fascinating may on occasion make their way into his paintings. One story Adamu heard a few years ago related that there had been a fight between lions and hyenas in the south of Ethiopia. The incident was reported in several Addis Ababa newspapers as well. The "battle" actually occurred in the Gobele Desert in southeast Ethiopia, near the city of Harar. Six lions and thirty-five hyenas were killed. Adamu notes, "I didn't see this, I just heard about it on the radio, and I painted it because it's a new thing." Qes Adamu created a visual narrative of the episode in much the same way that he has interpreted numerous religious and historical events.

The press likened the confrontation to a military battle, and it is interesting that Adamu has used some of the same devices seen in his representations of the Battle of Adwa in his imaginative rendering of the event. Recalling the story, he remarks that the lions and hyenas each stood to one side, and when they were tired from fighting, others would step forward to take their places. In the end, the lions won and the hyenas retreated. Adamu comments, "Of course, the lions would win. The hyenas are powerful but not like the lions, they [hyenas] just bite, they don't have force [strength]." Adamu attempted to demonstrate the discrepancy in strength by depicting the lions as very muscular and big "to show they won." On the right side are the lions watching and waiting to fight, and on the left are the retreating hyenas. "They were all fighting, not just the males. The animals whose eyes are closed are dead." Adamu notes, "It looked like a fight between humans."

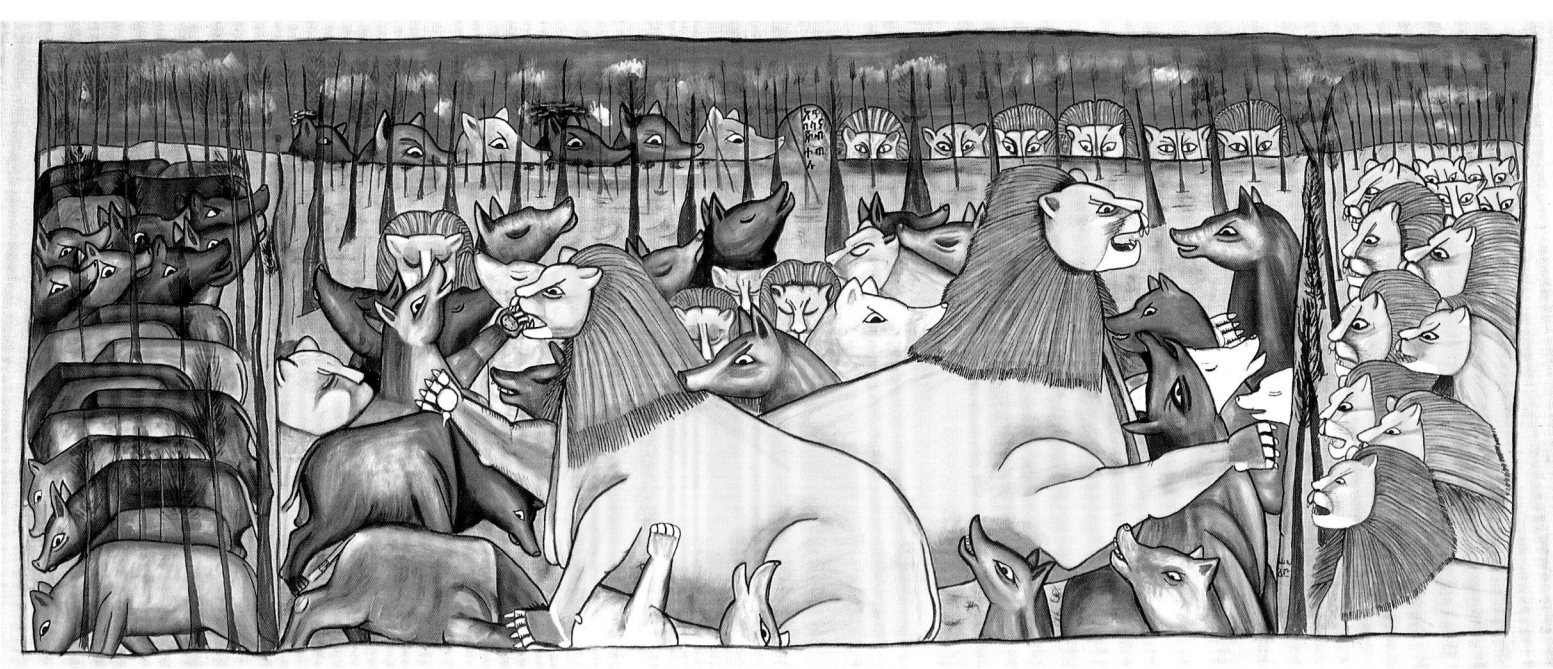

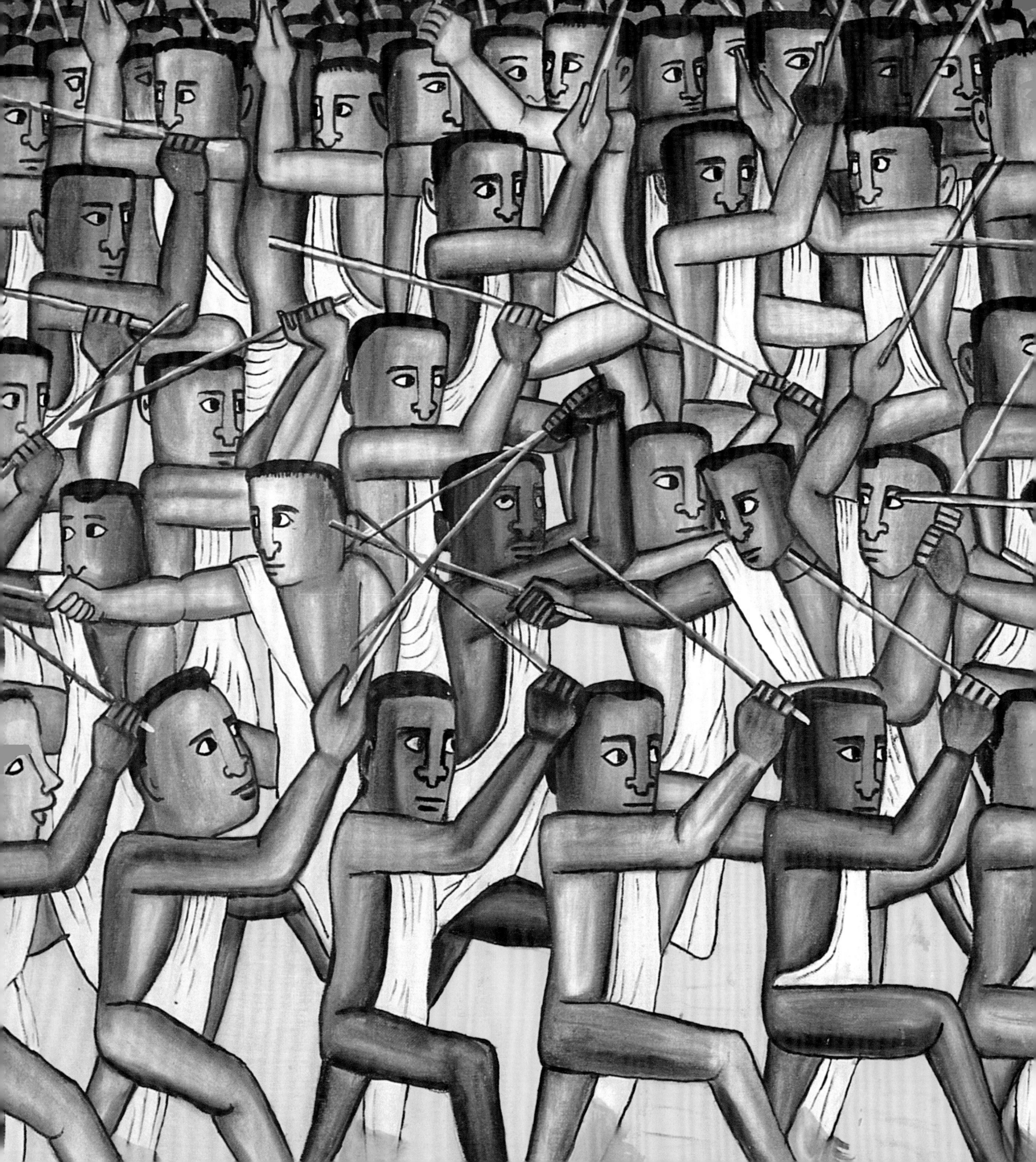

Reflections on Life in Ethiopia

Though Adamu believes his paintings of religious subjects are his most important work, he would rather produce compositions dealing with secular themes. His reason for this is quite simple: they allow him more opportunities to exercise his imagination and to be creative. After Adamu's arrival in Addis Ababa in the early 1960s, his godfather, Yohannis Tesemma, encouraged him to exploit what he had learned while studying for the priesthood and to continue to paint in a traditional idiom while focusing on subjects specific to Ethiopia—to produce what Adamu refers to as "cultural paintings." Adamu heeded this advice, and for the last forty-five years has worked in a style grounded in the Ethiopian Orthodox Church tradition, producing paintings that are vignettes of life in Ethiopia, past and present, religious and secular.

Thus, while Qes Adamu paints monumental moments in the history of the country and of Christianity, he also often depicts the everyday experiences of Ethiopians. Even when interpreting events that occurred outside Ethiopia, or in another era, Adamu is prone to "localizing" the subject. Actors in a religious narrative associated with the New or Old Testament may be presented wearing Ethiopian clothing. Adamu, for instance, often depicts Saint George (see cat. no. 8) wearing the attire and riding the festooned horse of an Ethiopian nobleman. Similarly, historical subjects may be interpreted with reference to Adamu's own experience, as may be observed in his painting *Retreat of the Italians from Adwa* (cat. no. 22) in which he depicts the soldiers not in the military garb of the late nineteenth century but of half a century later.

Unlike his religious and history paintings, however, which may incorporate ideas from earlier pictorial narratives, Adamu's interpretations of Ethiopian daily life are his own conceptions. Most of these paintings are in fact derived from firsthand experience. Adamu is particularly intrigued with recalling life in the rural areas of the country, especially the Ethiopia of his youth. One no longer sees brave patriots decked out in sumptuous warriors' attire, as in Adamu's *Jegnoch* (cat. no. 27), or legal scenes like the one depicted in *Court of Justice* (cat. no. 29). But sheep are still bought and sold in rural markets (cat. no. 30). Paintings such as these are based on careful observation and an exceptional visual memory.

This same visual acuity is present in Adamu's paintings dealing with aspects of contemporary life in Ethiopia. *Drought and Famine* (cat. no. 32) and *We Must Unite in Prayer to Fight HIV/AIDS* (cat. no. 34) are the closest that Adamu comes to making political statements in his work. These paintings deal with critical social issues that threaten the lives of millions of Ethiopians. Their fundamental message as well as that of *Unity* (cat. no. 33)—a recent painting that employs symbolic (instead of Adamu's usual literal) imagery—is that all of Ethiopia's diverse peoples must work together to overcome the challenges that face them.

Recently, Qes Adamu's sphere of experience expanded with the acquisition of his first television set. He is especially intrigued with programs that offer information about regions of Ethiopia with which he is unfamiliar. His painting *Southern Peoples' Stick Game* (cat. no. 31) was inspired by such a program. Adamu is capable of representing virtually any subject. Two years ago he was commissioned to paint Addis Ababa, although he had never before undertaken a cityscape. He took up the challenge and created a marvelous rendering of the sprawling modern city (cat. no. 35).

CAT. NO. 27

Jegnoch (Heroes)
circa 1980–1995

Paint on cloth
83 x 190 cm
Collection of the Institute of Ethiopian Studies,
Addis Ababa University, no. 9900

Depicting a scene from behind is one of Qes Adamu's hallmarks. In the painting *Jegnoch*, doing so allows him to celebrate the physical presence of the noble warriors of yesterday by emphasizing their ornate clothing, weapons, and horse trappings. Adamu explains that these are not old men going bald, but rather young men wearing a once-fashionable traditional hairstyle with a shaved spot at the back of the head. He adds, "I wore my hair like this when I was small." These are soldiers of "good build and strong youth," who come from the upper classes and ride sitting erect in traditional high-backed saddles. The red leather straps of the cruppers on the backsides of the horses give only a hint of the highly ornamented trappings that a full view of the mounts would display. The *jegnoch* wear richly embroidered tunics, and some sport animal skin cloaks and headpieces made of lion's manes. Their scabbards are held by distinctive cloth belts called *dig* that have been secured with leather belts known as *qebetto*. All are armed with spears, curved swords or straight swords, and flat shields. Adamu also indicates that the painting did not have a specific title and could have been called *To the Battlefield* or *Going to Visit a Prince.*

The explanation as to why he painted the *jegnoch* from behind is quite simple, "Horses, when they are seen from the front, are harder to paint; it's more beautiful when you look at them from the back." And in fact, as Adamu points out, very little is lost—the saddle's back support appears rather than the front support, and so too does "horse jewelry" or decoration that gives the riders such presence.

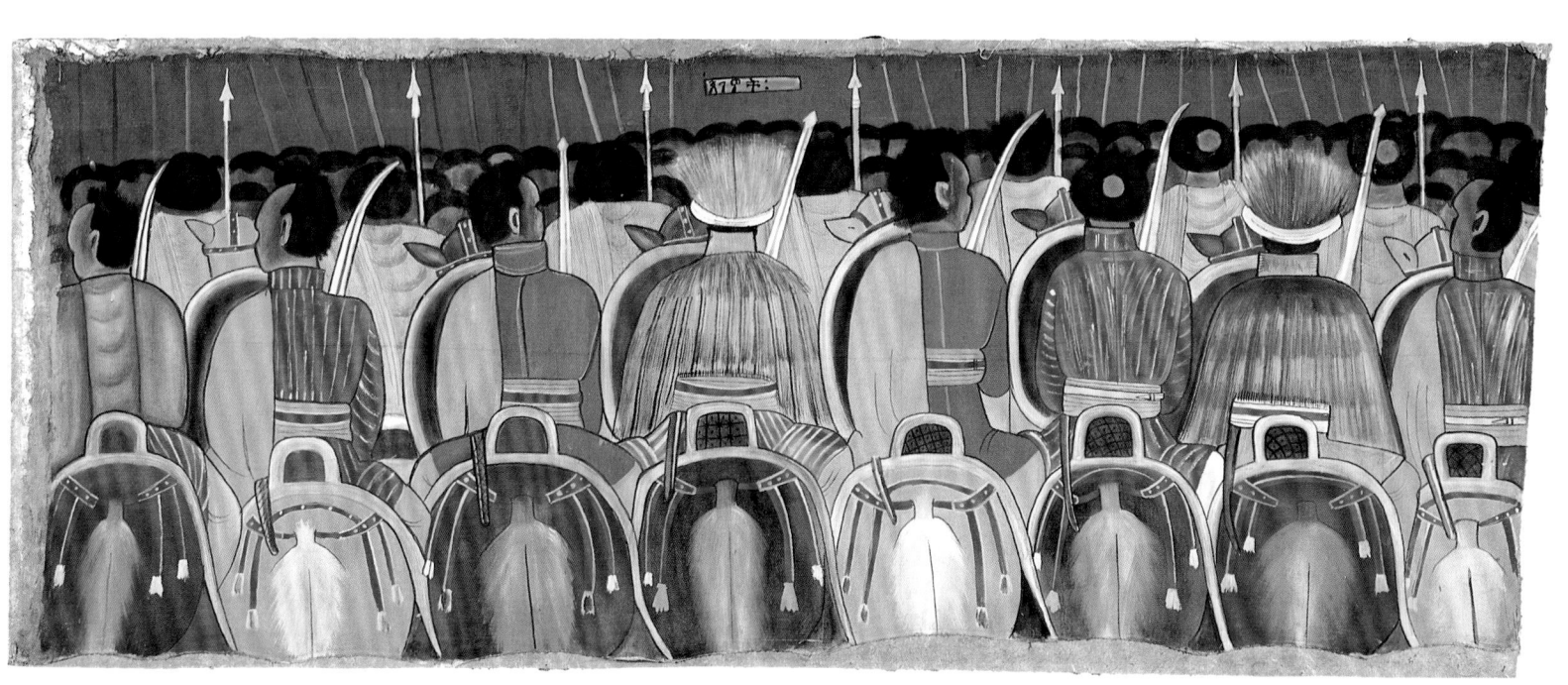

CAT. NO. 28

Gugs
circa 2000

Paint on cloth
76 x 109 cm
Collection of Neal and Elizabeth Sobania

This painting features mounted warriors involved in a traditional Ethiopian game of *feres gugs*, a mock battle once played to prepare men for war and to demonstrate their horsemanship. Riders raced at full gallop toward each other hurling wooden spears and protecting themselves with hide shields. As Adamu explains, "There are no teams; men fight for themselves. The number of players is determined by the size of the field and the number of interested riders." He adds that "Good players have to know how to protect themselves, turn and ride their horse, and attack.... When they play they move in one direction" and then another, "so I wanted to show them passing by each other." Adamu successfully captures the action of *gugs* by depicting the horses and their riders in a variety of highly animated attitudes. At the far right in the bottom register one horse and rider are shown falling, while another competitor disappears "off the canvas because he's riding so fast." Adamu has also included a number of spears on the ground where many end up in the fray.

Creating paintings of *feres gugs* allows Qes Adamu to indulge his enthusiasm for horses and express admiration for their riders, whether saints, warriors, or emperors. His representation of equestrian subjects is well informed, often based on his own experience. Adamu knows for example that the mounts used in *gugs* were specially trained to compete. Formerly, during festivals, people thronged the imperial parade grounds in Addis Ababa to watch the "nobility and those who know how to ride" demonstrate their military prowess in these exciting competitions. Adamu also relates that famous horses, such as those belonging to recent emperors, were known by name.

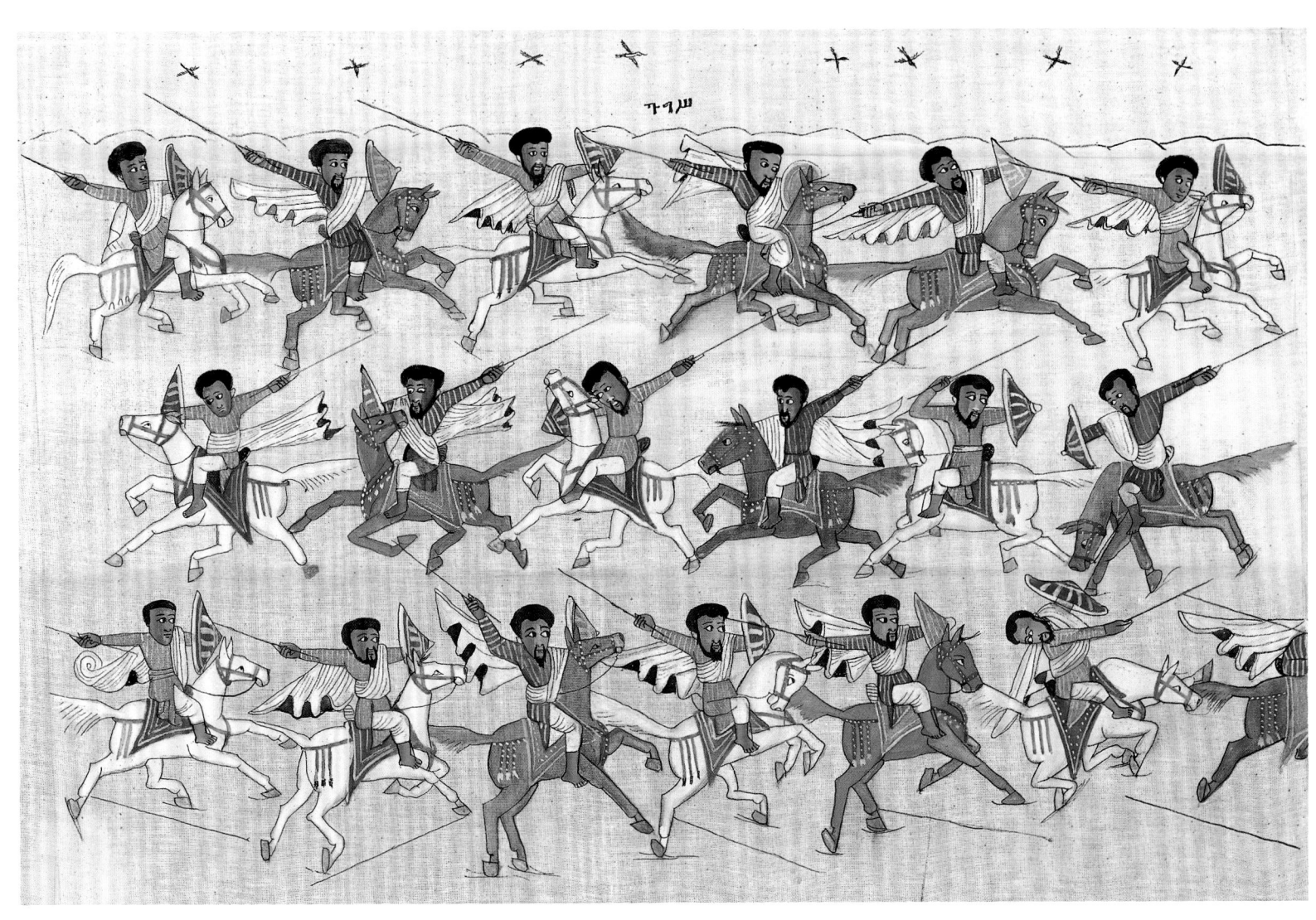

CAT. NO. 29

Court of Justice

circa 1980–1995

Paint on cloth
78 x 197 cm
Collection of the Institute of Ethiopian Studies,
Addis Ababa University, no. 10291

Today Ethiopian courts are found inside government buildings, and judges have legal educations. Historically, however, especially in rural areas, a court of justice was often held under a large tree or on a big stone. Petitioners presented their cases in envelopes held in cleft sticks, and these were received by a representative of the court. In Adamu's painting, the judges, highly esteemed members of local society, may be identified by their white beards and the flywhisks they carry, indicative of their age and wisdom. The two scribes on the right prepare petitions for the plaintiffs depicted at the far right of the composition, waiting for their cases to be heard. Adamu comments that these gatherings were often quite loud as people argued their cases before the judges. In front of the judges stands a mediator clad in blue, who could assist the petitioner. In common practice, however, the individual presented his own case, "using beautiful, strong words." Of note, in highland Ethiopia oratory employing poetic embellishment and the use of expressions with double or hidden meanings has long been and continues to be greatly admired.

When a decision is reached, the scribe on the left side of the painting will record the judges' decisions. In this particular painting, Qes Adamu has presented a rich man at the right, whose status is indicated not only by his being dressed in the same manner as the judges (i.e., in a *bernos,* or "cloak") but also by his horses and entourage of several men. Like everyone else, however, he must wait his turn to present his petition to the court using a cleft stick. There are no women present in this representation of a court of justice. Although Adamu recalls that as a youth he saw one strong woman who brought her petition to the court, he recognizes that this was rare and that women were generally represented by men at court. Once a decision was delivered, restitutions were often required, and those found guilty usually made promises to provide some form of compensation to rectify the offense.

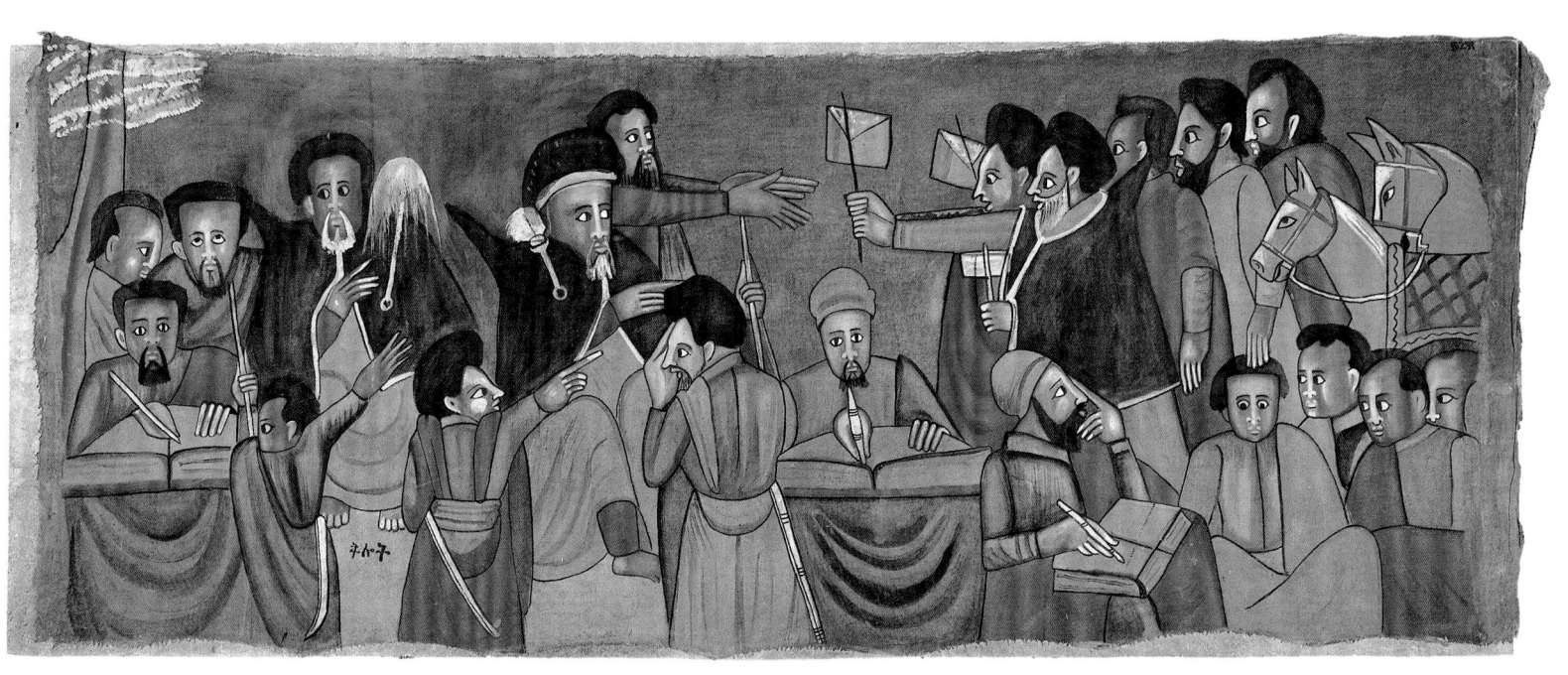

CAT. NO. 30

Buying and Selling Sheep
circa 1980-1995

Paint on cloth
71 x 178 cm
Collection of the Institute of Ethiopian Studies,
Addis Ababa University, no. 10280

Adamu recalls that "in the old days children couldn't go [and buy a sheep]; you didn't give them the money to buy for you [like now]. They talked too much. Only adults bought sheep and goats…[although] a boy might come to carry [an animal] for a male relative," as he illustrates at the far right of this composition. He adds that a woman went to the market to buy chickens, onions, or butter, but "if she had no male relative [to buy a sheep] she asked someone—a man—to help her because they knew the good quality."

This painting reveals Qes Adamu's careful observation. "If you see a sheep market, the sheep stand closely together to protect themselves from the sun and they hide their heads under each other's bellies." The market scene presents sellers on the left wearing traditional farmers' hats and numerous buyers, including a priest in the back, on the left side of the painting, peering over the shoulder of a boy holding a sheep. When asked about this, Adamu exclaimed, "What? You don't think priests buy sheep!" Some of the buyers hold large silver coins, which people usually carried tightly knotted in a corner of their cotton wraps. These silver coins, Maria Theresa *thalers*, were once widely used as currency throughout the Ethiopian highlands. Today, they can still be found in some rural areas. Adamu indicates, however, that times have changed and comments, "Now people use paper money." He also remarks that, when he was young, a sheep cost fifty cents, and you "had to go far to buy from the herders. Now, for holidays, for Easter, they bring the sheep to town to sell for two to three days." Of course, the cost of a sheep has changed as well.

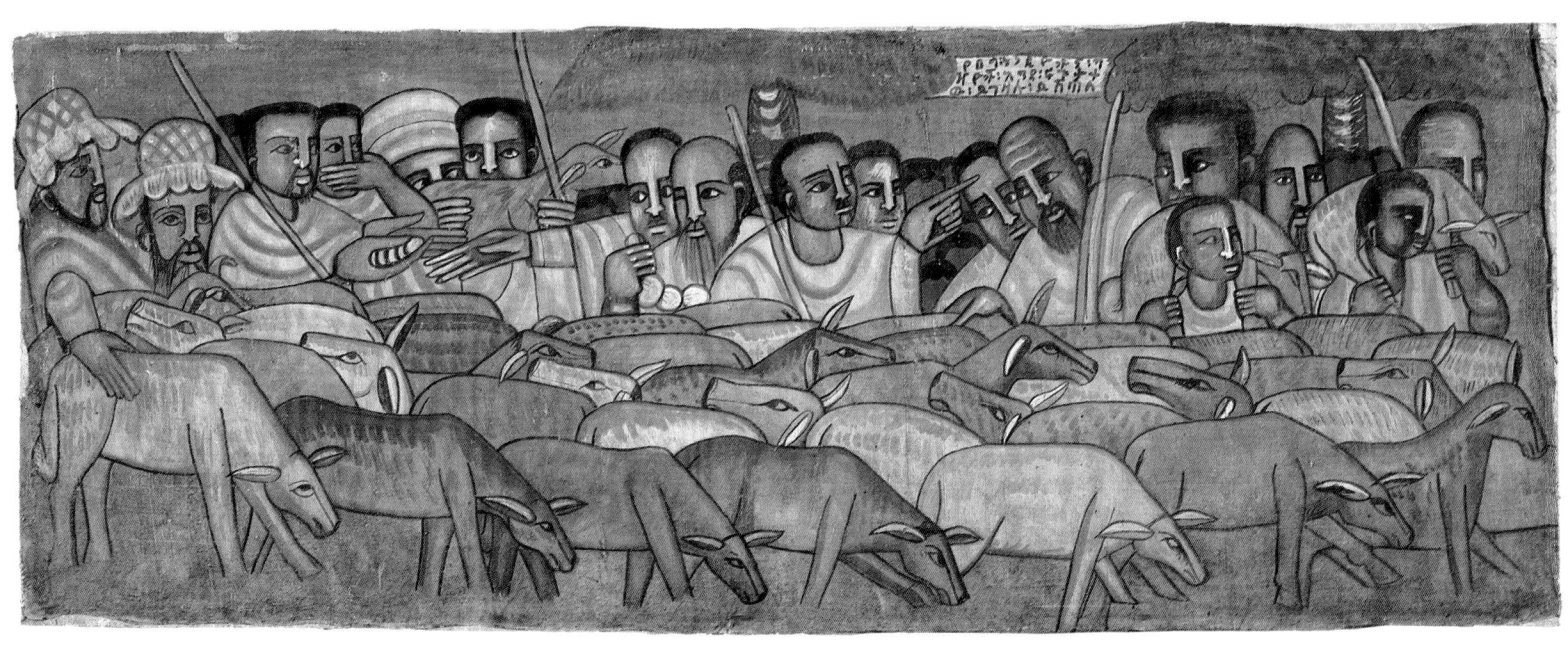

CAT. NO. 31

Southern Peoples' Stick Game
circa 2000

Paint on cloth
104 x 185 cm
Collection of Leah Niederstadt

One evening when Adamu was watching television he saw a program featuring peoples from the southwest of Ethiopia who are cattle keepers and whose women wear labrets that extend their lower lips. Both of these features are referenced in the panel at the right side of the composition, where cattle and herdsmen stand, joined by women, whom Adamu identifies as their "lovers or fiancées." The focus of the painting, however, is the stick fighting that is practiced by a number of peoples in this region. Qes Adamu comments, "The stick is very powerful; it is a serious game." He further explains that "There is no game like this in the north." As Adamu understands it, such stick fighting is an annual event in which the young men form two sides. One is victorious when those on the other side fall down or say, "it's enough." According to Adamu, "The winner is the hero and gets respect in the society." The women do not play, but "they make the men fight," and "they praise [the winners] and accept them in marriage." Qes Adamu also points out that the men do not fight all at once. In fact, only two men—the two on either side of the U-shaped void at the top of the painting—actually fight at one time.

Adamu further elaborates that "everyone is carrying sticks." Indeed in such herding societies most men carry a herding stick. He has portrayed some men as ready to fight and others, in the back, as spectators. Adamu observes that the men hold their sticks upward because they need to be ready to fight, and "if the stick is [pointed] down they would look like they are travelers." Qes Adamu was intrigued that the men wear only a single piece of cloth over their shoulder. He is also quite conscious that the people of southwest Ethiopia are physically different than the peoples of the central and northern highlands. Their skin is dark, but Adamu points out that he "used different [shades of gray] to give them beauty…. It was an artistic decision…. If I make them all dark it's not beautiful."

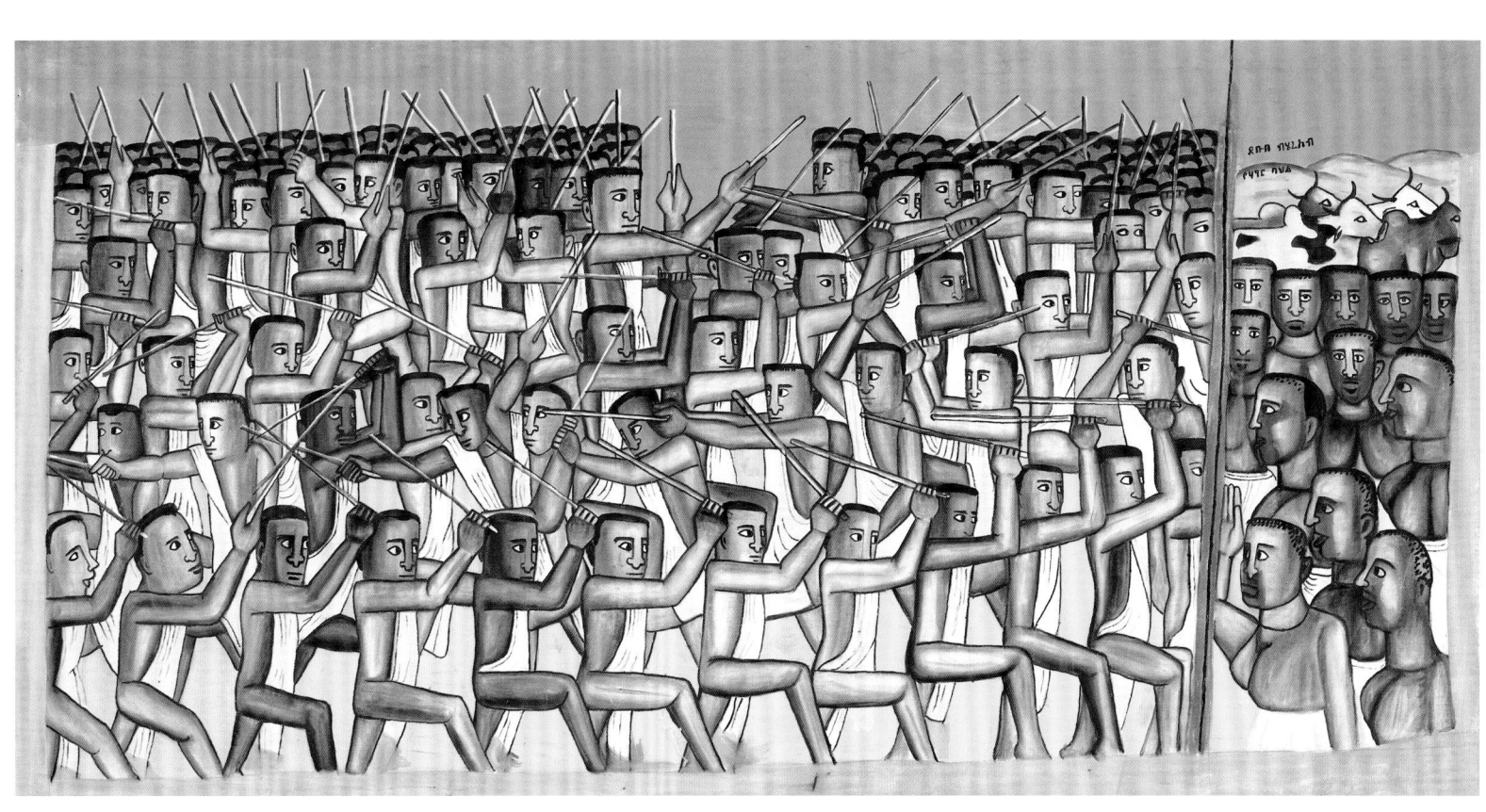

CAT. NO. 32

Drought and Famine

2001

Paint on cloth
153 x 100 cm
FMCH X2003.13.6; Anonymous Gift

Here Adamu confronts a theme with which Ethiopia is all too familiar, the suffering of its people from drought and famine. He says of his subject, "The famine time began in the past, and it is not a particular famine. It is to show that the poverty of the country is longstanding." In this representation of the Ethiopian countryside (note the flag), Adamu shows that everything is affected by drought—the land is dry and sandy, the trees are without leaves, and the cattle and people are emaciated. It is especially the children and old people who suffer. "I've seen people like this just with skin and bones. It's like their faces are empty." With their arms raised, the people ask for help, but "everything is in the hands of God."

In the 1970s and 1980s, television coverage played a dramatic role in bringing Ethiopia's plight to the attention of the world. Aware of this, Adamu comments, "If they come from outside, they film it to show it to the foreigners because if they don't see it, they don't help." At the same time, however, he recognizes that Ethiopians themselves need to take action, and so he has painted two men whom he identifies as *jegnoch, or* "warriors, patriots, guards of the country," observing the famine. Dressed in garments of a type once worn by nobles and warriors, they are clearly wealthy and not suffering. Armed with shields, spears, and swords and garbed in finely embroidered cloaks, Adamu notes "they represent the elder men of Ethiopia, who are asking for help to aid the people.... They are heroes and elders, begging for the rest of Ethiopia to help on behalf of the people, the cattle, the land, and the trees." Adamu believes that "like HIV/AIDS, drought and famine can't be solved by human beings.... We must seek God's help, but we also have to work and not just sleep, leaving our hopes on God [alone]." The inscription in the lower left corner of the painting reads, "Your eyes will see, and your heart will judge." Adamu explains, "If you see someone fall, your heart tells you what to do."

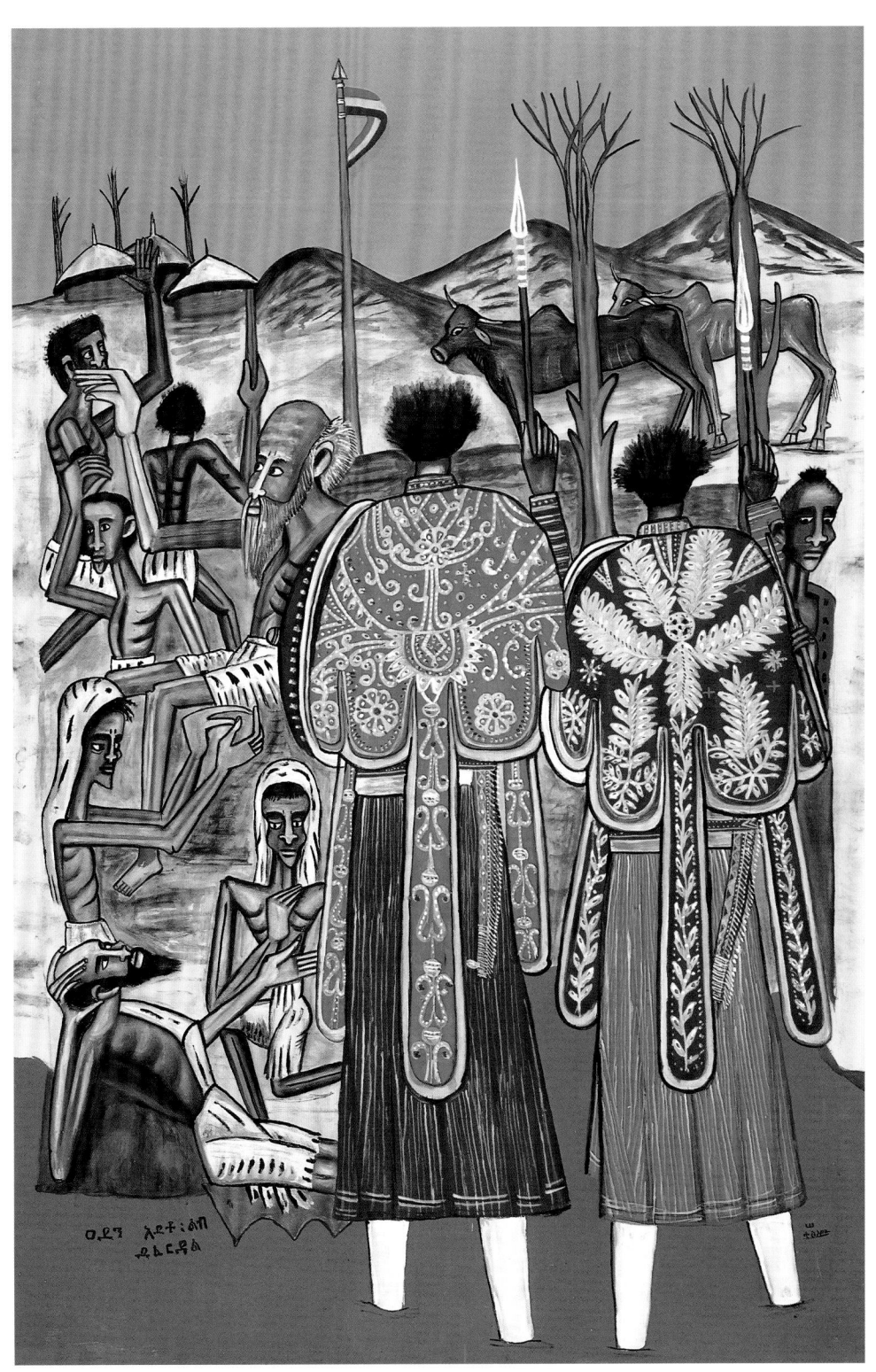

CAT. NO. 33

Unity

2003

Paint on cloth
101 x 150 cm
FMCH X2004.4.2; Anonymous Gift

Qes Adamu recently began experimenting with a more abstract approach to developing a narrative. This painting depicts an adversary who has fallen on the ground, weighed down and defeated by diverse symbolic objects. The inscription in the painting reads, "Unity will bring respect to the country and will defeat the enemy." Adamu explains, "If we unite as one we can build the country and defeat its enemies." When questioned as to the nature of Ethiopia's enemies, he responds, we "the people must fight against all enemies.… If all people unite, they can defeat the enemy from any country. For development as well, we must unite [as] we are constantly faced with challenges."

The objects on the fallen adversary represent the range of people who make up Ethiopian society and who must work together to overcome the country's difficulties. Weapons of war—spear, sword, shield, and rifle—are references to warriors; other symbols include a scissors to indicate tailors, a shuttle for weavers, a spindle for women who spin thread, a book and pencil for students and teachers, a prayer stick for the clergy, a hammer for construction workers, a *masinqo* (bowed instrument) for *azmari* (traditional minstrels), a tire for drivers of busses, taxis, and trucks, a hoe blade for farmers, and a scale for traders.

In elaborating further on the painting, Adamu is careful to explain that the enemy he painted is not any particular person or representative of a group. He offers a critique of his own work noting that, "The clothes are similar to what the Italians wore, but the enemy is not Italian; it is not even *ferenji* [foreign]. It would have been better to paint [the enemy] with Ethiopian features and clothes. I just didn't paint shoes, and painting the tie was a mistake. I should have put a torn *mahiteb* [a black string worn around the neck] to show the religion [of Ethiopian Christians]. It was traditional in the old days to wear the *mahiteb* to signify a promise [*qal kidan*] to God. A torn string means he's not respecting his promise [to God] so he becomes an enemy."

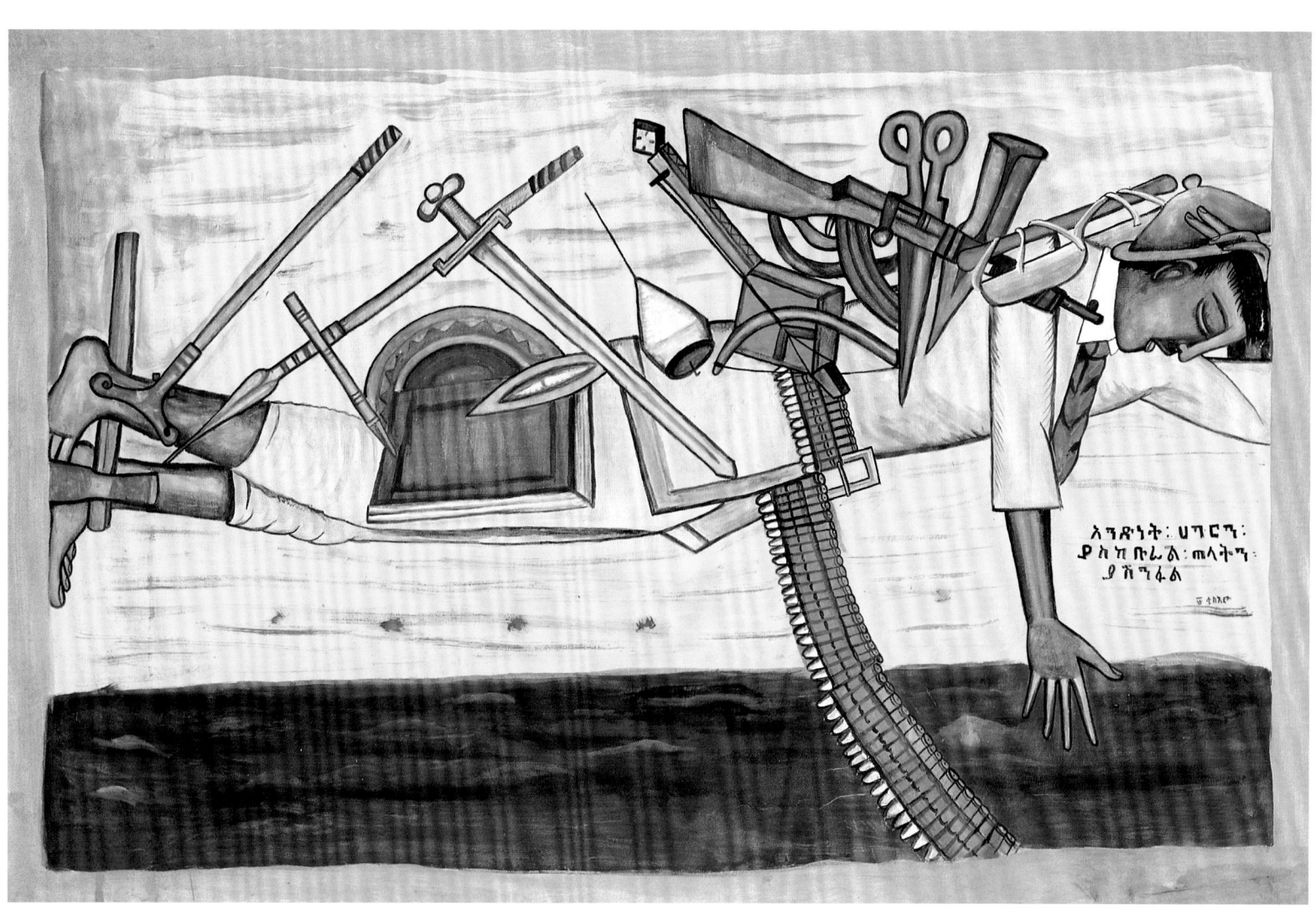

CAT. NO. 34

We Must Unite in Prayer to Fight HIV/AIDS
2003

Paint on cloth
154 x 96 cm
Collection of Leah Niederstadt

Qes Adamu is very much aware of the challenges facing Ethiopian society today. When we spoke to him about including this painting in the exhibition, he asked, "Don't you think this is too scary to show? In the media they recently said don't portray scary things about HIV/AIDS. The people with HIV/AIDS say that the paintings and posters [currently being used to educate people] give people a biased view… because they show them sick and thin, and with a skin disease… but they also say we should teach people about HIV/AIDS.… They are teaching in the church, in all areas of the country, and I am teaching though my paintings. This painting is my gift to help teach. I am a painter, so I teach though my paintings."

In this dramatic work Adamu represents the disease as a demon. He explains, "I haven't seen the disease, but I think it is the work of Satan or a demon…so I painted it skinny with a skin disease because then you don't dare touch it." Adamu notes that "For the people, it is a bad situation.… HIV/AIDS affects people all over the world, and until we discover the medicine [to cure or prevent the disease] we must join together to pray." Thus the painting shows Christians and Muslims reading their holy books and praying. God is portrayed "stretching out his hands…protecting the world." The young men without beards at the right of the painting are a comment on how the disease affects young people. Adamu notes that "some young people are careless and think HIV/AIDS doesn't exist even if someone close to them dies. So the only thing we can do is take care of ourselves and not think [that] it cannot affect us."

Qes Adamu points out that though his painting does not include foreigners, he knows that the disease affects everyone, "When you translate the idea [of the painting], it applies to all human beings.… There is no difference between people when it is about HIV/AIDS.… Everyone should take care to protect themselves."

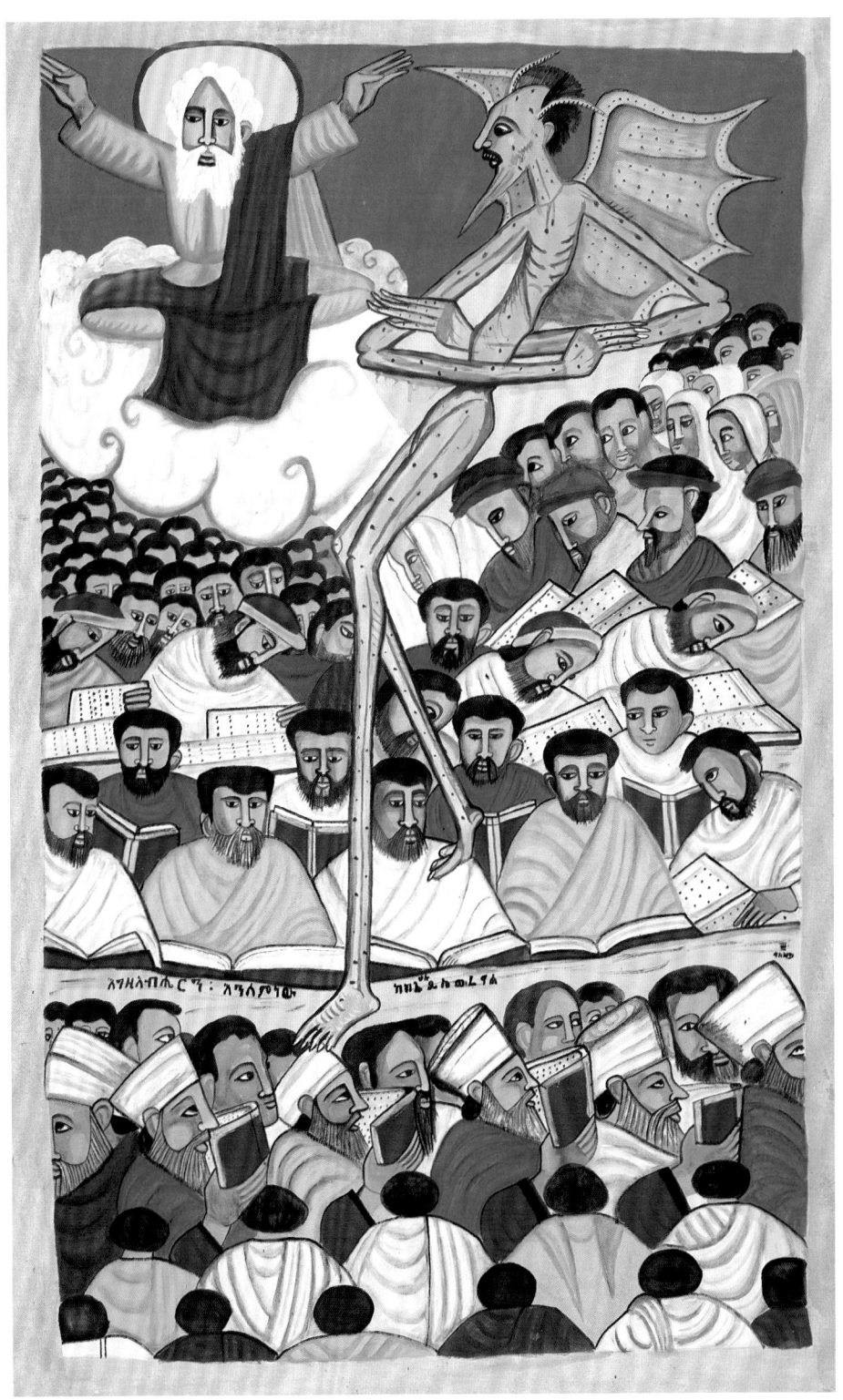

CAT. NO. 35

The City of Addis Ababa

2003

Paint on cloth
98 x 150 cm
FMCH X2004.4.1; Anonymous Gift

In the early 1880s Emperor Menilek moved his residence to the range of mountains known as Entoto, located on the northern edge of the plains that would soon become the site of Ethiopia's capital and its first modern city, Addis Ababa. Though founded in 1886, Addis Ababa did not become the country's capital until 1892. It quickly grew into a large cosmopolitan city that today supports a population estimated between 3.2 and 4.4 million people.

Qes Adamu had never painted a cityscape, and Raymond Silverman commissioned this painting to see how he would approach the challenge of representing Ethiopia's capital. Adamu's bird's-eye view is oriented to the north, toward Entoto. The city is surrounded by hills covered with the ubiquitous eucalyptus tree. Here, Adamu is not concerned with painting to scale or placing buildings in their exact locations. To those who know the city, however, all the principal landmarks are present. Depicted at the bottom—the south end of the city—is Bole International Airport and city hall with two cars on the road in front of it. Immediately to the right is a large mosque, and, in front of that, the train station with a three-car train. On the far right is the distinctive tower-like monument at Arat Kilo, one of the city's major traffic circles. The next tower to the north marks the parliament building, with Trinity Cathedral just to the left, while at the top right is the entrance gate to Addis Ababa University at the Siddist Kilo traffic circle. The two statues in the center, also situated at traffic circles, depict Abuna Petros (on the left) and Emperor Menilek II (on the right); between them is Bet Giyorgis, the Church of Saint George.

Scattered throughout the painting are various mosques and churches, as well as domestic architecture. Adamu depicts a dynamic city where one encounters a mix of old and new—mud-walled, thatched-roofed houses next to ultra-modern high-rise buildings. Indeed, Adamu's Addis Ababa is full of structures. Adamu remarks, "The city is getting very big.... There are always new buildings." He notes that the area surrounding his house used to be countryside, a place for collecting wood, "but now it's a city!" Asked why there are no people in his painting, Adamu replied, "The people are in the houses, it [the painting] would be very crowded if I put in people!"

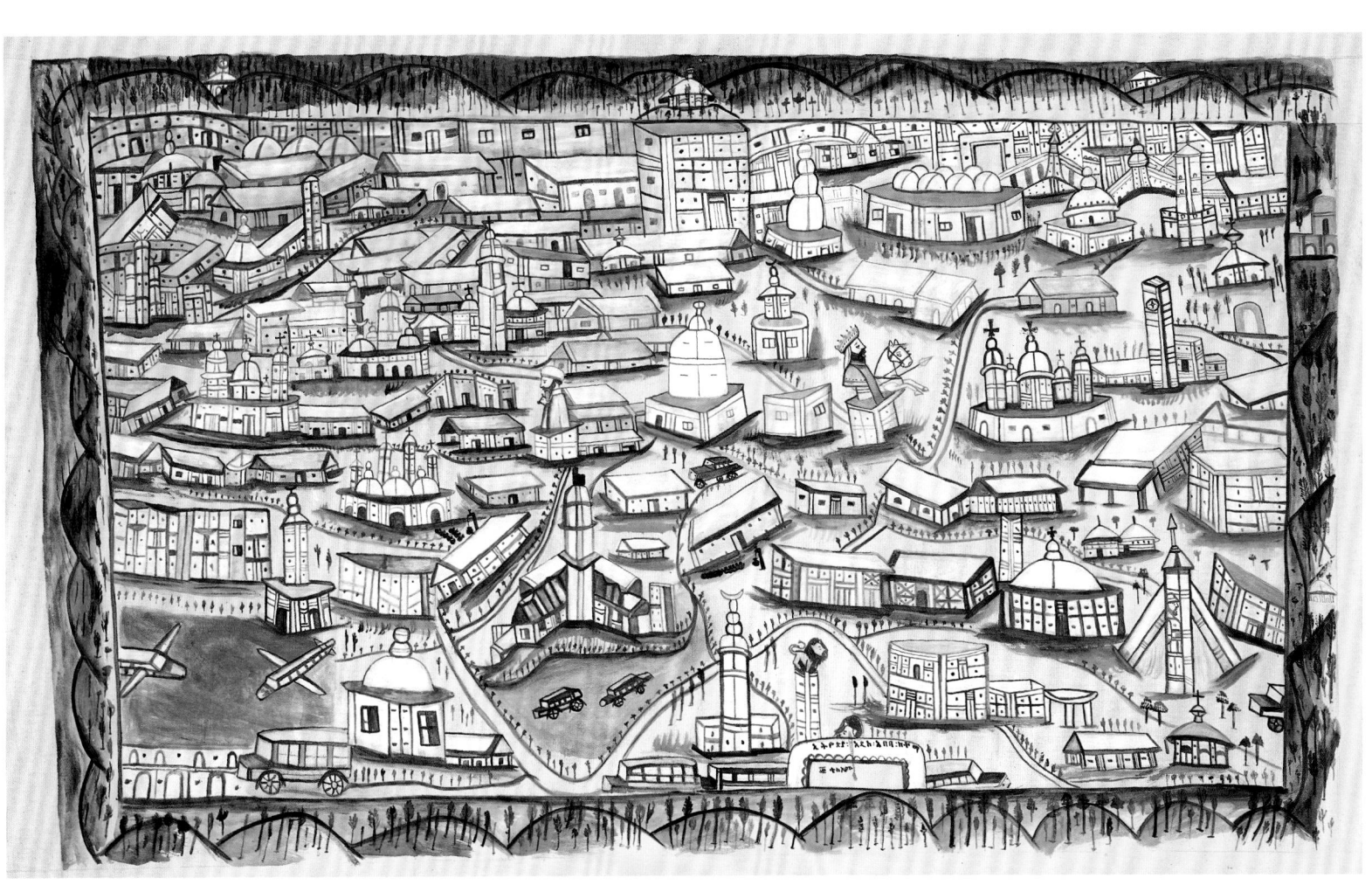

References Cited

Abebaw Ayalew Gela

2002   "A History of Painting in East Gojjam in the Eighteenth and Nineteenth Centuries: A Study of the 'Second Gondärine' Style of Painting in Selected Churches and Monasteries." M.A. Thesis, Addis Ababa University.

Björnesjö, Brita

1980   "Yohannes Tesemma: Un pittore etiopico tradizionale." *Quaderni di studi etiopici* 1: 54–57.

Chojnacki, Stanislaw

1983   *Major Themes in Ethiopian Painting: Indigenous Developments: The Influence of Foreign Models and Their Adaptation from the Thirteenth to the Nineteenth Century*. Wiesbaden: Franz Steiner Verlag.

1996   "Introduction." *Santi guerrieri a cavallo: Tele di Qes Adamu Tesfaw. Warrior Saints on Horseback: Paintings by Qes Adamu Tesfaw*, by Osvaldo Raineri, 9–58. Clusone, Italy: Ferrari Edizioni.

2000   *Ethiopian Icons: Catalogue of the Collection of the Institute of Ethiopian Studies, Addis Ababa University*. Milan: Skira.

Comaroff, John

2002   "Governmentality, Materiality, Legality, Modernity: On the Colonial State in Africa." In *African Modernities*, edited by J.-G. Deutsch, P. Probst, and H. Schmidt, 107–34. Oxford: James Currey.

Girma Fisseha and Raymond Silverman

1994   "Two Generations of Traditional Painters: A Biographical Sketch of Qangeta Jembere Hailu and Marqos Jembere." In *New Trends in Ethiopian Studies. Papers of the 12th International Conference of Ethiopian Studies*, vol. 1, edited by H. G. Marcus, 369–79. Lawrenceville, N.J.: The Red Sea Press.

Girma Kidane

1989   "Four Traditional Ethiopian Painters and Their Life Histories." In *Proceedings of the First International Conference on the History of Ethiopian Art*, editd by Richard Pankhurst, 72–77. London: The Pindar Press.

Haile Gabriel Dagne

1970   "The Ethiopian Orthodox Church School System." In *The Church of Ethiopia: A Panorama of History and Spiritual Life*, edited by Sergew Hable Selassie, 81–97. Addis Ababa: Ethiopian Orthodox Church.

Heldman, Marilyn, with Stuart Munro-Hay

1993   *African Zion: The Sacred Art of Ethiopia*. New Haven: Yale University Press.

Holbert, Kelly, Getachew Haile, et al.

2001   *Ethiopian Art: The Walters Art Museum*. Baltimore: The Walters Art Museum.

Kasfir, Sidney Littlefield

1999   *Contemporary African Art*. London: Thames and Hudson.

Leroy, Jules, Stephen Wright, et al.

1961   *Ethiopia: Illuminated Manuscripts*. Greenwich, Conn.: Graphic Society.

Levine, Donald

1965   *Wax and Gold: Tradition and Innovation in Ethiopian Culture*. Chicago: University of Chicago Press.

Mercier, Jacques

2000   *L'arche éthiopienne: Art chrétien d'Ethiopie*. Paris: Pavillon des Arts.

Messay Kebede

1999   *Survival and Modernization—Ethiopia's Enigmatic Present: A Philosophical Discourse*. Lawrenceville, N.J.: The Red Sea Press.

Pankhurst, Richard

1966   "Some Notes for a History of Ethiopian Secular Art." *Ethiopia Observer* 10, no. 1: 5–80.

1989   "The Battle of Adwa (1896) as Depicted by Traditional Ethiopian Artists." In *Proceedings of the First International Conference on the History of Ethiopian Art*, edited by Richard Pankhurst, 78–103. London: The Pindar Press.

Picton, John

1992   "On the Invention of 'Traditional' Art." In *Principles of "Traditional" African Art*, edited by M. Okediji, 1–10. Ibadan: Bard Books.

2002   "Tradition and the Twentieth Century." In *An Anthology of African Art: The Twentieth Century*, edited by N. G. Fall and J. L. Pivin, 329–33. New York: D.A.P./Distributed Art Publishers.

Raineri, Osvaldo

1996   *Santi guerrieri a cavallo: Tele di Qes Adamu Tesfaw. Warrior Saints on Horseback: Paintings by Qes Adamu Tesfaw*. Clusone, Italy: Ferrari Edizioni.

Silverman, Raymond

1994   *Qes Adamu Tesfaw* [Artist profile prepared for the exhibition, *Ethiopia: Traditions of Creativity*.] East Lansing: Michigan State University Museum.

1999   "*Qes* Adamu Tesfaw—A Priest Who Paints: Painting in the Ethiopian Orthodox Church." In *Ethiopia: Traditions of Creativity*, edited by Raymond Silverman, 132–55, 261–66. Seattle: University of Washington Press.

Silverman, Raymond, and Girma Fisseha

1999   "Jembere and His Son Marcos: Traditional Painting at the End of the Twentieth Century." In *Ethiopia: Traditions of Creativity*, edited by Raymond Silverman, 157–81, 267–71. Seattle: University of Washington Press.

Sobania, Neal, and Raymond Silverman

Forthcoming   "Patrons and Artists in Highland Ethiopia: Contemporary Practice in the Commissioning of Religious Painting and Metalwork." In *Proceedings of the 15th International Conference of Ethiopian Studies, Hamburg University, July 2003*.

Contributors

Steiner, Christopher B.
1994   *African Art in Transit*. Cambridge: Cambridge University Press.

Zervos, Adrien
1936   *L'empire d'Ethiopie: Le miroir de l'Ethiopie moderne, 1906–1935*. Alexandria, Egypt: Impr. de l'Ecole professionnelle des frères.

Interviews

Qes Adamu Tesfaw
    May 27, 1993 (Addis Ababa)
    June 7, 1997 (Bichena)
    November 13, 2001 (Addis Ababa)
    November 19, 2001 (Addis Ababa)
    December 15, 2001 (Addis Ababa)
    November 16, 2002 (Addis Ababa)
    June 8–9, 2003 (Addis Ababa)
    February 6, 2004 (Addis Ababa)
    July 9, 2004 (Addis Ababa)

Gebrekristos Solomon
    June 12, 2003 (Addis Ababa)

Benedetta Riva
    May 13, 2003 (Rome)

Raymond Silverman is a professor in the Department of the History of Art and the Center for Afroamerican and African Studies at the University of Michigan, where he also serves as the director of the Museum Studies Program. Initially, his research focused on interaction between West Africa and the cultures of the Middle East. For the last twelve years he has been working in Ethiopia with Neal Sobania, examining the social values associated with creativity in the northern part of the country, as well as the contemporary visual culture of the Ethiopian Orthodox Church. In addition to numerous articles and essays based on this research, he has edited a volume dealing with the visual cultures of the country titled, *Ethiopia: Traditions of Creativity* (1999). He has curated a number of museum exhibitions, most recently, *"Drinking the Word of God"—Expressions of Faith and the Search for Well-Being in Two West African Communities* (2001), *African Connections: Perspectives on Collecting Culture* (1999), and *Ethiopia: Traditions of Creativity* (1994). In addition to his research and teaching, he serves as a consulting editor for the journal *African Arts*. He is also on the editorial boards of *Northeast African Studies*, *Ghana Studies Journal*, and the *International Journal of Ethiopian Studies*.

Neal Sobania is a professor of history and director of International Education at Hope College in Holland, Michigan. He commenced his relationship with Ethiopia in 1980 as a Peace Corps Volunteer and later received his doctorate from the School of Oriental and African Studies at the University of London. His past research and publications—based on the extensive collection of oral tradition—have focused on ethnic identity and the formation of pastoralist societies in precolonial northern Kenya and southern Ethiopia. His present research interests are the ethno-historical identity of Ethiopian gold and silversmiths; the place of religious painters in contemporary Ethiopian society, an area in which he and Raymond Silverman continue to collaborate; and the use of historical photographs as research documents. His recent book, *Culture and Customs of Kenya* (2003), is a general introduction to the cultural, geographical, ethnic, and linguistic diversity of this dynamic country.

Leah Niederstadt is currently completing her doctorate in Social Anthropology at Oxford University. Her dissertation focuses on performance, creativity, and identity in Ethiopian children's circuses. Her broader research interests include cultural performance and traditional and contemporary art in Africa. She has published and lectured on representations of the Queen of Sheba in Ethiopian art and on Addis Ababa's contemporary art market. She served as a curatorial assistant for the present volume and has previously worked as a consultant for several performing arts organizations.

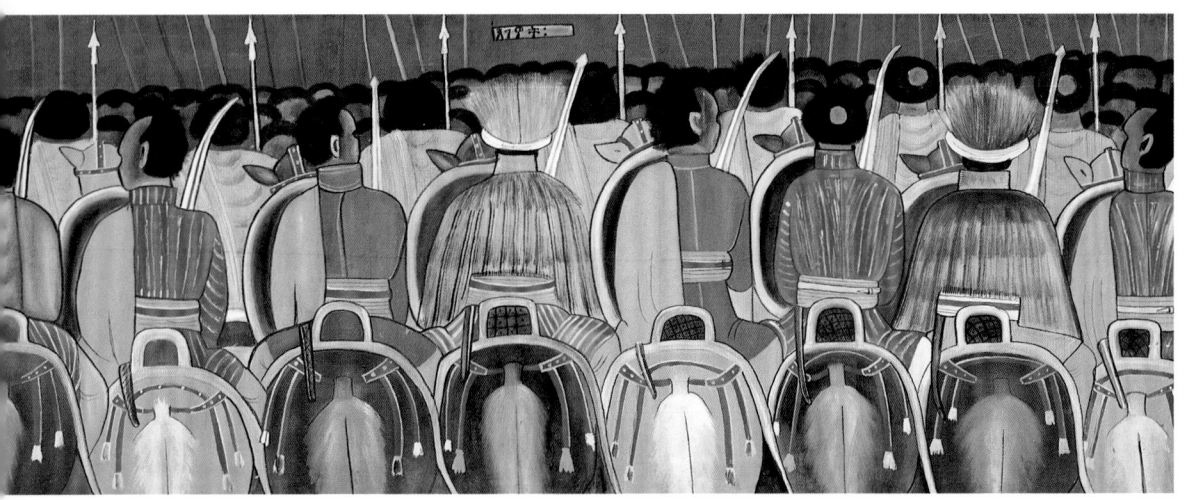